NPIC: Seeing the Secrets and Growing the Leaders

NPIC: Seeing the Secrets and Growing the Leaders

A CULTURAL HISTORY OF THE NATIONAL PHOTOGRAPHIC INTERPRETATION CENTER

Jack O'Connor

With a foreword by Carl W. Ford Jr

ISBN: 0692454535
ISBN 13: 9780692454534
Library of Congress Control Number: 2015908116
Acumensa Solutions, Alexandria, VA

"History never looks like history when you are living through it. It always looks confusing and messy, and it always feels uncomfortable"
John W. Gardner
No Easy Victories

TABLE OF CONTENTS

PREFACE

I n my first fifteen years of government service, I was fortunate to work at the National Photographic Interpretation Center (NPIC) and even more fortunate to witness firsthand a number of events chronicled in this book. I worked with the world's best finders of secrets. In part, this book describes how the people at NPIC found a large number of critical discoveries that altered the course of the Cold War. At the time of the events I witnessed, I never took notes or thought about capturing what was happening. Additionally, I don't think anyone else working at NPIC in the 1980s recorded these events either. We were all busy getting imagery-derived intelligence out the door to the military, intelligence, and policy communities; and figuring out how to deal with the director's new challenges. NPIC was a great place to start a career in the Intelligence Community to learn the tradecraft of an intelligence officer.

I also wrote this unclassified book to highlight what a well-led government organization and a committed workforce can do, and how an effective leader can reinvigorate an organization. While many of the attributes and manifestations of effective leadership are describable, every book definition seems to be unable to explain why some organizations produce leaders while others cannot, even under the same set of conditions and situations. Out of the group of people who started their careers and worked at NPIC in the middle 1980s, more senior executives emerged than from any other office in the Intelligence Community. This book also tries to explain that mystery— how and why NPIC produced more leaders and executives over a 20-year period than any other CIA office. Publically available stories about success in the Intelligence Community are rare, and only now can some of the NPIC story be told. Nearly all the technology in use during NPIC's "life" has become obsolete. Only the venerable U-2 remains today. All the satellite systems, the cameras, sensors, ground infrastructure, and the computer systems are gone. Even Building 213, the long-term home of NPIC, was demolished in the summer of 2014. Each of the intelligence stories I use has been declassified previously, and most of the details were obtained from documents or information made public after the fall of the Soviet Union. All the Soviet weapon systems I describe have been scrapped or destroyed by agreements defined in arms control treaties.

I've limited my discussion to former Soviet issues. This is not meant in any way to slight the excellent work NPIC accomplished on other issues in other parts of the world. There were many more NPIC successes, but most of these stories remain classified. The complete history of how NPIC analyzed the thousands of aircraft missions flown and the many hundreds of thousands of satellite images will not be told here. Nor will the stories of the important intelligence finds in the Middle East, North Korea, and China be addressed. Much of the Cold War took place in Third World proxy states, and those stories will also be untold. This is a selective cultural history rather than an exhaustive organizational study. The comprehensive unclassified history of NPIC remains to be written.

Along with NPIC's successes, there were intelligence failures in which NPIC played a part, sometimes a large part. I chose not to discuss these for two reasons. In some cases, the tradecraft involved was done in concert with another agency, and describing the failures would involve either revealing tradecraft still in use, or apportioning blame among multiple organizations. If this book were a comprehensive history of NPIC's efforts throughout the Cold War, that would have been appropriate.

In writing this book, I have had the gracious help of scores of former NPIC veterans who have shared experiences and memories. Many of these people helped me make connections with others who played important roles in this story. Their help was invaluable, and their encouragement sustained me while writing this book. But, to those of us lucky enough to have worked at NPIC, this willingness to help is no surprise. Some have asked to remain anonymous, and I have respected their wishes. I also received assistance from the Oral History Project at the Butler Library of Columbia University, where

Arthur Lundahl's reminiscences are kept, and from the American Society of Photogrammetry and Remote Sensing in Bethesda, Maryland.

While my attempts to get the sequences of events as accurate as possible were assisted by many former NPICers, the interpretation of the events and their outcomes is mine alone, as are any errors of fact or interpretation. Today these stories of intelligence challenges and particular technologies are old and unclassified. Nonetheless, they illustrate what made NPIC unique. While some details need to remain secret, the NPIC story deserves telling.

FOREWORD

J ack O'Connor's *NPIC: Seeing the Secrets; Growing the Leaders* takes you on a journey into the Intelligence Community (IC) that few other than those of us who worked there ever see. The insights should prove useful to both the general reader, as well as students focused on intelligence studies. For me, it brings back pleasant memories of my earliest days as an analyst at the Defense Intelligence Agency charting developments in China's People's Liberation Army. For my colleagues and I, satellite photography was key to everything we did. As all-source analysts, signals intelligence, open source information, and human intelligence also played an important role. But, without NPIC, we would have been blind to what was happening on the ground in China both literally and figuratively.

I heartily agree with Jack's praise of the IC's workforce then and now. Over educated, overworked, and underpaid, the members of the IC labor behind the scenes to protect America's interests. To be fair, most of us would admit that we could never have found jobs as fascinating and rewarding anywhere else. Being blessed with more than our fair share of exceptional leaders was a bonus. I did not know Art Lundahl personally, but his accomplishments speak for themselves. I experienced many of Rae Huffstutler's accomplishments first hand, and rate him right up there with Bob Gates, the only CIA analyst ever to be named director of the Central Intelligence Agency.

Jack's focus on the Soviet Union highlights many of the strengths and weaknesses of the IC that I observed as a China specialist, and I am certain that they will be familiar to others focused elsewhere and on different substantive issues. For one, we still complain about the lion's share of resources going to the Soviet problem leaving us to operate on a shoestring. We understood the strategic reasoning, but couldn't help be jealous of the resources going its way.

The dispute between single-source and all-source analysts that Jack describes in *NPIC: Seeing the Secrets; Growing the Leaders* is all too true and, if anything, may have gotten worse since he and I were actively involved. On most counts, I side with the single-source analysts even though I come from a different background. The imagery analyst for example has knowledge and skills that an all-source analyst can never duplicate. The same is true for signals and HUMINT analysts. They are true experts, being more narrowly focused on their primary responsibility—imagery, signals, or human reporting. To do their job effectively, however, they must also be knowledgeable of the latest in their colleagues' specialties. The role of the all-source analyst is to meld, if possible, all this information into a coherent whole. If any of the analysts attempt to do the others' jobs the quality of the information sufferers.

Most of the abuses I have witnessed have been all-source analysts who get into their head that they can interpret imagery better than NPIC or some other imagery agency; the same for NSA or the Clandestine Service. They start thinking: we see the whole picture; we know more than you. When that happens watch out. Trouble is bound to follow. One of the worst abuses I experienced was all-source analysts demanding that imagery analysts measure the size of Chinese ground force barracks--an enormous time consuming task that, because of its sheer size, would become the number one priority for hundreds of analysts. Some might argue what's wrong with that, if it answers an important question. But it didn't. Two or three analysts at CIA decided that they could determine the size of the PLA by using the square footage of buildings. Everybody else at the time thought it was the craziest idea they had ever heard. Even if you could determine a building was used for housing troops, square footage wouldn't take into consideration single beds or double bunks, or whether a unit was at full strength. Despite being wrongheaded, it took several years to fully discredit the idea.

When you hear complaints about "stovepipes" in the Intelligence Community, this is what is being talked about. Analysts with various specialties, working miles apart, belonging to completely different bureaucracies, often barely knowing who the other people are, struggle to answer the same complicated questions as if the others hardly existed. As some might say: It is no way to run a railroad. But that's is exactly how we do it. That was the experience of analysts at NPIC, and it certainly was mine.

Indeed, working in teams with each specialty represented is a rare occurrence. I've only seen it done once. It involved a serious discrepancy in our understanding of North Korea that caught all of the stovepipes by surprise. To resolve the problem, analysts from the US Army, CIA, DIA, NSA, and NPIC were thrown together in one building with the task of resolving the discrepancy. All hailed the effort a great success; there was unanimous agreement among the participants they had found a much better way of analyzing difficult problems. They didn't want to go back to the old stovepipe way of doing analysis. But of course they did, and they are still laboring separately in inflexible bureaucratic bastions.

Over time, one clear area of success has been technology. As the story of *NPIC: Seeing the Secrets and Growing the Leaders* unfolds, Jack gives the reader a rare peek into how much the technology available to imagery analysts then, and now, has changed. By the time you are finished reading, you will better understand and appreciate the capabilities of the Intelligence Community and the sophisticated tools available to today's imagery analysts.

Carl W. Ford Jr.

(In addition to many years as an all-source intelligence analyst, the Honorable Carl W. Ford Jr. served as a professional staff member of the Senate Foreign Relations Committee; as the National Intelligence Officer for East Asia on the National Intelligence Council; as Principal Deputy and Acting Assistant Secretary of Defense for International Security Affairs; as Deputy Assistant Secretary of Defense for East Asia and South Asian Affairs; and as Assistant Secretary of State for Intelligence and Research.)

INTRODUCTION

The National Photographic Interpretation Center, N-PIC as it was called and pronounced within the US Intelligence Community, came into being in the 1950s so that the United States could uncover what the Soviet Union and its allies were trying to hide. NPIC's analytic successes in the 1950s, 1960s, and 1970s, led to the possibility of, and the reality of arms control treaties with the Soviet Union, and these analytic successes helped end the Cold War.

NPIC was created and affixed to CIA to manage and to meet an urgent American national security need—strategic information about the Soviet Union during the Cold War. During its existence, it was little known outside the Intelligence Community, but inside the Intelligence Community, NPIC exerted a large and substantive influence on US policy and military decision-makers. Early in its history, NPIC was successful at finding the locations of the Soviet Union's strategic weapons—this period has been characterized as NPIC's age of discovery. As satellites improved, NPIC's analysis provided the basis for understanding the composition of those forces. This was known as the age of comprehension, and enabled the US to negotiate successful arms control treaties and agreements in the 1970s and 1980s. Finally, in the 1980s, NPIC began its age of tracking, which enabled the United States to follow strategic, re-locatable targets.

NPIC gained its influence by discovering secret facilities, and by providing accurate and actionable intelligence about the USSR, Cuba, China, Vietnam, and North Korea; and on global conflicts from the 1950s through the 1990s. In 1996, NPIC was removed from CIA to become a part of the

Defense Department. It, along with other organizations, became the National Imagery and Mapping Agency, renamed the National Geospatial-Intelligence Agency (NGA) in November 2003. Although NPIC has ceased to exist as an organization, its influence continues to this day.

This residual NPIC "influence" within the Intelligence Community is the human element. The young men and women who comprised the NPIC workforce in the mid-1980s went on to fill more senior executive positions than any other office in the Intelligence Community. This large number of future leaders emerged from one office as a consequence of the efforts of two men, Arthur Lundahl, NPIC's founder and first director; and its fourth director, Robert Macrae (Rae) Huffstutler. Each led NPIC through unforeseen intelligence crises that led to unanticipated, but successful outcomes.

For Art Lundahl, the Cuban missile crisis was his surprise. The successful outcome of the crisis, resulting from NPIC's two months of round-the-clock work during November and December 1962, proved that photo-interpretation could reliably monitor negotiated arms agreements with the Soviet Union. For Rae Huffstutler, the unanticipated event took place in April 1986, soon after Prime Minister Gorbachev's January 1986 announcement that he would eliminate all Soviet SS-20 medium-range ballistic missiles. NPIC had two months to search sixty percent of the Soviet landmass in order to verify the size of the SS-20 force. It succeeded by creatively figuring out how to answer this critical intelligence question with limited collection resources. The successful resolutions of Lundhal's surprise and Huffstutler's unanticipated event helped shape the outcome of Cold War and the direction of the post-Cold War Intelligence Community's analytic efforts. This book hopes to show how the first outcome—support to arms control negotiations—grew out of Art Lundahl's shaping vision, and the second outcome—future leaders—evolved from Rae Huffstutler's refocusing of an organization.

At its largest, NPIC had about 1,300 government employees. Of those working at NPIC from 1984 through 1988, more than ten percent became senior executives. NPIC turned out to be the training ground for a large number of future senior executives for CIA, the Defense Intelligence Agency, the Department of Homeland Security, and the Office of the Director of National Intelligence. NPIC produced executives who have gone into the intelligence components of the New York City Police Department, the National Archives and Records Agency, and the National Oceanic and Atmospheric Agency.

Many of the National Geospatial-Intelligence Agency's senior executives started their careers in NPIC. Other NPIC imagery analysts and leaders went on to lead the intelligence staff of the House of Representatives, to become senior congressional staffers, and to help start the US commercial imagery business.

Other NPICers who did not become senior executives had significant analytic and technical influence in the Intelligence Community serving on the National Intelligence Council; as senior all-source analysts, managers, and teachers of analysts in DIA and CIA; as technical innovators or as senior project and program managers in the National Reconnaissance Office; and in the CIA's Directorate of Science and Technology. And a few even went on to do the Lord's work as priests and ministers.

Throughout its history, NPIC had extremely challenging missions: seeing the secrets of other countries, and solving strategic puzzles after seeing only a few pieces. NPIC looked at vast areas of the world and, on critical occasions, when it focused on Cuba, Chernobyl, and the SS-20 treaty negotiations, it made a critical difference to US policy. Even on many less dramatic occasions, its discoveries and analysis had an impact on US policy.

NPIC's imagery analysts all participated in the high-stakes, high-pressure crucible of search. Search is the painstaking, mundane work of looking at aerial or space imagery for anything new that might be strategically important. Search was "shared" throughout the NPIC workforce. While difficult and sometimes tedious, it sometimes made a significant difference to national security. Success at the challenges of discovering, comprehending, and tracking what was going on in the world was possible only by developing and sustaining a workforce that could manage very large amounts of non-verbal information, and communicate it effectively.

The NPIC workforce never stopped learning. More importantly, it connected what it was learning with what had gone before. This thread of intelligence history allowed it to provide the context for what photo-interpreters and imagery analysts were seeing in their day-to-day analysis. And, of necessity, NPIC used cutting edge technology to accomplish its mission. It constantly adjusted and refined how it used digital technology that was far ahead of what was used in other parts of the US government.

NPIC had characteristics that fostered the growth of leaders. It grew future leaders because its leadership made clear and demanding expectations of its workforce; provided guidance on what it would take to succeed; directed a young, hard-working workforce to take on large responsibilities; and it gave these people a strong voice in how all of this would be accomplished. These experiences shaped NPIC's young officers, giving them early exposure to the challenges of analytic, organizational, substantive, and technical leadership in the Intelligence Community.

In the 1980s, NPIC underwent a number of complex transitions. Changes in satellite reconnaissance; unanticipated world events (mainly in the Soviet Union); the transition from film-based photography to digital imagery; the arrival of Rae Huffstutler in 1984; and the unique "photo interpreter/imagery analyst" culture that had developed since the 1950s were just a few of the milestones that had a substantial impact on the organization.

Rae Huffstutler, made significant changes in hiring, mentoring, training, and managing. He incorporated new technologies and methodologies into the analytic work, and gained access to other sources of intelligence not previously shared with NPIC's analysts. By combining the best elements of the existing NPIC culture, restoring some original NPIC practices, and introducing new challenges and ideas, Rae refocused NPIC. He created a way to listen to his entire organization, and to give them an opportunity to lead and influence it. His efforts, based on a deep understanding of the culture of Lundahl's original organization, energized and inspired a large number of NPIC's young intelligence officers.

This book covers NPIC through Rae Huffstutler's departure in February 1988. NPIC continued to provide essential imagery-derived intelligence to the nation until it was incorporated into the new National Imagery and Mapping Agency in October 1996. And it continued to develop future leaders under the tutelage of its next three directors, Frank Ruocco, Leo Hazlewood, and Nancy Bone.

Although NPIC is gone, a number of NPIC officers still influence the Intelligence Community widely and effectively today. Those who served in the NPIC "culture" found innovative solutions to hard problems; created approaches to managing risk by "finding" new information; handled and applied strong peer pressure to perform good analysis, solve problems, and take responsibility for the outcomes. They are still among the Intelligence Community leadership today, though near the ends of their careers.

In large part, though most of them are not specifically mentioned, this is their story.

CHRONOLOGY

1 Apr 1915	Arthur C. Lundahl born in Chicago
1942	Lundahl commissioned as officer in US Navy
1943	Lundahl posted to NORPACFLT in Attu in the Aleutian islands in Alaska
27 Dec 44	Lundahl marries Mary Hvid at University of Chicago chapel
Jan 45	Lundahl begins work at Navy Photographic Interpretation Center in Anacostia preparing amphibious landing charts for Operation Olympia (Invasion of Japan)
Mar 46	Lundahl becomes a GS-13 navy civilian and begins work on Operation CROSSROADS, first postwar atomic test at Bikini atoll
1949-55	Lundahl begins taking leadership positions at American Society of Photogrammetry; serves as board member, editor of *Photogrammetric Engineering*, vice president, and president
13 May 53	Lundahl moves to CIA, retains title at Navy
13 Dec 54	Lundahl directed to turnover CIA Photographic Intelligence Division and work on U-2 project under Richard Bissell
Jul 55	President Dwight D. Eisenhower learns of new Soviet bomber seen by US air attache at Soviet Aviation Day parade
20 Jul 55	Eisenhower proposal for Open Skies overflights over US and USSR is rejected by Nikita Khrushchev in Geneva
1 Jul 56	Photographic Intelligence Division moves to Steuart building at 5th and K NW Washington D.C.; assumes HTAUTOMAT internal address

4 Jul 56	U-2 begins first of eight successful penetration overflights over Eastern Europe and USSR. Flights continue until 10 July when Soviet Union protests
29 Sep 57	First Soviet nuclear accident at Kysthym, near Sverdlovsk (Yekatrinburg) contaminates area equal to Massachusetts. Precise accident location unknown until 1968
Aug 58	Photographic Intelligence Division becomes Photographic Interpretation Center, the first step in Lundahl's vision of a national center
21 Jan 59	First attempt at launching CORONA photo-reconnaissance satellite
1 May 60	U-2 overflight of USSR shot down over Sverdlovsk; pilot Francis Gary Powers captured; Kysthym on target list for the mission
18 Aug 60	First successful CORONA mission. Film returned and sent to PIC by August 19. More Soviet targets covered than all previous U-2 missions
25 Jan 61	President Eisenhower, in final days of his administration, signs NSCID-8 which creates the National Photographic Interpretation Center, administered by CIA
17-19 Apr 61	Bay of Pigs fiasco. Disastrous invasion of Cuba causes President Kennedy to fire DCI Allen Dulles. Richard Bissell resigns in disgrace
19 Oct 62	NPIC discovers SS-4 IRBM canisters in Cuba; Cuban missile crisis begins
1 Jan 63	NPIC moves from upper floors of Steuart building to Building 213 at western end of Washington Navy Yard in SE Washington
12 Jul 63	KH-7 high-resolution satellite launched
Aug 63	KH-4a, begins operations with twice the amount of film as KH-4
1964	NPIC creates model shop
1965	DoD and CIA/IG inspection of NPIC done; both recommend establishment of DIA and CIA departmental organizations
29 Jul 66	KH-8 high resolution satellite series launched
1968	SS-9 Silo construction analysis done by Kress and Merritt; beginning of transition to imagery analysis

15 Jun 71	KH-9 large area collector satellite launched
Jul 73	Art Lundahl retires; succeeded by John Hicks
6 Oct 73	Beginning of Arab-Israeli war (6-25 October)
Jan 77	KH-11 near-real-time digital satellite begins operation; start of Priority Exploitation Group (PEG) operations
1978	R. P. (Hap) Hazzard succeeds John Hicks as fourth director of NPIC
1982	CIA IG inspection of NPIC begins
Dec 83	NPIC cable announces third TYPHOON submarine launched at Severodvinsk
Feb 84	R. M. (Rae) Huffstutler succeeds Hap Hazzard as fifth director of NPIC.
May 84	Third TYPHOON confirmed at Severodvinsk
Dec 85	NPIC reorganization announced
Jan 86	In January surprise, Premier Gorbachev announces Soviet willingness to eliminate entire SS-20 IRBM force
18 Apr 86	Last KH-9 satellite destroyed in launch explosion at Vandenberg AFB
26 Apr 86	Chernobyl nuclear accident
May-Jul 86	SS-20 search of sixty percent of USSR
11 Oct 86	Reykjavik summit. INF treaty is agreed to in principle by President Reagan and Premier Gorbachev
Jan 87	Arthur Lundahl's last visit to Building 213
May 87	National Exploitation Laboratory created
8 Dec 87	INF treaty signed in Washington D.C. by President Reagan and Premier Gorbachev
Feb 88	Rae Huffstutler becomes Director of Administration at CIA; succeeded at NPIC by Frank Ruocco
Feb 91	Leo Hazlewood succeeds Frank Ruocco as seventh director of NPIC
22 Jun 92	Arthur C. Lundahl dies in Washington D.C.
Oct 93	Nancy Bone succeeds Leo Hazlewood as eighth and final director of NPIC
1 Oct 96	NPIC becomes part of National Imagery and Mapping Agency

CODA

TWO LEADERS, ONE STAGE

Late in January 1987, two men shared a stage in a packed auditorium at Building 213, a large six-story rectangular factory building at the northwest corner of the Washington Navy Yard. The younger, Rae Huffstutler, was the current director of the National Photographic Interpretation Center. The older man, with a full head of silver hair, was confined by arthritis to a wheelchair. The occasion was the dedication of the refurbished auditorium to the career of the older man, Arthur Lundahl, who had envisioned and realized the National Photographic Interpretation Center, and who twenty-seven years earlier, had become its first director.

The auditorium held many imagery analysts and support people in their twenties and thirties who had never seen, but had heard stories about Mr. Lundahl. Some were CIA employees, some DIA employees, and some were active duty military officers. All worked together at NPIC.

Art Lundahl had been invited back to speak to the newest generation of NPIC imagery analysts, and the auditorium was packed forty minutes before his scheduled arrival. It would be Art Lundahl's last visit to Building 213.

Rae had asked Mr. Lundahl to come back to tell the younger people the stories of the early NPIC years and of Mr. Lundahl's role in them. Rae also wanted to honor Art Lundahl and to show him the changes that had occurred since his last visit. On that one day, those in the audience saw the two leaders who had helped bring about the most significant outcomes of the Cold War, but the two men on stage were looking at an audience full of future leaders.

CHAPTER 1

Nearly Missing Chernobyl

In a dimly lit corner, in a dimly lit room of a ground station that housed NPIC's Priority Exploitation Group (PEG), a young Navy Lieutenant sat in front of an IDEX 1A workstation (an early digital television monitor). She was waiting for an image to appear on its screen. Soon, she would be looking at a target that she and her colleagues at PEG knew little about, as they usually did not look at, or pay attention to this target. Imagery analysts usually know what they are likely to see when looking at a frame of imagery or photography. They have worked a target or an issue long enough to know what is "normal." This was not one of those times.

By April 1986, the Priority Exploitation Group had been in existence for nine years. Its primary mission was to look at "high current interest targets" collected by US imaging satellites. The ground station provided imagery and analysis to all the military services, the Department of Defense (DoD) intelligence centers, and CIA. PEG was staffed around the clock, everyday of the year. It was located at a ground station to enable imagery analysts to look at satellite imagery as soon as it could be received and processed. As part of the National Photographic Interpretation Center, the Priority Exploitation Group was the first in the Intelligence Community to receive that imagery. PEG imagery analysts were the first to see what was happening at targets of strategic interest to the United States.

PEG was the first organization to see the results of the recent US air strikes on Libya. And its preparatory work on Chernobyl over the previous three days, the details of which were unknown to the Navy Lieutenant, would enable the United States to know what was going on at the exploded reactor nearly as rapidly as Mikhail Gorbachev.

NPIC was a bureaucratic anomaly. Most of what it produced was strategic military intelligence, but it was not part of the Defense Department. NPIC was managed by and part of CIA, but it was physically separated from the Agency. Although only a few miles down the George Washington Memorial Parkway from Langley, many CIA all-source analysts refused to visit or consult with their imagery analyst brethren. NPIC often produced intelligence based on imagery analysis that did not agree with and sometimes contradicted CIA's all-source analysis. One of these "disagreements" resulted in Chernobyl being imaged that night in April.

The previous Saturday, April 26, 1986, at 1:23 in the morning, during an equipment test, one of two operational nuclear reactors at the Chernobyl Nuclear Power Plant about seventy miles from Kiev in the Ukrainian SSR exploded. The explosion released radiation equivalent to hundreds of times the amount released by the atomic bomb dropped on Hiroshima. On Sunday, the first indications of the Chernobyl accident came from increased atmospheric radiation measured by safety devices more than six hundred miles away at a Swedish nuclear power plant. Initially, the Soviet Union provided no information on, or confirmation of the accident. After the recordings of higher than usual radioactivity were verified that weekend, the US Intelligence Community wanted to know what was happening.

The Intelligence Community had questions. Where was the radiation coming from? Was it a leak, an accident, an explosion? How much area was contaminated and how badly? What were the Soviet government and the Soviet military doing in response? These questions stirred the Intelligence Community.

The Chernobyl accident exposed some operational challenges faced by the Intelligence Community. However, it also showed how first-line managers at NPIC made decisions when no other information was available and took initiatives that resulted in an intelligence success. As a result of their actions, the Intelligence Community was able to use analysis gathered from satellite imagery to force the Soviet Union to admit what happened at Chernobyl, to admit its shortcomings in its disaster response, and ultimately to accept foreign medical and scientific assistance in response to the disaster.

After NPIC received its first news on Sunday about a radiation leak, it responded in two ways. Externally, NPIC had Phil Lago, an experienced imagery analyst on a rotational assignment at the DCI's Arms Control Intelligence Staff (ACIS). Phil got a secure-line call on Sunday April 27th that a Swedish nuclear station was recording increased radioactivity. Most NPIC personnel did not have a secure phone in their homes. Phil had a secure phone at his home because his wife, a former NPIC imagery analyst, was on a rotation to a counterterrorism team. Phil called PEG at the ground station to alert the analysts there, and he also called the Committee on Imagery Requirements and Exploitation's (COMIREX) collection branch. (COMIREX was the organization responsible for planning and tasking the collection of satellite imagery.)

Phil's call to COMIREX was not well received. COMIREX thought Phil was attempting to circumvent its collection voting process. The COMIREX watch officer told Phil that imagery collection was not really necessary, as the United States already knew through other sources that a radiation leak had occurred in the Soviet Union. When Phil reported back to Doug George, his ACIS boss, that COMIREX was not planning to change its collection plan to find the source of the radiation leak, this news went to CIA's Director of Intelligence, and then to his boss, Bob Gates, the deputy DCI. These calls eventually resulted in COMIREX reversing its decision.

On Sunday afternoon, PEG imagery analysts belonging to the Navy/Nuclear Branch began to answer the first question: where was the radiation coming from? They used the NPIC database to list the potential locations to search, and they prioritized this list in light of the little information they had. That they had a list at all was a result of efforts that started in 1956, when NPIC's predecessor organization began to develop its initial database of Soviet strategic and nuclear facilities. The PEG imagery analysts also called their NPIC counterparts from the Imagery Exploitation Group (IEG) Nuclear Branch at their homes. These IEG imagery analysts, specialists in nuclear energy issues, drove to Building 213 at the Washington Navy Yard in Southeast Washington D.C.. There they could talk on secure telephones with the PEG analysts at the ground station. By doing so, they were able to review and augment the PEG list of potential nuclear targets where a radiation leak might have occurred.

Initially, the challenge was to bound the problem. This was not easy. In the western Soviet Union, nuclear power plants existed at Kursk, Kola, Leningrad, Obninsk, Kalinin, Smolensk, Zaporozhye, Kuzneskovsk, Chernobyl, and Yuznoukrainsk. Based on weather information about prevailing winds and the nuclear facilities in the NPIC database, the imagery analysts included Chernobyl as a possible site. To get ad hoc (special emphasis) imagery collection, NPIC would have to make its case on Monday to the COMIREX committee that had already told Phil Lago that it did not plan to collect against this issue. The initial COMIREX decision not to collect imagery of Chernobyl was not entirely irrational. The imagery collection budget was very lean, in large part due to a recent launch failure.

Eleven days earlier, immediately after launch, a rocket exploded at Vandenberg Air Force Base in Southern California. Its payload was the last KH-9 film return satellite. As a consequence of the launch failure, COMIREX had to be very conservative in its collection decisions, as imagery collection was as constrained as it could be. But the PEG imagery analysts persisted in requesting collection.

The PEG imagery analysts at the ground station and the IEG nuclear analysts at Building 213 knew that this accident was important enough to change the collection plan. Even the possibility of a false radiation report was important enough to investigate. And if true, NPIC imagery analysts knew that they would be expected to locate, comprehend, evaluate, and track events quickly.

By the time the imagery analysts knew enough to make a list of potential targets on Sunday, they also knew that they might not get imagery of Chernobyl on Monday. And, as frequently happened, other parts of the Intelligence Community had different ideas about what NPIC should collect and analyze.

On Monday, two PEG managers, Mike Rains, the Navy/Nuclear Branch Chief, and Tom Wahl, chief of the Imagery Science Branch, went to the COMIREX collection meeting. PEG managers often attended COMIREX meetings when they wanted collection that would disrupt the standing plan, or when NPIC thought that it needed to make a special case to the Intelligence Community representatives for why it needed either a certain resolution or a certain number of images. (Resolution is the technical measurement of what can be seen on a photograph. It is measured in units of distance. A three-foot resolution means that the camera or sensor will detect any object that measures three feet in length.)

PEG's managers had prepared in two ways. Collectively, the PEG and IEG imagery analysts had agreed on the most likely targets, and Rains brought this nuclear analytic perspective. Additionally, in anticipation of the technical information that COMIREX would demand, if there had been a serious nuclear accident, the imagery analysts had consulted with the image scientists about how to task the satellite to get the best possible images of the location. Wahl, who understood the properties of the sensor and the orbital geometry, had worked with the NRO and NPIC image scientists, and he brought this perspective. Prepared with analytic and sensor expertise, both branch chiefs attended the meeting. Usually only one manager would make the case for collection, but the NPIC imagery analysts had been thinking hard about the potential source of the radiation, and they and the imagery scientists were probably the most knowledgeable people in the Intelligence Community about how to obtain a high-quality image of Chernobyl or the other possible targets.

PEG imagery analysts usually did not look at civilian nuclear power plants, but NPIC had kept target folders of information about these power plants for precisely this kind of accident. One of the earliest questions about the Soviet Union that US photo-interpreters had tried to answer was the location of a 1957 Soviet nuclear accident. Locating and characterizing this accident had taken more than ten years. Since its inception, NPIC had tracked the construction of the Soviet nuclear infrastructure. After consulting with the experts at Building 213 and looking at the target folders, the PEG imagery analysts knew that four RBMK reactors were at Chernobyl, although only two were in operation. The PEG imagery analysts had been talking with the IEG Nuclear Branch to see what additional information they had about this particular power plant, and to find out which imagery analyst knew the most about Chernobyl, as imagery analysts frequently had information that was not recorded in the data base. They also spoke with the military analysts who worked Ukraine to determine what Soviet military units were nearby and which might respond. All this was done to prepare for the Monday meeting.

At the Monday collection meeting, another component of the Intelligence Community surprised the NPIC managers. The CIA representative made the case that NPIC should not try to take a picture of the reactor at the Chernobyl nuclear power plant. Instead, CIA wanted to take a picture of Pripyat, the

Ukrainian city closest to Chernobyl, to see if they could observe activity that indicated that the Soviet Union had enacted its civil defense plan for nuclear war. For nearly forty years, this secret Soviet civil defense plan had been a subject of much intense speculation in the Intelligence Community. In the mid-1970s, it had been the center of a very contentious argument between CIA and the US Air Force about how much civil defense activity had been observed and reported.

Additionally, CIA's collection representative argued that the existence of the Soviet radiation leak was already known, and that a radiation leak might not even be visible. The largest US nuclear accident, Three Mile Island, had no unique visible signatures. CIA and the Intelligence Community considered the implementation of the Soviet civil defense plan as an indicator of their secret preparations to survive a nuclear attack. In their way of thinking, to understand that possibility was more important than finding an unlocated and undefined radiation leak. The Chairman of the COMIREX/OPSCOM, the operations subcommittee, initially agreed with the CIA all-source analysts.

As was the custom, contentious collection issues were put to a.community vote. The NPIC representatives, who had prepared for a combative meeting, made the case that it was more important to quickly locate the radiation source to determine the cause and extent of the radiation. They also argued that the lack of information from the Soviet government made ascertaining the potential physical damage at the reactor more important than the civil defense plan.

Finally, they argued that after the location of the radioactive leak was known, opportunities would still exist to see how or if the Soviet Union enacted its civil defense doctrine. The NPIC analytic and technical preparations, along with the leadership pressure from Doug George at ACIS, and Bob Gates, the CIA deputy director, persuaded the Intelligence Community collection managers to try to image Chernobyl on Tuesday. As Ukraine is seven time zones ahead of Washington, D.C., it would be before dawn on Tuesday when PEG could see the image. Late that Monday, Phil Lago called NPIC from ACIS with information from a sensitive source that Chernobyl was the likely site of the radiation leak, but there were no more details. He was relieved to find that it was included in the target list for emphasized collection.

All the work done at PEG on Sunday and Monday would have to be communicated to a group of imagery analysts and managers unaware of the crisis in progress. PEG had been organized to work seven days a week, and Tuesday was known as "overlap day." The weekend and weekday imagery analysts on the night shift both worked on Monday night into Tuesday morning. This schedule resulted in an overlap with the day shift on Tuesdays. This overlap schedule facilitated the coordination of intelligence issues that had changed or emerged in the three days and/or nights since the imagery analysts coming onto day shift had last worked. The imagery analysts who came in that Monday night learned about the analytic and collection preparations made since they had left on Friday morning the week before. The shift change meeting was how these returning imagery analysts learned about the planned collection that had not yet occurred. And the weekend imagery analysts who had done all the preparation for collection "passed on" their work. They would not return for another three days. Only on the subsequent Friday night or Saturday morning, would they learn what had happened as the result of their collection plans.

On that Monday, April 28ᵗʰ before the image was collected, other NPIC imagery analysts were preparing to "identify" what they might see. In preparation, the IEG Nuclear Branch analysts reviewed all their information about Chernobyl, and graphics support people at PEG and IEG were tipped that there might be a need for extra priority production support. Some of the IEG imagery analysts who worked the Kiev Military District were alerted without being told why to come in early on Tuesday.

In the first hours of Tuesday April 29ᵗʰ in Washington, later Tuesday morning in Ukraine, an image was taken. When the imagery came to the IDEX 1A softcopy workstation, a navy lieutenant was the first person to look closely at the damaged Chernobyl reactor and to not die or become seriously ill from the experience. Through the haze, the first image clearly showed the blown-out dome roof of the reactor, scattered debris, and evidence of still burning fires. Fire trucks and helicopters were visible, and the PEG imagery analysts and managers who saw the image knew that most of the people near the reactor would shortly be seriously or fatally ill from radiation poisoning. Yet, none of the PEG analysts or managers who made possible the observations and analysis were there to see the imagery. They would only learn about what the lieutenant saw either the next day, or when they came back to work on Friday night or Saturday morning.

The NPIC collection turned out to be critical, as the official Soviet response continued to be silence. No other information was available, and it was now three days since the explosion. The Soviet media made no reporting or broadcast of the accident, nor was there any announcement or warning of any potential danger from the radioactive leak. Western news organizations had reported the story that workers at a Swedish nuclear power plant at Fosmark had high readings of radiation on their clothing on the morning of 28 April; it was the first public media awareness that some release of radiation had occurred somewhere. But the world media had no other information. As the Soviet government continued to say nothing, NPIC was reporting regularly.

NPIC imagery analysts, looking at the nearby town and military facilities, did not see evidence of any closure areas or evacuations on that first imagery. According to open sources, the first evacuations did not begin until two o'clock in the afternoon on the 27th, more than thirty-six hours after the explosion. But visible evidence of the large-scale evacuation was not observed until early in May when analysts at PEG saw hundreds of trucks and buses in Pripyat.

In subsequent days, NPIC tracked the response on the scene as the Soviet government began to use helicopters to photograph the damage and to drop boron on the exposed reactor hall. Even after the Soviet government began to report the accident publically, its severity was not acknowledged. By taking later satellite images at a higher resolution, the full extent of the catastrophe was shown to experts at the Department of Energy, Nuclear Regulatory Agency, Atomic Energy Commission, and various health organizations, so these groups could begin to calculate the health and radiation risks to the people, the crops, the environment, and foreign countries.

Not everything at NPIC went smoothly that day. As part of the reporting process, PEG made two special videos of the damage on 29 April. One cassette was sent to CIA so Bob Gates, then deputy DCI, could carry it down to the White House to show it to President Reagan. The other was sent to the director of NPIC, Rae Huffstutler, at Building 213 to show to senior officials. As it happened, two members of the Senate intelligence committee had heard that NPIC had imagery of the disaster. The Senators drove the short distance down from the Capitol to Building 213. But, April 29th was a lovely spring day in Washington, and it was also when the Building 213 Support Group scheduled its spring picnic. In the haste to rush the special video to Building 213, no one told the courier or the registry desk that this video was special, and that it was to be rushed to the director of NPIC. As the courier had no other instructions, he dropped the video onto the empty counter in the Building 213 Registry and went to the picnic.

Meanwhile, the director of NPIC, with two waiting Senators, was calling the chief of PEG about the video, as no one was answering the phone in Registry. It took a few hours to find the tape, and a little while longer than that for the director to calm down. But, eventually, the videotape was taken to the Capitol where a total of fifty-seven members of the House and the Senate came to watch it.

The Soviet Nuclear Branch in the Imagery Exploitation Group (IEG) in Building 213, where most NPIC nuclear experts worked, did valuable work on this issue, but their initial reporting was text only, and far less dramatic than the text, pictures, and videos done at PEG. These analysts worked "second-phase analysis," a slightly slower-paced, follow-up analysis that was as important as the current "first phase" reporting. Over the next few months NPIC produced more than fifty electronic intelligence cables and eighty briefing boards to report the ongoing events at Chernobyl, their effects on the region, the progress of the disaster response, the pace of the evacuation, and the extent of the newly uninhabitable area. The area of contamination was a 30-kilometer circle from the power plant, slightly less than 1,100 square miles or ten times the area of Washington, D.C. Later in the year, NPIC, with the Department of Energy, produced a longer video that summarized the event.

The Chernobyl reporting was NPIC's first major video intelligence story. Many US senior officials first saw Chernobyl on an NPIC video. The use of video technology to report intelligence had not been in any organizations' program. From its beginning, NPIC imagery analysts and managers had been focused only on accelerating the production of the intelligence. Continually, they focused on cutting the time between taking the photos or images and communicating what the imagery analysts saw to their customers. The PEG videos were only one recent example.

In PEG, at the ground station, the awareness of the advantages of the digital nature of the daily imagery led to a sense that all of the time-consuming conversions of digits to film, and of film to paper products might not be the best way to produce timely intelligence. The speed with which an image could be acquired, processed, and sent to a softcopy workstation slowed greatly when the intelligence production process began. Even at PEG, where the process was measured in hours, the multiple steps to convert digits to photographic prints and paper took most of the time. The challenge of how to accelerate getting intelligence out the door occupied much of the PEG managerial thinking.

Prior to the use of the videos at PEG, the production challenge had led to the use of the point-to-point secure fax machines so that images could be gotten to Langley for inclusion in the President's daily brief, to the Pentagon for the Joint Chiefs of Staff, and to the White House for the National Security Council. One of these secure fax machines was later installed in Building 213.

But the inherent production delays continued to challenge the PEG managers—secure fax machines were not enough. Late in 1984, three managers, John Wawro, Steve Irish, and Tony Perrillo, began thinking about a different way to present imagery-derived intelligence. They made a pilot intelligence summary video with borrowed training equipment.

When the PEG group chief, Gordon Duvall, saw the prototype video, he liked it and wanted funding and approval for trial production. He called Rae Huffstutler, the director of NPIC, that morning. Rae agreed, and that same morning he called Evan Hineman, director of CIA's Directorate of Science and Technology. Hineman in turn called the CIA Director, William Casey, who was looking for innovative ideas. That afternoon, Evan Hineman brought the video to the Casey's office and showed it to him. Casey approved, funded the pilot, and the next day, PEG began figuring out how to make a daily video summary from satellite imagery.

The DCI's approval enabled NPIC to divert existing funding to invest in the technology needed to produce overnight intelligence. At first, only a few copies were made, but the success and novelty of the classified television tapes soon caused the video audience to grow.

Chernobyl brought a larger audience to the PEG video reporting. The experiment that led to the PEG videos opened up the possibilities for digital transmission of finished intelligence. Chernobyl created a developing market every morning for images and stories throughout the Intelligence Community. The video reporting created the expectation for rapid visual information such as bomb damage assessment, environmental disaster reporting, and frequent daily updates on unfolding events of significance. The cleared audience began to want images and movement along with words, and NPIC began to feel this pressure.

This technology also introduced the beginning of a reality that would change NPIC. The imagery analysts who produced the daily video for the Intelligence Community were the first to recognize that not every day brings exciting images. Also, by the mid-1980s, the Intelligence Community was expecting visual news with two characteristics that satellite imagery lacked—movement and sound. CNN had started its twenty-four-hour news operations in 1980 and, after its coverage of the Challenger disaster in January 1986, its audience grew quickly. In recognition of its influence, cable televisions and CNN were installed at PEG to make NPIC imagery analysts aware of breaking world events.

In the Intelligence Community, the Chernobyl accident resulted in the recognition that in the first days after the disaster, NPIC was the only source of reliable information. NPIC alone in the government had reliable information and a way to bring this information to bear quickly. NPIC also understood how to get more information to trained and experienced imagery analysts who could interpret and report quickly. It was an organization that expected to have to overcome resistance to get what was needed, that expected to risk its credibility to get results, and that had a long tradition of cooperative work. CIA, the director of NPIC and his exploitation managers knew that NPIC might not have gotten its collection if its officers had not taken the initiative to request collection without waiting for orders. This experience made them recognize the need to change the collection planning process.

The Chernobyl analysis and reporting illustrated NPIC's responsiveness, teamwork, and innovation; and its ability to do rapid accurate research, and to challenge the bureaucracy. These characteristics had their beginnings more than thirty years earlier in the vision of Arthur Lundahl.

CHAPTER 2

ART LUNDAHL—THE FIRST TO SEE THE SECRETS

In December 1954, Americans were going to the movies to see White Christmas with Bing Crosby and Rosemary Clooney, or dancing to Bill Haley's "Rock Around the Clock." Senator Joseph McCarthy was censured by the US Senate for "conduct that tends to bring the Senate into dishonor and disrepute." On December 13th, Arthur Lundahl was called to a surprise Monday morning meeting with Allen Dulles and Richard Bissell in the Central Building of CIA in downtown Washington.

Dulles was the director of CIA, and Bissell was his Assistant for Special Projects. Arthur Lundahl led CIA's 13-person Photographic Interpretation Division (PID). Dulles, who had a flair for the dramatic, told Lundahl that he was relieved of his duties and that he was to turn over the Photographic Interpretation Division to his deputy. Only then, on that December day in 1954 was Lundahl, who had been with CIA for less than two years, briefed about the classified program that would build the U-2 spy plane. Less than a month earlier, Bissell had learned that he would be running this program after President Eisenhower authorized the CIA to build the aircraft and to manage the program. Lundahl was told to work full time on building the organization needed to interpret, exploit, and analyze the photos that were to be taken over the Soviet Union.

Much has been written about the history of the U-2 program and how America began high-altitude and space reconnaissance. On the other hand, the story of the unique organization created by Art Lundahl to look at U-2 photographs has not been told. After that surprise Monday meeting, Arthur Lundahl created a part of CIA that became independent of CIA, an organization predominantly focused on the military forces that was not itself military. He infused a culture into his organization that would later grow a disproportionally large number of leaders for the US Intelligence Community. More than any other man, he changed how the United States used intelligence to fight the Cold War with the Soviet Union.

In December 1954, Art Lundahl was 39 years old. Although he had only been at CIA for less than two years, he had worked on aerial photography for more than seventeen years. Lundahl had grown up in Chicago where he attended Tilden Technical High School and the University of Chicago. As one of the best students at Tilden, he was a class officer, and played varsity football. Initially, after struggling at the University of Chicago, he withdrew and worked at a distillery, but within a year he returned to college. At the time Lundahl attended the University of Chicago, Maynard Hutchins revamped its curriculum and broadened the general education requirement. By his own admission, Lundahl was a better student in the sciences than the arts, and he majored in geology.

Lundahl had developed one skill that brought him to the attention of the geology faculty. At Tilden, he had taken several courses in technical and mechanical drawing. His artistic and lettering skill, of which he was proud, caused him to be requested to prepare artwork for his professors' academic papers and textbooks. In the summers of 1937-1939, one of his professors invited Lundahl to accompany him on fieldwork to prepare maps of remote backwoods areas of Canada that had interesting geologic formations.

Every summer, Francis W. Pettijohn would go into northern Ontario to map areas for his own pioneering work on sedimentology. The Canadian government subsidized his efforts. Pettijohn would obtain aerial photographs of the areas he was interested in and then, after analyzing them with Lundahl, they would hike the terrain and more precisely note, survey, and map these geological formations. Their work became the basis for some of the first accurate maps of this area. In his reminiscences, Lundahl described how they would search the photographs before they would hike into the region that they would be mapping and surveying. They did fieldwork in the Patrician County, in the northern part of Kenora district, near Hudson and Jones Bays. The geology of this region is taiga characterized by discontinuous permafrost, but the northern part of this region is the only part of North America characterized by tundra and permafrost. This very remote terrain was difficult to search on aerial photography, and yet Lundahl was able to pick out terrain and man-made features, which were mostly unimproved logging roads.

The fieldwork and his class work caused Lundahl to be nominated to a scientific fraternity, Sigma Xi, and he was awarded a scholarship to work on his doctorate in geology. During this time, he taught undergraduate classes and continued to illustrate other students' dissertations. Lundahl's photographic interpretation and Canadian fieldwork shaped his own academic pursuit. He completed his masters in geology and all the coursework and examinations for his PhD. His master's thesis dealt with the geology and petroleum deposits underneath Cedar Point, Ohio. His Chicago professors thought highly of him and recommended him for academic and industrial positions before and after the war.

During the summer of 1939, Lundahl worked as a tour guide for the Department of the Interior at the new National Park at Mammoth Cave, Kentucky. In the caves each day and evening, he would brief multiple groups of tourists. He credited this experience with improving his public speaking and for teaching him how to explain, simply, his knowledge about the cave geology to all kinds of people.

After Pearl Harbor, Lundahl joined the navy, which sent him to Dartmouth for basic officer training. From Dartmouth, he went to advanced communications training in Millington, Tennessee. As an officer, Lundahl was expected to lead and organize the enlisted men's schooling while participating in his own training. During World War II, Millington was a large naval training facility with more than 30,000 people stationed there. In his account of his time there, Lundahl described three events that illustrated his leadership characteristics.

One challenge was sorting out and organizing the hundreds of sailors and marines who would arrive on the trains. Lundahl devised a process that was academic, practical, and quick in order to select platoon leaders to help organize the groups of about six hundred men. He devised a general knowledge test and administered it right after the group would arrive. While the test was being graded, the men were run through medical processing, fed, and assigned barracks.

Lundahl's criteria for selecting platoon leaders were simple: he chose men with intelligence, with military experience, and with above-average height. After scoring the tests, all men with scores above ninety were culled out. From this group, those from this group with prior military experience of any sort were separated, and then Lundahl would select the taller ones as platoon leaders. He would identify them early to the group and enlist their help in keeping order and in communicating with the other groups of men. After this selection was made, he made himself available to answer any questions that the sailors had on their first night.

The other anecdote had to do with the schooling. He and another officer looked for statistical patterns among men who did well with Morse code. From their analysis, they could determine which navy basic school produced better than average scores. The training commander was impressed with this work and visited the schools to see what made their students distinctive. Lundahl's other effort dealt with individual students. He made it a practice to notice when good students would have a drop in test scores. He would call these men in and, often, would find out that a family or financial issue at the root of the change. He would then arrange for a cash advance or some intervention to allow these men to focus on their work. For those who enlisted early, he also worked to have their navy training credited toward their high school diplomas. Lundhal would write and petition the principals to grant diplomas in absentia. Nearly every principal Lundahl wrote to was amenable and many of his students were grateful.

After training in Tennessee, Lundahl went to the Naval Photographic Interpretation School in Anacostia, in Washington D.C. He then went on to school in Chapel Hill, at North Carolina. (At North Carolina, two of his classmates were Ted Williams and Johnny Pesky of the Boston Red Sox.) In Anacostia, even though a student, Lundahl was called on to teach photogrammetry—the accurate measuring of photographed objects—to his classmates.

On completing his training, Lundahl was posted to PACNORFLT in Adak, Alaska in October 1943. Adak was in the Aleutian Islands, some of which had only been recaptured earlier in 1943. His particular responsibility was preparing all of the fleet's maps and charts, and he also led and managed a small, deployed, headquarters photo-interpretation unit. Lundahl had a wide array of wartime intelligence responsibilities. He was planning reconnaissance missions, building targeting packages for air and naval strikes against the Japanese mainland, as well as providing for the other officers and enlisted men under his charge. He demonstrated an ability to work with all ranks and to bound and solve complex problems. In his reminiscences, his memories of Adak illustrate his natural curiosity and abilities. While many of the officers would drink in their spare time, Lundahl explored the island and Mount Moffett. He had gotten an aerial photograph of the island. On the image, he identified a large circular mound with more vegetation than the surrounding area. When he hiked there, he discovered that it was a burial area for the indigenous tribes from thousands of years earlier. He also discovered underwater volcanic springs that, when active, could make the Arctic Ocean water hot. More importantly to his men and colleagues, he found where he could collect large sacks of clams, where to catch Dolly Virden trout and salmon in season, and where to catch king crabs. The catch from these expeditions was a welcome change to their rations and made him popular with his men.

As part of his duties, he made some special charts that included angles of deflection that improved fleet gunnery when they shelled the Japanese coast. His own area of expertise was photographic analysis of Japanese airfields, but his most recognized effort was for his assistance in anti-submarine work.

He received a commendation medal for his analysis of the mathematics behind a submarine search model. Lundahl and a colleague, Allan Kramer, recognized that the mathematics of an anti-submarine search plan were in error. Their find led the navy to reissue the procedure. This effort illustrated Lundahl's interest in designing aerial search strategies. When they recognized the error, Lundahl and Kramer designed a new pattern of aerial search that would work more effectively at far northern latitudes. This experience also gave him an important first experience with bureaucratic rivalry when a Japanese submarine was reported to be coming to their area. When Lundahl and Kramer briefed their new method to the air wing commander, the response was, "I'm not flying my planes that way," and he dismissed them. Shortly afterward, a captain from the air wing persuaded his commander to fly Lundahl's plan. On their second set of radar contacts, the air patrols passed information about the submarine's location to the surface fleet that recorded a confirmed submarine sinking. Lundahl and Kramer each received the Navy Commendation Medal, but the memory of the intra-service rivalry stayed with Lundahl.

The navy brought Lundahl back to Washington D.C. in January 1945 to work on planning for the invasion of Japan. On route, Lundhal stopped in Chicago where he married his fiancée Mary Hvid in the University of Chicago chapel on December 27th.

In Washington, Lundahl was preparing charts of Japanese beaches in preparation for the planned US invasion, and then he also worked on photo-interpretation keys for the school at Anacostia where he worked with the Army Corps of Engineers and other military units. He made contacts in other military photo-interpretation intelligence units, and he was working on determining water depth measurements from aerial photography.

After the Pacific war ended in August 1945, Lundahl decided to stay in the navy as a civilian at the Photographic Intelligence Center in Anacostia. One of his former professors recommended him for a position as the head of the geology department at Beloit College in Wisconsin. Another recommended him to the Socony Vacuum Oil Company (now part of Exxon/Mobil) to lead their exploration in Venezuela. Lundahl also chose to remain in the naval reserve. In March 1946, after the navy converted its Naval Photographic Intelligence Center to a civilian and military staffing organization, Lundahl was honorably discharged as an officer and later that day reported to work as a civilian.

Operation Crossroads

The first task for this new organization was a unique event. In March 1946, the navy was pulled into the planning for the aerial photography for the world's first nuclear weapons effects test. A joint army-navy task force had decided to test two atomic weapons identical to the one dropped over Nagasaki. The first test, named Able, was to be exploded in the air over a lagoon and eighty-eight obsolete ships at Bikini Atoll in the Marshall Islands. The second test, named Baker, was to be exploded underwater in the lagoon. The army's planning for the aerial photography had begun the previous January, but the navy was not brought in until March. While both tests were designed to see the effects of the nuclear weapons on a fleet, the Army Air Force took on most of the planning for the aerial photography.

At the 1947 Conference of the American Society of Photogrammetry (ASP), Colonel Paul Cullen described the US Army Air Force's preparations, and Lundahl described the navy's preparations. The two descriptions, which were sequential at the conference, clearly pointed out the lack of coordination between the two services. Colonel Cullen contrasted the after-effect of both tests: "The impression of terrific unused force being expended in the upward surge of the cloud will always stay with me. The Able Day cloud had a beautiful, ethereal, though awesome, aspect. In contrast with this, the Baker Day explosion presented a dirty brutish upheaval. It looked like a steaming caldron. The impression of strength was still there; the beauty of form and color was gone. "

At the ASP conference, Lundahl was to introduce the navy's film titled "Operation Crossroads," which was released to the public. In his introduction, he described the efforts of the Naval Photographic Interpretation Center in the three months before the test. Lundahl also spoke about being on "a so-called composite panel," which reviewed the photography and provided expert advice to senior officials about what the photographs would reveal about the tests, and which photographs should not be released. Lundahl was proud of the results that the Naval Photographic Interpretation Center was able to achieve, but his language indicated that the environment was more competitive than cooperative. He said, "I am not bragging, and I am not trying to list the results for you, because I cannot, but I might say that that the results which were derived by the Naval Photographic Interpretation Center agreed very closely with the army and very closely with the results which were derived by other technical means that I am not at liberty to disclose. These results were placed in the hands of the technical director of Task Force One and have been used in their compilation of the final report."

Colonel Cullen, in his talk, also spoke of the challenges of photographing the test. He spoke of being unable to get a P-80 jet fighter for photographic purposes, and of getting a new photographic requirement three days before the Able test. He concluded that, "some of the studies are continuing while others are temporarily suspended for the want of personnel and funds." Colonel Cullen also spoke of the difficulty of getting the inter-service requirements defined, and mentioned that the services' work could have been better if they had been brought into the planning earlier. Operation Crossroads, Lundahl's first experience as a navy civilian with a joint task force, taught him how inter-service rivalry would impede and sometimes preclude getting optimal results. Lundahl's participation in Operation Crossroads taught him that even with critical national issues, inter-service rivalry would impede the requirements definition, create conflict over capabilities and roles, and diminish the effect of good intelligence. In his most important civilian work for the navy, he learned a lesson he never forgot about cooperation and coordination. From his description of his contributions, it is clear that Lundahl thought the results would have been better if the services were cooperating rather than competing for control. Even though the Army Air Force was unable to get a jet fighter and resources to complete its work, it did not think of working jointly with the navy until very late in the planning.

Lundahl's post-war experiences in naval intelligence were not fulfilling. Personally, he was busy developing and promoting the tradecraft of photo-interpretation. The navy selected him to represent the service on a number of geographic, research, and intelligence committees and working groups. His participation on the Pentagon Research and Development committee on optics, the Arctic, and geodesy caused his reputation to grow beyond the military services into State, Interior, and the CIA. His scientific reputation in the photogrammetry community also grew as the navy selected him to attend national meetings on this subject

Through his weekend navy reserve duty, Lundahl also made many more contacts and developed his reputation. He traveled to New York and Chicago to speak to military groups about the intelligence value of photo-interpretation. His briefing and writings increased his reputation in the academic community, particularly through his work with the American Photogrammetry Society, where he started the committee on photo-interpretation. In 1948, the navy selected him to attend the first postwar International Photogrammetry course in Europe, in Zurich, Switzerland. There, Lundahl was one of dozens of students from more than twenty countries, including some behind the Iron Curtain. From this experience, he learned the current state of technology, research, and national capabilities in the world photogrammetric community. Some of the relationships he made in Zurich were to be helpful later. In 1951, on his return to the United States, he shared his knowledge inside the government, and with the ASP outside the government. Lundahl's continuing professional accomplishments were doubly recognized when the navy selected him to attend the Commonwealth aerial photo exhibition, and the American Society for Photogrammetry selected him as the publications editor for *Photogrammetric Engineering*, its professional journal.

While Lundahl was becoming widely known throughout the US government, academia, and in the international aerial photography community, he learned, to his dismay, how little the navy was investing in photographic intelligence. His immediate boss, his former commanding officer in Alaska, not a gifted speaker or writer, could not persuade the navy to invest in photo-intelligence. Consequently, in spite of Lundahl's efforts, the Naval Photographic Intelligence Center was put into the Bureau of Aeronautics. The Bureau of Aeronautics focused nearly exclusively on naval aviation, so this move did not bode well for the future investment in aerial photography. Photo-interpretation would never be a navy priority, and Lundahl recognized that no matter how good his personal reputation was, he would continually struggle for resources. At the beginning of the Korean War in 1950, the navy had the best organization, and it had restored its photo-interpretation faster than other services. However, Lundahl saw that it lacked the leadership, vision, and resources to realize the potential intelligence gains that he could envision from photo-interpretation. While the navy was reducing its photo-interpretation efforts, CIA was deciding to invest in photo-interpretation. It had become aware, mostly from Lundahl's talks of the potential benefits, of getting more intelligence from aerial photography, and the CIA began to recruit him. So, after much lobbying by CIA, as well as the air force and the navy, Arthur Lundahl joined CIA on May 11, 1953.

Working Out of a Briefcase

After his December 1954 meeting with Dulles and Bissell about the U-2, Lundahl was, in his own words, "working almost out of a briefcase. He was flying across the United States and back, visiting the factories and laboratories where the camera, shutter, lenses, film, tools, and aircraft were being designed and built. The history of the rapid innovative development and the risky missions of the U-2 has been told frequently. The huge advances in aircraft technology were the best-known parts of the story. Under Kelly Johnson's leadership, and CIA program management, the Lockheed Skunk Works built a prototype in eighty-eight days and, in nine months, delivered twenty aircraft that could fly 20,000 feet higher than any other aircraft in the world. Lockheed was able to build the U-2 ahead of schedule and under budget because of its skilled workforce, unbureaucratic program management, and

President Dwight Eisenhower's willingness to be unconventional by letting the CIA manage the program against the wishes of the US Air Force.

In 1954, President Eisenhower had nearly no strategic, nuclear, or military intelligence on the Soviet Union, and he was willing to take large risks to obtain it. Since the attaché's discovery of the Bison bomber when it flew over the 1954 Soviet Aviation Day parade, the president had focused on the Soviet Union. At that time, no one in the US Intelligence Community could tell the president where these bombers were built, or how many had been produced, much less where they were deployed. Eisenhower, who had learned firsthand the worth of new technology in World War II, enlisted the finest scientific minds in America to advise him. The Technological Capabilities Panel included two of the most innovative scientific researchers in photography and optics, Edwin Land, who developed the Polaroid Camera with self-developing film, and James Baker, who pioneered the use of the computer in designing and creating lenses. Land's advocacy of the U-2 design was instrumental in Eisenhower's decision, but it was James Baker's work that was essential to the success of the new U-2 cameras.

James Baker had been designing lenses and cameras for aerial photography since the mid-1940s. By the early 1950s, aerial photography cameras had a resolution of about twenty-five lines per millimeter (mm). (Resolution is the ability to distinguish objects of a certain size on an image or photograph.) This limited the magnification of the film. To meet the altitude requirements of the U-2, the cameras would need much better resolution, which meant an increase in the focal length of the camera. But the diameter of the U-2 fuselage limited the potential focal length of the camera. Baker used the IBM CPC computer at Boston University, with its 2,174 calculations per minute, to design an improved lens. With this approach, he was able to increase the resolution of the first camera he designed to sixty lines per mm. In his second design, completed before the U-2 went operational, he achieved one hundred lines of resolution per mm. This enabled the camera to achieve a ground resolution of less than twelve feet from an operational altitude of 68,000 feet. Baker's new camera would detect any object larger than twelve feet, from nearly thirteen miles away.

Baker's camera design also addressed the critical issues of size, weight, and stability. Weight mattered, as every pound of camera weight limited the amount of film that the aircraft could carry. The stability issue came from moving the weight of thousands of feet of film through the camera. That film movement would, at the high altitude, affect the trim and stability of the aircraft. Instability introduced vibration into the camera, and vibration ruined the photographs. The technological problems of focal length, vibration, weight, and film load that Baker and the other engineers and scientists at Perkin-Elmer faced remained challenging for the next thirty years of film-based strategic reconnaissance.

While the U-2 testing and production were ongoing, President Eisenhower attempted to begin a dialogue with the Soviet Union. Acutely aware of the risk inherent in each country's ignorance of the other's strategic intentions and capabilities, President Eisenhower agreed to meet the Soviet leaders in July 1955 as part of the Big Four (United States, Great Britain, France, and USSR) conference in Geneva. The president did not wish to attend without a proposal so, to address the superpowers' lack of knowledge about each other; he proposed a treaty agreement to allow open aerial reconnaissance over each other's military facilities. President Eisenhower could make this proposal confidently as, if it was accepted by the Soviet Union, the United States and the Western powers would be more informed about the Soviet capabilities. Even if the Soviet Union rejected the proposal, Eisenhower went to Geneva, knowing in advance, that the U-2 program would enable him to see the Soviet secrets.

Nikita Khrushchev, whose first Western appearance was at Geneva, vetoed Eisenhower's Open Skies proposal instantly. In the next five years, the West would learn why, but on that rainy Wednesday afternoon of July 20th, there was no real news story from the Four Powers meeting in Geneva. Lack of news about a diplomatic breakthrough meant that the waiting journalists and couriers outside the League of Nations buildings didn't have any stories or photos to courier to the only photofax machine in Geneva. So an American college student from California, Rae Huffstutler, working in Geneva in the summer of 1955 as a motorcycle courier, did not have to drive across town that rainy afternoon.

While the president was attempting his diplomatic initiative, a third revolutionary development was underway in Washington. This did not involve a new aircraft or improved cameras. It was an organizational redesign that would last longer than the revolutionary technology. While Arthur Lundahl was involved with and reviewing the work of James Baker and Kelly Johnson in 1955 and 1956, he was also creating a unique organization to take the film product of their technology and turn it into strategic intelligence.

Seeing the Soviet Union First

Lundahl's design for an enlarged Photographic Intelligence Division grew out of his wartime and postwar photo-interpretation experiences, and his belief in how this tradecraft could penetrate the Iron Curtain. Before anyone else, he knew the potential for aerial photography to see the Soviet secrets. And, he also knew, from his Operation Crossroads experience, how the inter-service rivalry could limit the effectiveness of this source of information.

To preclude the rivalry, Lundahl designed an organization with joint staffing and management. While CIA would provide support, administration, security, and cover; the staffing would be blended among CIA and all of the military services. More importantly and progressively, all participants would share in the management of the operation.

Lundahl had seen rivalries limit the possibility and utility of good intelligence, even in critical nuclear tests. In his post-war experiences, he had seen how each of the military services used its own priorities to reduce its aerial photographic capability. Their collective reduction meant that, at the start of the Korean War, the US had a shortage of trained photo-interpreters. In particular, the air force did not address the national need for reconnaissance over the Soviet Union. US ignorance of the Soviet Union and its strategic capability was a national priority, and Lundahl envisioned a photo-interpretation center that would solve this problem. By keeping a national focus, this organization would also be able to support each service and to diminish the rivalry among the services and CIA.

Lundahl designed his new organization, even when it only had thirteen people, to become a national center. From the beginning, he insisted on joint staffing, and he overcame resistance from both CIA and the air force to make this happen. From his knowledge of photo-interpretation and his awareness of the capability of the U-2, he knew how much potential information would come from his center, and how valuable it would be to many parts of the US government, including all military services. From the onset, he focused on meeting all the service obligations for information, rather than issues of ownership. He was able to do this because he was aware of the president's interest;

he had CIA support; and he knew more about this tradecraft than anyone else in the US government. He knew that U-2 photographic information would have to be treated as TOP SECRET, with high security, and he insisted that his workforce and the intelligence it created be subject to the demands of CIA security, including special handling for the information, and polygraphs for the people. The special handling channel was called TALENT.

Before the first U-2 overflight, Lundahl personally made most of the recommendations for the organization, its specialized equipment, and the people it should hire. As he likely knew more about photo-interpretation than anyone else in the United States, he was able to do this with nearly total autonomy. But autonomy meant work. Lundahl was solely responsible for writing the hiring requirements, position descriptions, technical specifications, organizational tables, and budgets. He also advised on the security, logistics, infrastructure, hiring selections, information policy, and operations concepts. He even identified the water, electrical, size, and ventilation requirements for the facility. Because he knew the capabilities of foreign technology, especially when it was demonstrably better than American equipment, he personally wrote the justifications to obtain it, instead of American technology. The initial stereoscopes were from Wild in Switzerland, and the computer he purchased, the first in CIA, was an ALWAC II, from Sweden.

Lundahl received much CIA support, even though most of its people were not then cleared for the U-2. The Agency rented a 50,000 square foot facility, which he needed for the equipment, the photo-interpreters, their support materials, film storage, the required technology, and photo lab. This decrepit facility was on the top four floors of the Steuart Motor Building, a Ford dealership, at 5th and K streets, in a run-down area of northwest D.C. Between the decrepit working conditions inside the building, and the more decrepit neighborhood outside the building, it was a perfect cover location. It was also auspicious for another reason. One of the tenants on the lower floors was the original Toys R'Us store.

CIA provided Lundahl's organization with sixty support positions from its reference organization, and seventy additional positions for a total of ninety photo-interpreters. CIA gave Lundahl complete autonomy in selection for these positions. In his reminiscences, Lundahl praised the quality of the people that CIA sent to him initially. But he also spoke about how CIA tried to control the operation exclusively, and how he had to persuade them to work jointly with DoD and to share reporting responsibility and authority. Lundahl's knowledge of the photo-interpretation communities, both military and academic, enabled him to fill positions with talented men from the navy, the Army Map Service, air force intelligence, and the demographic branch of the Library of Congress. As so much of this program was new, it would require energy and initiative. So, he selected many young men for this group, with one exception, Alice Davy Sheldon, a CIA photo-interpreter whose work Lundahl had admired since her postwar study of World War II German photo-interpretation. Lundahl hired other women, but only in support positions.

During 1955 and the early months of 1956, Lundahl was briefing his new organization to army, navy, and air force intelligence organizations. From the onset, he was open about his intention to have a jointly managed organization with shared responsibilities. After his briefings, the army committed ninety photo-interpreters and support personnel, and the navy committed ten to twelve photo-interpreters, but the air force did not send any. It did send a few liaison officers, but their initial unwillingness to cooperate with reporting, dissemination, and security procedures would be troublesome. The trust and reciprocity displayed by the other military services was not initially matched by the air force, which thought that all reconnaissance ought to be under its control. Not all the promised positions had been filled when the U-2 first became operational, but the people arrived shortly afterwards.

Lundahl designed PID to have shared management and leadership. In the planning and training for the U-2 missions, before the first Soviet overflight, he stipulated that all missions would be worked by joint teams with members from each organization. Each successive U-2 mission would be led by a team member from a different organization who would be in charge of the exploitation and initial reporting for the entire mission.

Lundahl's vision of the potential value of the U-2 information to many government agencies and services, and the need to share to meet national needs, caused him to take a participatory approach to management. His initial concept of a national center, with shared management of the operation worked very effectively. Although his organization held only about sixty people when the U-2 missions started, it would become influential very quickly.

CHAPTER 3

THE MOST VALUABLE SLUM PROPERTY IN AMERICA

In spring of 1956, before the Steuart Building was ready for occupancy, training missions started for the mission planners, the U-2 pilots, the film developer, and the photo-interpreters. Even on the training missions, Lundahl rotated responsibility for managing the missions among the services and CIA. All received equal responsibility; none were given primacy. From this start, with training missions that photographed US military facilities, his organization built cooperative processes. From its earliest days as the Photographic Interpretation Division (PID), Lundahl's organization effectively combined people from CIA and all branches of the military (PID became PIC in August 1958 and PIC became NPIC in January 1961).

Outside the Steuart Building, winos often slept in the vestibules; muggings and other street crimes were common. There was no dedicated parking so carpooling was encouraged, but riders often had to clear broken glass from neighborhood parking spaces. Inside the Steuart Building, working conditions were rudimentary—no cafeteria, no amenities, and no air conditioning except for window units in rooms with sensitive mensuration equipment. The building smelled from the chemicals used to develop the photographs, and there were no environmental or air handling devices. The gallons of fixer and developer were dumped down the drains. It was a great cover location as, to all outward appearances, little of value would be going on in such a decrepit slum building in this bad neighborhood. Nearby were a diner where neighborhood policemen ate, and a market where Steuart Building workers could get coffee and food in the morning. Carpooling was necessary, but from the beginning, it presented a managerial challenge when priority missions forced carpool riders to stay late. Culture was a word not heard or used much in the neighborhood where photo-interpretation started to develop into imagery analysis. Run-down was a much more accurate and common adjective. But part of the way Lundahl's employees dealt with the Steuart Building was communal. They commuted together, worked together, waited for missions together, celebrated together, and shared the whole experience.

Inside the Steuart building, the other challenge was logistical. As nearly everything about the U-2 program was new, nearly all the equipment in the Steuart Building had to be either created or modified. Much of the equipment, tools, and storage had to be built from scratch. And, because so few people were cleared into Lundahl's organization, self-reliance became a fundamental part of its problem-solving culture. Because of the strict secrecy and security, there was little reaching outside for assistance. Anything would be considered, tried, or changed to accelerate or simplify getting information and intelligence from the film to the customers. The eventual inclusion of a model shop in 1964, and later a machine shop, helped this process. While these shops were intended to repair equipment and to make products for use in briefing customers, photo-interpreters and support people would frequently have an idea and use one of these shops to make a prototype. Over the years, Lundahl's workforce would generate many innovations, such as additional light sources for the light tables, motorized cranks for the roll film, dark-toned glare diffusers for the scopes, and Polaroid microscopes. The equipment manufacturers eventually adopted many of these prototypes.

Art Lundahl led the technology procurement for his new organization. Lundahl's original vision—a metaphor for the center—was the automat. In the CIA cable traffic system AUTOMAT became the identifier address for Lundahl's organization. But for him it was not simply a catchy slogan. In all his briefings to the military services and the Intelligence Community, Lundahl inserted a phrase that described his operating concept. He envisioned the operation of the national center as a "service of common concern" for the federal government, open twenty-four hours a day to all who were cleared, and he instilled this service mindset into his organization.

Neutrality About Collection

Lundahl recognized that while he could control the output of photo intelligence, he would have to keep his organization neutral about the collection of this information. Among the military services and the Intelligence Community the competition was fierce for which areas and targets to photograph. The scarcity of the U-2 photography created a great demand. Lundahl took measures to separate his organization from the collection and prioritization process. He advocated creating a staff that would adjudicate collection requirements outside his organization. He participated in the creation of the ARC, the AdHoc Requirements Committee, later renamed the Committee on Requirements (COMOR), to adjudicate requests for collection. So little was known about the Soviet Union that the Intelligence Community formed this committee to manage this shortcoming. Lundahl's insisted on being neutral about collection because so much was unknown about the USSR, and he sensed that his organization would likely be providing the preponderance of information about an area or a target. Because he correctly intuited that his organization's reporting would have a great deal of influence, he knew that staying out of the collection conflicts would help his organization maintain credibility. As well as being neutral about what would be photographed, Lundahl also did not want to merely be a "photo lab" for the rest of the Intelligence Community. From the onset, he was content to let Eastman Kodak do the photo processing.

The Highest Possible Approval Authority

Jim Reber chaired the Ad-hoc Requirements Committee. The military services, CIA, and the rest of the Intelligence Community nominated targets to be photographed, and the chairman of the committee adjudicated each request, ranked the critical priorities, and decided which targets would be collected on which mission. This information would be used to determine the flight track of each mission. In the U-2 program, these criteria were based on whether a target was important enough to be collected if there were to be no more U-2 missions over the Soviet Union.

As an indication of the risks, no U-2 mission flew without the President Eisenhower's approval. Before each mission the president was briefed about which part of the Soviet Union would be overflown. The risk of a shootdown was part of every mission, and the Intelligence Community wanted to be sure that if there were a shootdown, the most critical targets would already have been photographed. And President Eisenhower wanted to be sure that the political and national risks had been mimimized, as he knew that each mission could be interpreted as an act of war.

In the spring of 1956, with the U-2 program ready, Richard Bissell petitioned President Eisenhower for permission to overfly the Soviet Union. The first U-2 detachment deployed to West Germany in April. June and July were considered the best possible weather for collection, and Eisenhower approved the first mission on June 20, 1956.

Proof of TALENT

Over the next thirty days, the first eight of the twenty-four U-2 penetration overflights of the Soviet Union and the Warsaw Pact countries took place. From the first overflights there were two important developments. One was promising in that the film quality was good; the other was threatening. As soon as the U-2 crossed into Eastern Europe, Soviet air defense radars detected and tracked it.

Between 20 June and the middle of July, film from the eight missions was flown back to the United States, processed and duplicated in Rochester, New York, and delivered to the Steuart Building. These eight deliveries challenged Lundahl's organization in that the Steuart Building was not fully ready for operations until 9 July.

Of the eight missions at the start of the U-2 program, the first three covered Warsaw Pact countries—East Germany, Poland, Czechoslovakia, Hungary, Bulgaria, and Romania. These missions provided much useful intelligence that was melded with other sources of information, called collateral information by the photo-interpreters, about these countries. Lundahl's researchers in PID had gathered refugee reports, railroad schedules, World War II German aerial photography, and other sources of information about these countries and the Soviet Union. But the most significant strategic intelligence came from the five 1956 overflights of the Soviet Union between the 4th and 10th of July.

These five overflights answered President Eisenhower's questions about the number of Soviet bombers. They also reduced critical information gaps in our understanding of Soviet nuclear testing locations, missile development facilities, and submarine construction facilities. The film clearly showed all of these targets, and it also showed MiG-15 and MiG-17 fighter planes trying to shoot the U-2 down. The Soviet Union sent a note of protest to the United States that arrived on 10 July; and that note ended the first series of overflights.

The successful Soviet radar tracking of the U-2 flight paths from the outset of the program heightened US awareness of the risks. This unexpected vulnerability accelerated thinking about other ways to collect intelligence over the Soviet Union. These risks also increased the pressure on Lundahl's photo-interpreters. Their response to the early missions created an essential element in the NPIC culture.

When the U-2 completed a mission, its film was transferred to fighter planes and flown as quickly as possible to the United States for processing. If a crisis was underway or a time-sensitive critical question was pending, as was the case with the early missions, teams of Lundahl's photo-interpreters often were sent to Rochester, to scan the imagery as quickly as possible and to report telephonically. When the film arrived at the Steuart Building a short time later, photo interpreters worked around the clock until all of the film had been reviewed. From the first overflight in June 1956, overtime work was constant. The photo-interpreters worked sequentially, and this work pattern shaped the process, practices, and culture of Lundahl's organization from those early days and throughout NPIC's entire history.

The first order of business was a quick review of the new mission, called first-phase analysis. Most first-phase photo exploitation looked for changes at known targets or for new discoveries related to known intelligence gaps. In the early missions, very few targets were known. Once the first look was completed, the interpreters undertook a slower, more in-depth look at the "known" targets they were updating, or at any new targets found during the quick scan. This more in-depth work was called second-phase analysis. During this "phase" the photo-interpreters wrote up reports about the most significant changes to known targets, and started new write-ups about intelligence "finds."

After the second phase effort was completed, the routine re-looking or general search started. This effort often led to additional discoveries. With the scarcity of information about the Soviet Union, particularly east of the Ural Mountains, finds were plentiful.

General accountable search was the extensive locating, categorizing, and indexing of all targets found when photo-interpreters scanned the coverage of denied areas for any object or activity with possible strategic or military value. In the earliest missions in 1956, the photo-interpreters saw areas that had last been looked at, if at all, by German photo-interpreters during World War II, fourteen years earlier. Searching all the film, while not necessarily as focused a process as first-phase analysis, often turned out to be more important. In the 1950s, 1960s, and early 1970s, so little was known about what was present in the Soviet Union. (This later proved to be the same for China.) For this search process to be effective, photo-interpreters had to be briefed in advance on what little was already known about a specific geographic area.

The significant installations found during the search became targets and were assigned unique numbers. The earliest missions contained hundreds of finds. The equipment at these targets—to the degree that it could be identified—was described, counted, and named. The targets that could not be defined or identified absolutely were called "enigmas," and studied on successive coverages until their function could be defined. All these installations, objects, and "enigmas" were accounted for in a database.

All of these "phases" relied on analysts who were gifted in the "art" of photo-interpretation. However, those most capable of the "find" or discovering the "new," distinguished themselves as the best. These "best" photo-interpreters combined traits of trained observation; visual acuity; a spatial awareness; practiced memory; a specialized knowledge of either a region of the world or of a strategic manufacturing or military process; and an ability to "construct" a military organization from the number and types of equipment, or patterns of billeting. And, the best had a fierce curiosity.

Intellectual preparation and visual acuity were not enough to succeed. Photo-interpreters were required to make the "call," often with images partially obscured by clouds, haze, or shadows. It was not enough to report a vague "find." The interpreter was expected to identify, as best as possible, the observed equipment or activity. So the art of qualification, or how much certainty could be attached to a "find," became important. And after the find, the support people brought their skills to assist the interpreter.

Photogrammatists and mathematicians were brought in to take measurements from the images. Geographers helped determine the precise location and elevation of new targets. Indexers put the target, now with a unique indicator called a BE (bombing encyclopedia) number, into a database. Secretaries typed up the photo-interpreters' notes, and collateral researchers helped them find additional information about either the target's region, or other facilities that shared similar features with the new targets. Editors clarified the reports; photo lab personnel made and enlarged photographs; and graphic artists annotated briefing boards, mosaicked images together, and made three-dimensional drawings of the photo-interpreters' finds. The print shop printed and duplicated copies of their reports. The registry logged, traced, and transported reports to customers in the Intelligence Community. Because the aircraft and later the satellite photographic collections were so highly classified, all these functions remained at NPIC throughout its history, and the criticality of good support never diminished. Until all of the intelligence had been gleaned from a mission, all this work would go on seven days a week, twenty-four hours a day.

From its earliest days, PID and then NPIC, relied on its own staff to research other sources of information—called collateral information—to learn everything available about the areas the photo-interpreters anticipated they would be looking at.

When the U-2 program was being planned, CIA supplied most of Lundahl's research staff. From its earliest days, Lundahl's organization had about three support people for each photo-interpreter. These researchers would often reach out to the Library of Congress, academia, industry, or to other countries for any additional information. The United States and its allies had known that the USSR had moved a great part of its military infrastructure east of the Urals in the late 1930s and during the early part of World War II. More than 1,500 factories were relocated. While the fact of the massive relocation was known, the exact location of each of these individual industrial facilities still needed to be found. More importantly, the newer nuclear and missile-related locations also needed to be found.

After the initial eight missions, the U-2 missions over Russia were suspended on account of events in Egypt and Hungary. In late July 1956, the Egyptian leader, Gamal Abdel Nassar, seized the Suez Canal, then under the control of the British and French. U-2 missions were flown over the eastern Mediterranean in August to assess the British and French military preparations. A second detachment of U-2 aircraft was deployed in Turkey in September 1956. It also was used to monitor the British and French troop buildup until 29 October 1956, when the U-2s were used to monitor the activity during ten-day war between Egypt and Israel.

The second event was the October 1956 Hungarian revolution. The U-2 did not overfly Hungary, but Soviet actions there increased the Intelligence Community's need to know more about the Soviet military, in particular its nuclear forces. In the middle of these two world events, Richard Bissell again petitioned President Eisenhower for permission to overfly the USSR. Bissell did not get permission until after the two conflicts were over. The reaction of the West to these two conflicts increased tensions between the USSR and the western powers. Inside the US, President Eisenhower was reelected in November, and Bissell did not receive permission to resume overflights until after the election.

After the US presidential elections in late 1956, President Eisenhower approved only three missions over the periphery of the USSR. But in 1957, eleven missions were flown from Turkey and Pakistan that went deep into the USSR east of the Ural Mountains to photograph the nuclear- and missile-related targets. Three flights covered the missile test centers at Tyuratam (Baikonur) in Kazakhstan, Kapustin Yar, and Sary Shagan, as well as the nuclear test area at Semipalatinsk. Another two missions collected photos of the Chinese nuclear test area. These eleven missions kept Lundahl's photo-interpreters busy for more than a year.

These missions also presented the first real collection management challenge for the Intelligence Community. Strategic photography of the USSR was extremely scarce, but the Intelligence Community now had to decide whether it was more important to look for new, unknown targets, or to relook at newly discovered strategic targets.

The August 1957 missions provided the last significant gains in US intelligence about the Soviet strategic programs. They photographed the major missile and nuclear test facilities and the warhead impact area on the Kamchatka peninsula northwest of Japan. Once again, Soviet air defense radars detected all these flights, and the Soviet air force attempted unsuccessfully to intercept and shoot down every flight.

President Eisenhower's sensitivity about a U-2 shootdown reflected his awareness of public trust in American leadership, and of the public and international mistrust of aerial spying. Yet, the national need for accurate information and intelligence about the Soviet Union resulted in a number of secret initiatives other than U-2 overflights. Among these was an ineffective program to attach small, 35-millimeter cameras to balloons. The risk of public disclosure of the U-2 program was high, and growing with each overflight, but the United States had no other reliable source of hard intelligence about the Soviet Union. The United States' development of its own strategic weapons had an unintended effect that resulted in the development of an intelligence collection system that turned out to be as strategically valuable as the development of the actual weapons themselves.

Breakthrough in Space

By 1955, the United States had achieved the technical possibility of putting a thermonuclear warhead on a missile. As the propulsion requirements to launch a warhead from a rocket were nearly identical to those to launch a satellite into polar orbit, this made satellite photography technically possible. In October 1956, the plans for a photoreconnaissance satellite started, but the air force program was behind schedule by the end of 1957, and it became a subject of interest to the press that focused on what the government was attempting to launch into space. CIA was also studying the feasibility of space reconnaissance, but a presidential review board, in its look at the air force and CIA efforts, judged that neither program could be ready before mid-1959 at the earliest. After this study, the National Security Council requested a joint status report from the director of CIA and the secretary of defense.

Between December 1957 and March 1958, the White House secretly decided to have CIA and the air force jointly manage a new reconnaissance project called CORONA. Richard Bissell and his air force deputy from the U-2 program, Colonel Ritland, would manage this new satellite program. The program took the best developments from the previous programs, and increased its security by cancelling the public contracts of the existing programs, and reissued new, secret contracts restricted to many fewer people. Bissell also devised a cover that made the program appear like a series of missile launches for scientific discovery. To the public, the missiles would be known as the DISCOVERER series.

During this time, Lundahl's interpreters were still gleaning valuable intelligence from the August 1957 U-2 missions. President Eisenhower began to send Lundahl abroad to brief the photo intelligence to selected allies. In 1957, Lundahl travelled to Great Britain and West Germany to brief them about the new discoveries in the Soviet Union. Before his briefing to Konrad Adenauer, despite the significance of the photo-intelligence, Lundahl had to wait until the chancellor shared what he learned about the Soviet civil defense system on his recent trip to the USSR. Soviet civil defense was of great intelligence interest to the United States and the Allies who knew almost nothing about the Soviet emergency civil defense plans. The U-2 missions, although they made many discoveries, were only capable of photographing a small amount of the Soviet Union, and their focus on strategic and nuclear targets meant that civilian and less important military targets would remain undiscovered and unknown.

The Unknown Nuclear Disaster and Another Intelligence Gap

In September 1957, when Buddy Holly's "That'll be the Day" was number one, and *West Side Story* opened on Broadway, the world's first large-scale nuclear accident happened. On Sunday, September 29, 1957, an explosion occurred at a plutonium production facility at Kysthym, about sixty miles south of Sverdlovsk (Yekaterinburg). This accident would cause the most serious release of nuclear radiation until Chernobyl in 1986. The explosion at Kysthym threw a 160-ton concrete containment lid into the air. It released liquid radiation that formed a radioactive cloud that extended 185 to 220 miles to the northeast, and more than 10,000 people had to be evacuated. The accident forced the creation of the East Ural Containment area, an uninhabitable area larger than the state of Massachusetts. That area in the Urals remains contaminated today and will be for thousands of years to come. But, the USSR kept this secret both from its own population and the West. In 1958, western intelligence services began to learn from émigré reporting about the disaster. The United States was not able to locate or verify any evidence of the accident from any other source. Consequently, it added Kysthym to its list of U-2 targets to be photographed. But the potential damage to civilians was not considered as important as finding either Soviet missiles or strategic targets.

The sole 1958 overflight focused on the Soviet Far East. Lundahl's photo-interpreters looked along the Trans-Siberian railroad, but they did not find any deployed missile sites. However, they did find nuclear storage locations. The United States also learned that its new U-2 anti-radar devices were not effective, as the U-2s were still tracked by Soviet radars.

Tensions between the United States and the USSR increased when the US Air Force started a series of balloon overflights over the Warsaw Pact, and increased again when the Soviet Union and East Germany signed a peace treaty that prompted the 1958 Berlin Crisis. These tensions influenced President Eisenhower not to approve any more overflights until July 1959, sixteen months later. This 1959 flight over Tyuratam indicated that the Soviet Union was expanding its missile launch facilities there.

The expansion observed at Tyruatam increased the Intelligence Community's concern about Soviet missile developments, but other events had already increased public concern in the United States. Starting with the Sputnik I launch in 1957, Soviet missile launches and public statements—many later proven to be false—created the perception that the United States was far behind the USSR in developing missiles. The anxiety and fear surrounding this missile gap resembled the bomber gap of four years earlier. To make matters worse, in September 1959, the Soviet Luna rocket reached the moon shortly before Premier Khrushchev visited the United States. On this visit Khrushchev publically boasted of the Soviet Union's great progress in its missile programs, and he claimed to have 250 missiles with hydrogen weapons in their warheads. The public's concern about the missile gap grew, and the concern became a political issue in the bitterly contested 1960 US presidential elections.

Secretly, the CORONA satellite photography program was making rapid progress. By using launch technology developed from earlier programs, the delivery system was ready. Bissell's program worked with a number of contractors who made significant advances in stabilizing the camera; designing a recoverable capsule for the exposed film; inventing a process to recover film from space; building a camera light enough to be launched and to achieve orbit; good enough to photograph the earth at an interpretable resolution; resilient enough for a rocket launch; and carrying enough film to justify the expense of the missions. By January 1959, the first DISCOVERER was ready to launch.

But these great technical achievements could not get "off the ground." If they got off the ground, they would not work well enough. If they worked well enough, they would not return from space. From January 1959 through June 1960, thirteen launches were attempted, and thirteen consecutive launches failed. Rockets failed, signals failed, cameras failed, film failed, parachutes failed, timing failed, retro-rockets failed. Each failure meant another period of retrospective analysis, followed by another period of intense work and deadlines. Each failure increased the pressure, and each failure increased the program's budget overruns. Yet everyone involved—government and contractor—persisted, because the pressure of not knowing, and not wanting to believe that the United States might be behind the Soviet Union in developing ballistic missiles and nuclear weapons, kept everyone focused, motivated, and working extremely hard. Lundahl's interpreters were among those who continued to work extremely hard.

Even though there was not a great deal of new aerial photography over the USSR, three types of activities kept the interpreters busy. While they had already reported on the new facilities and equipment that they had seen, Lundahl's photo-interpreters had other questions to answer. Scouring all of the collected U-2 photography led them to new questions. So little was known about the Soviet Union and, despite the risks taken by U-2 pilots, so little had been seen that Lundahl's photo-interpreters were building lists of questions.

The photo-interpreters were interested in what they could not see. As they looked at the targets they "knew," they saw rail lines and roads that extended to the edge of the photographic coverage, but they did not know where they led. At times they saw new buildings, and sometimes they knew their function. But often they did not know, and they wanted to see them again to help them identify their function. Photo-interpreters also saw ground scarring, and they wondered what was changing at those locations. They saw objects that made no sense at all, and they wanted to have their curiosity sated. They taped clear plastic-like overlays onto copies of the film and marked them up with their questions. In the early days, they did not know when they would see these locations or facilities again. They kept their questions to themselves. But, based on what they had learned, they re-prioritized what they wanted to see again. Their reasons would be added to the lists of questions that other intelligence analysts had. All of these inputs would be ranked for planning the photographic collection on the next mission.

By the middle of 1960, the Intelligence Community and Lundahl's photo-interpreters had prioritized collection for a total of 148 Soviet targets or areas of interest in thirty-two categories of intelligence. The top priorities were ballistic missiles, heavy bombers, and nuclear energy targets. The list also contained the anti-ballistic missile targets, as well as the surface-to-air missile locations. But the next to last paragraph of a COMOR memorandum reflects the lack of hard information, even after four years of U-2 overflights: "Many targets on the list, however, are supported by relatively little firm evidence. They are included here because, as a basis of deductive reasoning, they appear to be the most likely of all known targets to bear upon missile deployment and other highest priority matters at this time. This means that the receipt by the Intelligence Community of a modest amount of firm evidence on a number of problems could cause us to add targets not on the list, or withdraw targets now carried. "

Many of the known targets were areas near rail lines or sites that had not yet been seen by the photo-interpreters. In July 1960, before the initial CORONA success, CIA estimated that about a quarter of the Soviet land-mass was deemed suitable for missile deployments and was in need of being photographed. The U-2 program had only been able to cover about thirteen percent of the suitable landmass. That percentage may seem very small, but it covers nearly the area of India. In the eight priority areas for search, about twenty-four percent of the total suitable area, the U-2 missions had covered less than four percent.

TALENT is Not Enough

By 1959, the U-2 missions over the Soviet Union were fewer and fewer. Only two penetration missions were flown during 1959. Both overflew the missile test range at Tyuratam (Baikonur) and both tried to photograph Kysthym but it was cloud-covered on both occasions. These missions were flown to get in-formation on the missile gap, and to ascertain the extent of the development of the Soviet ICBM program and its nuclear infrastructure. From signals intel-ligence and from radiation sensors, the United States was aware of Soviet test launches. Although it was aware of nuclear tests, it did not know if any of the weapons being tested were deployed, or where they might be deployed.

The uncertainty about the number and state of the Soviet missile pro-grams was being used by some in the US government and military to justify enlarging and accelerating their own weapons development programs. As a result, the Eisenhower administration wanted to get verifiable facts about the Soviet missile program.

The risk that had been building with each overflight since 1956 became public on 1 May 1960, when a U-2 was shot down over Sverdlovsk. Its pilot, Francis Gary Powers, was captured and put on trial for espionage by the USSR. This event outraged some members in Congress who had not been briefed on the existence of the U-2 program. On 9 May, Allen Dulles went to Congress, and he brought Arthur Lundahl to give a briefing on the U-2 program and the intelligence that it had provided to the United States. While many members of Congress initially were irate, by the time Lundahl finished his half-hour presentation, he received a standing ovation.

The U-2 shootdown also ended hopes for any diplomatic progress in the 15 May meeting in Paris between Premier Khrushchev and President Eisenhower. On 25 May, President Eisenhower went on network television to explain to the American people that he had authorized these overflights for reasons of national security.

KEYHOLE

While the American public wondered what the Soviet Union would do to the captured US pilot, the CORONA program counted down toward the start of space photography. Discover XII launched on June 29, 1960 and failed to reach orbit. But thirteen was the lucky number for the Discoverer program. On August 10, 1960, the first successful capsule recovery took place in the air north of Hawaii, when a C-119 aircraft caught the ejected capsule in mid-air. In space program terminology, the parachute held a "capsule." But, Lundahl's interpreters called the capsule a "bucket," for it provided them information by the bucketful. The New York Times put this story on the same front page that described the sentencing of the U-2 pilot to ten years in a Soviet prison.

Eight days later, on August 18, with the launch of Discoverer XIV, space reconnaissance began. Two days later, on August 20th, the film from this first photo satellite arrived at the Steuart Building. As Lundahl's photo-interpreters looked at it, they identified hundreds of new targets east of the Ural mountains, and hundreds more possible targets. These were locations or facilities that the interpreters suspected to be strategic or military, but for which images with better resolution would be needed to make precise or "confirmed" identifications. As one interpreter said, "You would look at the film and find an airfield that no one knew about, and a short distance away on the film, you would find a city that also was not on any map."

The area covered by the first CORONA mission was about fifteen percent of the Soviet Union, an area slightly larger than India. But with every mission, the total imaged area and the amount of interpretable imagery was never the same. Some areas were always covered by clouds. Some other areas, such as swamps, deserts, or inaccessible mountain terrain, were unsuitable for any activity. But the amount of clearly photographed terrain provided a large amount of work for the photo-interpreters. Satellite missions had to be worked in a number of ways, and each way had a different mental demand and intensity.

The most important observations from the first CORONA Mission, Mission 9009, were negative. What the photo-interpreters did not see on that mission mattered more than the targets they did see. The number of deployed strategic missile sites, especially the SS-6 intercontinental ballistic missiles, was the most critical question that the photo-interpreters were trying to answer. No new SS-6 sites were observed. The knowledge from that first mission began to close the "missile gap" in the Intelligence Community. But it did not end the public's perception and the political charges of US military and scientific weakness relative to the USSR. CORONA information was so precious that before the 1960 election, President Eisenhower did not share it with either candidate. In one of his last official acts, two days before the Kennedy inauguration, Eisenhower signed NSCID-8, which made Lundhal's organization into the National Photographic Interpretation Center. This action codified Lundahl's vision and validated his concept for how to provide this scarce information to all parts of the government that needed it.

Even with this intelligence success, the CORONA program continued to have difficulties. Three more missions failed in that year, and the next successful mission was not until December 11th, 1960.

The initial CORONA success provided a substitute for the U-2, yet it lacked some of the U-2's technical attributes. The initial and lasting attributes of CORONA were the amount of coverage it could take in one day, and its invulnerability from Soviet air defenses. Its first mission, on August 18, 1960, photographed more of the Soviet Union than all twenty-eight U-2 penetration missions from 1956 through 1960. On the film from that one day, photo-interpreters were able to find more targets, than all twenty-eight previous missions of the U-2. They discovered sixty-four new airfields and twenty-six new SAM sites in the Soviet Union. Initially, the satellite imagery resolution was far worse than the U-2. Photo-interpreters could resolve objects from one to two feet on a side (about the size of a microwave oven) with a good U-2 photo, but objects on the CORONA KH-1 imagery were resolvable from only twenty to forty feet on a side (about the size of a cottage or a house). But, the satellite could not be shot down.

The initial CORONA mission also created tension within the small community of photo-interpreters. The U-2 images, photographed from twelve to fourteen miles up, were much clearer and more interpretable than the early satellite images taken from seventy to one hundred miles in space. So NPIC's photo-interpreters learned to qualify their findings to what they could actually see and confirm. Qualification led to a continuous debate among interpreters about whether an observation contained enough detail for an object to be renamed from a possible, to a probable object; or from a probable, to a confirmed object. These decisions, partially objective and partially subjective, caused much internal reflection and debate, as well as some shouting.

Photo-interpreters had to combine their experience and their judgment against the varying interpretability of an image or series of images. Inevitably, because of the variable image quality, some calls would later be proven wrong after they obtained imagery with better interpretability. On the other hand, many of the "calls" would be confirmed or proven right. But the expectation for imagery photo-interpreters was the same as for baseball umpires—make the call, the quicker the better. This is not to say that photo-interpreters did not consult with each other, particularly when the call was difficult or the issue significant. But, photo-interpreters who hesitated to make a call were not respected by their peers.

Photo-interpreters at PIC, and later at NPIC, developed a unique kind of peer pressure. Good searchers were esteemed. "Finds" were celebrated; "misses" were dreaded. Yet, as the volume of imagery continued to increase, every photo-interpreter knew that he/she would eventually miss something and have their call corrected by another interpreter. The norm of getting the calls "right" weighed on the photo-interpreters. For those respected for their accuracy, they worried about the correction process. For those who were frequently corrected, the process was neither gentle nor private. Skill in the art of photo interpretation came to be valued more than prior military service, rank, education, or seniority. The blended workforce of CIA, army, navy, and air force photo-interpreters added to the pressure, in that all were aware of the others' skills and backgrounds. From the start, the peer pressure shaped the NPIC culture.

Arthur Lundahl had been a trained geographer, a mapmaker, and a photo-interpreter. He understood the profession as well as, if not better than his interpreters. In the 1930s, he had searched and made maps from low-resolution oblique imagery at the same latitudes as he asked PIC employees to search twenty years later. His experience interpreting aerial photography allowed him to understand their challenges very well. Through the 1950s and 1960s, the photointerpretation process was nearly all manual. Photo-interpreters carried 7X tube magnifier lenses, and they used rear-projection viewers, microscopes, and light tables. Photo-interpreters cranked rolls of film across the viewers and light tables by hand, and each roll of U-2 film was five hundred to six hundred feet long. Files about each target were built individually and idiosyncratically. Photo-interpreters built personal files of locational information and construction chronologies, often with incomplete understanding of what they were looking at. Most of this work was captured on paper and only some was typed into reports.

From the beginning, Lundahl's photo-interpreters worked knowing that, as they learned their targets and regions, their knowledge would shortly be challenged or changed by more and faster arriving information. From its earliest years, the sensitive and TOP SECRET environment of PIC necessitated a self-contained support infrastructure. This autonomous environment, where the interpreters' expectations were that they would have resources to solve their problems, shaped the culture in a number of ways.

It promoted insularity. New people were expected to prove themselves, no matter what they had done in the military, in academia, or in the Intelligence Community before joining PIC. As PIC's earliest employees were selected by the director, and the community of skilled photo-interpreters was small, selection to work at PIC was neither made, nor taken lightly. The small size of the organization and the critically important mission fostered a sense of elitism based on skill, and on the restricted access to highly classified information. It certainly was not based on status or working conditions.

Because the community was small, and the work was so highly classified, PIC and NPIC fostered a culture that valued problem solving and performance under stress. And it was not a culture that particularly valued rank or external acclaim. The immensity of the ignorance about the Soviet Union, and the unanswered questions that remained, fostered a culture of continual learning. With each U-2 and KH-4 mission, PIC and NPIC developed its culture of experts. (The photo-interpreters generally called the CORONA missions by the shortened form of the name of their reporting channel—Keyhole. As the early camera models changed from KH (KEYHOLE) 1 through 4, the photo-interpreters referred to individual mission numbers and the collective program as KH-4.)

In the early days, when information about the denied areas was scarce, anyone who could add to that information, and who could help photo-interpreters was appreciated. PIC valued those who could help build its expertise, and who could perform in stressful environments any hour of day or night. Intelligence was expected, even if an individual lacked academic credentials. Where they went to school mattered far less than knowing what they were looking at and knowing the tradecraft. If an interpreter knew what he or she was talking about and could perform when it mattered, under the deadline of a new mission, he or she would be accepted.

For those who supported photo-interpreters, the "save" was valued nearly as much as the "find." Many times support people would find a small error, like transposed coordinates, switched place names, misspellings, inverted images, and misplaced annotations. When these were caught and brought to the photo-interpreters' attention, support's help was really valued.

The autonomous, performance-based culture placed great value on reputation. Although a person who could make "finds" or catches, was valued, the ability to work at a number of tasks and pitch in was equally valued. Photo-interpreters cut their own film, annotated their own maps, and did their own filing. The work environment also reinforced the PIC and NPIC cultures. Before NPIC moved out of the Steuart Building at the beginning of 1963, PIC/NPIC had worked more than 300,000 hours of overtime over six and a half years in that decrepit building. Considering that fewer than one hundred people worked at PID at its beginning in July 1956, and fewer than four hundred worked there at the end of 1963 after it had become NPIC, the amount of overtime—more than 150 work-years—indicates how hard and long this small group of people worked. The episodic nature of mission planning, photo processing, and film delivery meant that some number of photo-interpreters worked every hour of every day. And it meant that some had to come to work at odd hours, but it also meant that there would be slack time.

Reputations—both good and bad—were built and recognized quickly. Idiosyncrasies and eccentricities were tolerated if someone could read out film. And tolerance shrank if someone could not perform. Both photo-interpreters and support people learned to protect their reputation and their credibility.

This work environment led to a high social value on predictability and accountability. Nearly everyone felt a strong sense of not letting down the mission or each other. Peer pressure came with the PIC/NPIC badge. If someone had trouble keeping up or could not perform, this pressure worked against them. While it was generally not personalized, it was unavoidable. The pressure was identical for interpreters and support people. This atmosphere was stressful, and photo-interpreters in particular, from the beginning indulged in some creative ways to deal with the stress. For as hard and as long as they worked, they frequently played as hard and not always in healthy ways. Athletic leagues were present from the beginning. They started with softball and soon spread to football, basketball, bowling, and volleyball. And, after the games, many of the teams either drank in the parking lots or went to bars.

With film return systems, there was a built-in lag because of the sporadic mission scheduling and the time between the end of the film collection and the film delivery. Because of the time needed to recover and process spools of film from the aircraft or satellites, and to chemically process the film-based imagery, the photo-interpreters would wait multiple days to get at the most current imagery. And after that was received, scanned, and exploited, another interval of "down time" occurred before the next mission.

Stories

From the earliest mission, photo-interpreters would talk among themselves about what they "saw" on the imagery. These discussions or "stories" served as a way of teaching other interpreters about what they had seen, but had not written in their cables or reports. These branch "stories" also were used to bring the branch up to date before a new mission, and to keep track of the puzzles, enigmas, and observations that could not yet be put into context. The collective story was the sum of the "databases" that existed in the interpreters' heads.

Stories would persist as an informal information management system as these stories were a better and more accessible method than any paper database.

The lag time between the processed buckets of film provided interpreters a hiatus to do in-depth research. But some, generally the better interpreters, would make better use of the interval. For others, the cycle of stress and excitement resulted in a strong need to unwind. When the film began to come from satellites in addition to aircraft, the lag time remained, but the work changed.

The public's outcry and the Soviet trial of Francis Gary Powers after the U-2 shoot down brought much attention to the administration's policy toward the USSR, the U-2 spy plane, and the pilot. Over the summer of 1960, the subsequent trial, conviction, and sentencing of Francis Gary Powers, brought much attention to the US aerial reconnaissance program and to the administration, but PIC did not receive any publicity.

Inside the Steuart Building, even though the most important intelligence question was being answered, the overtime continued. The search for new developments at known strategic installations became the new focus. Some photo-interpreters studied the medium range ballistic missile (MRBM) or intercontinental ballistic missile (ICBM) systems in great detail. Others focused their attention on the missile test centers at Tyuratam, Kapustin Yar, Plesetsk, or Sary Shagan. This detailed analysis involved looking for often-minute differences from previous observations. Additionally, the photo-interpreters were tracking new and suspected construction sites.

Two databases generally aided photo-interpreters in this work. One was the written record of significant observations about targets previously recorded for the larger audience of intelligence analysts who did not have the clearance to see the film. The other database, kept informally in the interpreters' heads, contained the branch "story." These were the incomplete, partial observations; partial clues or indications; and curiosities that could not be explained. Even in the 1950s and 1960s, it was impossible to capture in writing all that was seen on the imagery. And much of what was seen did not make complete sense on the first observation. The "good" interpreters retained visual information in their memories from previous looks at a target or from previous looks at other similar targets. When a photo-interpreter saw a certain pattern of changes or activity, other interpreters could recall whether or not they had seen this information. The ability to recall many "images" was a defining characteristic of the good photo-interpreters, and this unwritten database fed a third type of mission work.

After specific questions had been answered, the general or non-specific search took place. Interpreters looked at every inch of the film to see every part of the terrain that had been photographed rather than looking for a specific target or object. With so much new area to see, and so little known or mapped in the Soviet Union, this general search really amounted to having to catalogue all the observed man-made activity. Search created anxiety among interpreters. They feared that they would miss some activity that would later turn out to be strategic and important.

The general search mission took a tremendous amount of effort. It involved locating, identifying, naming, and tracking tens of thousands of facilities and installations that had the potential to be military or strategic facilities. When an area of clearing or ground scarring was observed, it would be followed until it could be proven that the activity was agricultural, logging, mining, or civilian in nature.

All these analytic activities were done as quickly as possible, but this effort required a large amount of overtime. The photo-interpreters and support people worked nights and weekends until the review of the mission was completed. By 1961, the areas of the USSR searched by Lundahl's photo-interpreters "proved" that there were no more deployed SS-6 missiles. They did find, however, hundreds of other new targets.

In 1961, the National Intelligence Estimate had a much-reduced number of Soviet ballistic missiles. The "missile gap" had been narrowed. Even though the air force continued to disagree with the findings of the NPIC's photo-interpreters, the rest of the Intelligence Community contributors agreed with the information found by NPIC photo-interpreters in the Steuart Building. NPIC provided facts about the Soviet missile force, and those facts greatly reduced planned weapons procurements, particularly by the air force.

The kind and volume of new information that CORONA provided to the Intelligence Community brought many senior visitors to the Steuart Building. It also brought increased dissemination requirements for many military exploitation centers. NPIC, as Lundahl's organization became known in January 1961, helped many of them with specialized equipment purchases in order to meet these increased requirements.

Lundahl's intelligence automat never closed, and its work kept increasing. His vision of a national center came into being in January 1961. While it started in a slum, NPIC enabled the United States to make national policy and defense procurement decisions from a basis in fact, rather than a basis in fear. This resulted in budget savings of enough money to make the Steuart building the most valuable slum property in America. Although NPIC focused so much time and attention on the Soviet Union, Lundahl's organization would make its most visible contribution to the Cold War during its last months in the Steuart building through its work on Cuba.

CHAPTER 4

CUBA—OPPORTUNITY WRAPPED IN CRISIS

While Lundahl's photo-interpreters focused mainly on the Soviet Union, they also started to look at Cuba, a client of the Soviet Union. The Eisenhower administration started U-2 overflights of Cuba in October 1960. These overflights were intended to assist the CIA with planning for the Bay of Pigs invasion, a disastrous attempt to start a revolt against the new Castro government.

The failed invasion resulted in the resignation and firing of two men instrumental in Arthur Lundahl's successes. Richard Bissell, who had managed the U-2 and CORONA programs, resigned after the invasion; President Kennedy fired Allen Dulles, the director of Central Intelligence. But Arthur Lundahl and NPIC continued to build their reputations throughout 1961 and 1962.

The 1961 CORONA missions more than doubled the amount of information from the two successful 1960 launches. NPIC's reporting and analysis reduced the perception of the Soviet Union having vastly more Intercontinental Ballistic Missiles than the United States. The 1961 missions showed that the Soviets had constructed many more SS-4 medium range ballistic missiles (MRBM) than they had constructed SS-6 ICBM sites. The positive information about the SS-4 MRBMs and the negative information about the SS-6 ICBMs persuaded the new Kennedy administration about the increasing value of the KH-4 CORONA photography and Lundahl's interpreters.

With the exception of the émigré community in south Florida, most Americans were not paying attention to Cuba. In the fall of 1962, federal troops were sent to assist with the integration of the University of Mississippi, and the New York Mets were setting a record for most baseball games lost by a major league team. Johnny Carson was appearing on his first Tonight show, and the popular songs were 'Sherry' by the Four Seasons, and 'Sheila' by Tommy Roe.

The Cuba Missile Crisis in October 1962 was the most publicized event in NPIC's history. It has been the subject of at least a score of books, hundreds of articles, scores of television presentations, and at least one movie. But the daily grind of what went on in the Steuart Building on those days and nights from October through December—the time and effort invested in finding and breaking open an intelligence bombshell—is not as well known.

From August through the end of 1962, the efforts of the NPIC photo-interpreters proved the worth of Art Lundahl's vision. Their rapid observations and reporting demonstrated NPIC's ability to perform national-level strategic warning. The results of NPIC's analysis, shown for the first time on national television and at the United Nations, demonstrated NPIC's direct and unmistakable impact on a national security crisis. The intelligence successes in Cuba—identifying Soviet-supplied weapons systems—grew directly from the six years of effort and painstaking work on learning the makeup of the strategic forces and military organizations of the Soviet Union and the Warsaw Pact countries.

The strategic warning that NPIC photo-interpreters provided was the first intelligence success in Cuba. How NPIC worked during the thirteen days of the crisis, and what it accomplished over the two months after the Soviet decision to withdraw the missiles led to an outcome ultimately as significant as the discovery of the missiles.

Throughout 1962, military activity in Cuba had been increasing, and NPIC and other parts of the US Intelligence Community were tracking a number of Soviet military transport ships en route to Cuba. In any crisis, and this was rapidly becoming a national crisis, NPIC characteristically responded by surging some of its photo-interpreters from their usual accounts to the crisis area. It had done this for the Suez crisis in Egypt in 1956.

Because the equipment seen in Cuba was Soviet in origin, NPIC moved some photo-interpreters from working the Soviet Union to work U-2 missions over Cuba. But rather than surge, this was a more-permanent move. The work in Cuba combined looking for equipment in expected places, such as port facilities and military garrisons, and searching the entire island for signs of additional Soviet equipment. To get a sense of the scale of the task, Cuba is about the size of the state of Ohio, but the Soviet Union was a little more than two hundred times larger than Cuba.

In response to the DCI's concerns, President Kennedy authorized additional U-2 missions over Cuba. As a result, in August 1962, NPIC increased its efforts, and NPIC photo-interpreters saw a significant amount of military equipment. On August 30th, NPIC's photo-interpreters saw an SA-2 surface-to-air missile—the same kind of missile that in May 1960 had shot down the U-2 over the Soviet Union. This discovery had two immediate ramifications. One was additional risk to American pilots, as this air defense system was clearly capable of shooting down a U-2. The other was increased suspicion among the photo-interpreters. This advanced air defense system was likely protecting some strategic target, and they did not know what or where that strategic target was. To compound the risk, on 9 September, a U-2 flying over Communist China with a Taiwanese pilot was shot down by an SA-2. In response to this event, the United States ceased U-2 overflights of Cuba. Even though NPIC had discovered the SA-2 in Cuba, and requested more coverage, the president ordered a stand-down on Cuban overflights.

But the CIA all-source analysts did not share the suspicions of the NPIC photo-interpreters. At the direction of the DCI, they published a Special National Intelligence Estimate (SNIE) on 19 September. This assessment, coordinated throughout the Intelligence Community, did not support the judgment that the Soviet Union would deploy strategic missiles in Cuba. The day after the completion of the SNIE, John McCone, the DCI, dissented with this estimate, even though it reflected the thinking of his own all-source analysts. As a result, the combination of the lack of current information about what was happening on the island, and the DCI's concern about Soviet intentions caused the president to change his mind. He ordered U-2 flights over Cuba to resume on October 4th.

The SA-2 find in August ensured that NPIC photo-interpreters would pay extra attention to Cuban air defenses. The diligence with which they tackled those concerns influenced how they organized their work, and how they made a number of decisions in the process of their analysis over the next few days.

NPIC managers learned late in the previous week that a U-2 mission over Cuba would be flown on Sunday, October 14. They rapidly organized their photo-interpreters into teams to look at the film from this mission. Some teams would look at the specific point targets for new activity where previous military construction had been seen. Other teams would search all the imagery for new activity. But, early on Monday October 15th, when the developed U-2 film was delivered to the Steuart Building from the Navy Photographic lab in Suitland, the first priority was not deployed military units, or construction sites, or search. It was air defense. So, when the Cuba film arrived at the Steuart Building, the air defense team looked at the film first.

This was the first U-2 flown over Cuba in more than forty days. Flying manned reconnaissance missions was and is risky. Pilot safety made discovering the status of Cuban air defenses NPIC's first priority. For good aerial photography the flight paths are straight and level. Unfortunately, as these aircraft were unarmed, straight and level made it easy to track them on radars. When this particular mission came in, it was initially thought that because the aircraft flew a short track, across rather than along the island, it would be easier to get through all the film that day. Some of the Cuba team and some of their managers came in with their carpools and brought their lunches thinking that it would be an ordinary day. They were mistaken.

On the backup missile team, the four photo-interpreters: Dick Rininger, Vince DiRenzo, Joe Sullivan, and Jim Holmes were assigned to look for air defense equipment in the mountainous areas and farm country in central Cuba. Their effort took most of Monday. Air defense equipment was generally located to protect important equipment or sites of importance, and the presence of new air defense equipment was considered an indicator of other significant activity.

When the photo-interpreters found long canvas-covered cylindrical objects along the edge of a field, their concerns changed. Initially they did not know what these objects were. They also saw a large number of military trucks and transport vehicles. So, to accomplish their analysis more quickly, the team divided the work. One made rough measurements, while another looked at equipment keys and at earlier imagery to determine if they could identify precisely what they were seeing. A third looked at the last imagery collection of the area to see if any of the equipment had been there before. This process, called negation, helped determine the schedule and sequence of the interpreters' activity. The four photo-interpreters also talked to the Soviet ballistic missile experts to have them look at the equipment to get their opinions. The team also called in a photogrammatist to check their measurements. The four photo-interpreters then told their manager, Earl Shoemaker, that they thought that they found something important, and that they better tell Mr. Lundahl.

Art Lundahl listened to his photo-interpreters, and then he looked at the film himself. After reviewing their reasoning and analysis, he decided that evening to tell the CIA's director of intelligence and the DCI on a secure telephone call. He also told the senior military officers in NPIC—army, navy, and air force—about the find. One, the senior navy officer on duty, had to tell his carpool to go home without him, as did one of the four air defense photo-interpreters.

Measuring the equipment took most of the evening but, eventually, it confirmed the photo-interpreters' initial assessment that these canisters had the same dimensions as Soviet SS-4 missile canisters, but without their warheads. A later look at other equipment revealed that the missile erecting mechanisms—called strongbacks—were also present.

Despite the serious implications for the United States—the Soviet's intent to defy the Monroe Doctrine and to put nuclear weapons in Cuba—the team that made the find—although not missile experts themselves—continued to work the discovery. The effort was not turned over to other "expert" analysts or even managers. This was part of Lundahl's NPIC's culture back to its start in 1956. Those who found the equipment—the air defense team—did all the work on the observation. The strategic missile interpreters who usually looked at and reported on Soviet missiles, while consulted, did not get to brief the bosses, annotate the images, or write the cables or reports for the community. Although Mr. Lundhal briefed the team's work to the senior officials, the "call" was theirs to make. The value placed on the find and accurate information, and the teamwork exhibited by the photo-interpreters resulted in such strong bonds that no manager or other photo-interpreter intruded on their work. The premium NPIC placed on discovery, and the value placed on the "find" and the "call" meant that the first photo-interpreters to observe activity, even if outside their area of expertise, would get whatever recognition was given.

Throughout that Monday evening, a photogrammatist, Leon Coggin, used the Mann comparator—a primitive computer—to check the rough measurements provided by the photo-interpreters. The comparator, advanced for its day, was being affected by voltage fluctuations, which happened regularly in the old Steuart Building. Despite the fluctuating voltage, Coggin was able to measure the important find. When he finished, his measurements confirmed the photo-interpreters' estimates. The graphic artists were called back into work at 3:00 a.m. on Tuesday, and the courier was told to come in early on that morning so that Mr. Lundahl would be able to leave for the White House at 6:00 a.m. on that same day.

The heightened pace of activity at the Steuart Building increased. Already, NPIC photo-interpreters had been busy with the exploitation and production work resulting from CORONA KH-4 Mission 9045, which had been flown on 29 September. It had arrived in the building early in October. For two weeks prior to the arrival of the U-2 film over Cuba, the Soviet missile, air defense, and nuclear photo-interpreters had already been working extended days and nights on the Soviet Union. But the missile threat to the United States was found on the U-2 imagery of Cuba and not the satellite imagery of the USSR.

NPIC's success at finding the missile equipment in Cuba did not extend to locating their warheads. However, on Wednesday, 17 October, a photo-interpreter spotted precast concrete arches, which suggested that a nuclear weapons storage bunker was under construction. While indicators of nuclear storage bunkers were observed, neither the warhead vans nor the warhead containers were seen until October 25 after Khrushchev had ordered the missiles back to the USSR.

The low-level photography taken over Cuba after the discovery of the SS-4 missile canisters allowed NPIC's photo-interpreters to make a "qualified" association between the vans and the warheads. But the inability of Lundahl's interpreters to make the exact association illustrated the extra challenge presented by mobile equipment. Fixed targets and locations were easier to discover and monitor; re-locatable targets were easier to hide from aircraft or satellites. The failure to find the associated warheads illustrated a challenge for photo-interpreters and imagery analysts that would continue through the 1970s and 1980s. Not known then in October was the ominous fact that the missile warheads were not the only nuclear weapons in Cuba. Other shorter-range missiles with nuclear warheads were on the island and were never observed.

The risks taken to photograph the location of the missiles would soon result in tragedy. The prioritization of the photo-interpretation, which put air defense first, was sadly prescient. Two weeks later Major Rudolph Anderson, USAF, a U-2 pilot, was shot down and killed by an SA-2 missile over eastern Cuba while on a reconnaissance mission. By then, the NPIC photo-interpreters had been working around the clock, a pace they sustained through the end of the year.

Opportunity Out of Crisis

Most Americans believe that the Cuban Missile Crisis ended after thirteen days when the Soviet ships en route to Cuba turned around. But, US reconnaissance aircraft missions continued to be flown over Cuba, and NPIC continued working around the clock to make sure that the Soviet missiles and aircraft were removed. Because of NPIC's comprehensive searching and researching of Cuba after the discovery of Soviet missiles, the US government had confidence that the Soviets had done what they agreed to. This work, in which aerial photography tracked the removal of a strategic force, would have significant consequences for NPIC and the Intelligence Community. For the first time, aerial and satellite reconnaissance provided the information that could verify that a deployed strategic force had been withdrawn. This kind of information would be needed to monitor any future arms control agreement. In the case of Cuba, NPIC's efforts provided the preponderance of information for the US Intelligence Community.

While the area in Cuba to be searched was not as large and not as effectively denied to US reconnaissance, and although the Soviet missile force in Cuba was small, NPIC proved the effectiveness of using photographic reconnaissance to verify a diplomatic agreement. This was a first in the Cold War, and this mission would grow.

An immense amount of intelligence gathering, analysis, overcoming technical challenges, and expense would be entailed, but NPIC proved the concept of using photographic interpretation to track the compliance of a negotiated agreement. As a result, the US was now able to "trust," and to verify that the Soviet Union did what it said it would do.

During the Cuban missile crisis, NPIC's work validated the persistence and foresight of Art Lundahl. By the end of 1962, twenty-one successful photographic satellite missions had been flown over the Soviet Union and China, and the discoveries in Cuba were being duplicated by the dozens, less dramatically, but more comprehensively as the result of every satellite mission. NPIC established its track record of discovery based on search. But the Intelligence Community did not universally admire the success of Lundahl's organization.

Lundahl's direct access to White House policymakers was envied as much as it was admired by his CIA and Intelligence Community colleagues. In particular the all-source analysts at CIA and in the Intelligence Community were not happy to have their coordinated national estimate overturned by his photo-interpreters. The CIA owned the process of creating the President's Daily Briefing, but their finely crafted and heavily edited documents sometimes had all their words trumped by one dramatic NPIC photograph. Also, some CIA all-source analysts who had made claims about the strong Soviet strategic prowess had their assessments overturned by the information first seen by Lundahl's photo-interpreters. As Lundahl had predicted, NPIC attracted the interest of powerful officials in both the administration and the national security community.

While the Cuban Crisis was ongoing, so was the around-the-clock renovation of Building 213 in the Washington Navy Yard. In 1961 and 1962, visitors to the Steuart Building became more senior, including the attorney general and the secretary of defense. Their presence contrasted with the increasing squalor of the neighborhood, and their new government limousines were out of place. The Kennedy administration began to pressure CIA to find a better location for NPIC. In 1962, this became a priority. As the story had it, the impetus to move NPIC had its origin in the vestibule of the Stuart Building when, to get inside, Bobby Kennedy had to step over a sleeping drunk. Building 213 would increase the NPIC workspace from 50,000 to 200,000 square feet.

From a decision in the middle of 1962, Building 213, a former gun turret factory in the Washington Navy Yard, was refitted on a twenty-four-hour/seven-day-a-week schedule. The $17 million expense for refurbishing Building 213—two thirds of that year's NPIC budget—was not questioned, although the use of marble in the lobby was.

Lundahl's vision—the secret automat that, as a national center, would provide intelligence to the entire government—came to life in the Steuart Building. His organization began the era of discovery through locating, identifying, and naming the Cold War Soviet threats. While other intelligence sources could provide some evidence of activity, NPIC's photographs provided locations, numbers, and information that could be compared against statements by the Soviet Union. The combination of photographic intelligence, cutting edge technology, a self-reliant and knowledgeable workforce, the peer pressure created by a jointly staffed organization, an excellent leader who marketed his organization effectively, tight internal security, and a slum, all shaped the early NPIC culture. The very last work NPIC did in the Steuart Building—the search that monitored and verified the Soviet agreement to withdraw their strategic forces from Cuba—would become how NPIC would bound the Cold War at its new location in Building 213.

CHAPTER 5

BUCKETS OF DISCOVERY

W hen NPIC, with about four hundred people, moved into Building 213 on January 1, 1963, it brought with it round-the-clock intense work. The practices and culture created in the Steuart Building continued. The new building, in a different but still bad neighborhood, was at the western end of the Washington Navy Yard, at First and M Streets in Southeast Washington. When NPIC moved there, the Southeast/Southwest Freeway was not yet completed, and the 11ᵗʰ Street Bridge had not been built. Building 213 shared the corner of First and M with two liquor stores and the Washington Star's newspaper garage. Brick row houses and small businesses were outside the western end of the Washington Navy Yard. A poorer part of Washington, it was not one of the worst neighborhoods in the District of Colombia, but it was not a place where those who lived there or those who worked there felt safe after dark.

As with its old location, NPIC was in a neighborhood in which most of its employees did not live. While Building 213 had more amenities—a cafeteria, air conditioning, break rooms, and a fenced parking lot—neighborhood parking was still unsafe. Initially, all employees could park in the front lot, but that did not last. So the tradition of employee carpooling continued and grew.

NPIC's record of success in Cuba, and the increased amount of imagery from the satellites drove a hiring surge. The constant engineering inventions and improvements by the contractors building new satellites increased the amount and interpretability of the film. NPIC needed more people to succeed. NPIC's intelligence success, helped greatly by Art Lundahl's renowned briefing skills, persuaded CIA, the military services, and congress to double the size of NPIC's workforce in 1963. The discoveries NPIC found in the first handful of successful satellite missions persuaded the government to invest, and NPIC's first decade in Building 213 would make discovery commonplace. As a result, comprehension of the Soviet strategic forces was starting to become possible.

In 1963, NPIC hired young people out of the military, right from college, and from other government agencies. Three years earlier, George Kistiakowsky, in his recommendation to President Eisenhower to have CIA manage NPIC, noted the youth and energy of the NPIC workforce as major factors in NPIC's successes. Lundahl believed in staffing with younger people and giving them considerable responsibility as soon as they demonstrated the ability to handle it. And youthful energy was needed to work the long hours required when buckets of imagery would come to Building 213. Lundahl's organization, in 1959, averaged less than thirty years of age, and this trend would continue after NPIC moved to Building 213.

The year 1963 marked the greatest change in satellite photography since its inception. While 1962 had sixteen successful launches, all were KH-4 or the lower-resolution KH-5s. In 1963, the number of launches was the same, but late in that year, the KH-4a, which carried twice the amount of film with two buckets (individual canisters of film), was first launched. Although the resolution of the KH-4 did not improve greatly, the three KH-6 and four KH-7 launches that year provided higher resolution photos, with much greater detail for the NPIC interpreters.

In the three years since the first successful KH-4 launch, the NPIC search mission, or locating new or unknown targets, had already been defined successfully for the Intelligence Community. The knowledge that NPIC gained from locating Soviet strategic targets shrunk the bomber and missile gaps, discovered Soviet missiles in Cuba, and tracked the Soviet compliance that resolved the crisis. NPIC's record of accomplishment had won the trust of the policy and intelligence communities.

NPIC had proven that it could identify large strategic targets using this lower resolution photography. In the three years after it began identifying these targets in 1960, its photo-interpreters had requested, and the engineers had built satellites and cameras that produced pictures with better resolution. These KH-6 and KH-7 satellites were designed to take photographs of known targets at a much higher resolution. When the film from these systems came to Building 213, it enabled a different kind of photo-interpretation. Better resolution meant that more interpretable details could be seen, and seeing these details meant that NPIC could look at known targets repeatedly and answer more intelligence questions. Higher resolution meant that photographs could be taken repeatedly and studied more frequently. The higher resolution allowed the photo-interpreters to monitor small changes at important targets and to learn even more about the capabilities of the weapons planned, built, stored, or tested at these targets.

NPIC used the higher resolution satellites to look for details and characteristics that would give the photo-interpreter precise target measurements, information about its components, smaller weapons systems, and objects two to three feet in size. This capability from space, which with the best of the KH-6 and KH-7 was as good as or better than the U-2, began to change how NPIC thought about collection management. The improved resolution meant that the NPIC photo-interpreters would become the best advisors on how to collect strategic targets. By this time, the all-source analysts in the Intelligence Community recognized that getting advice from NPIC photo-interpreters was a very effective way to plan future collection. The NPIC role in collection began to shift from strict neutrality to sought-after advisor. Increasingly, Lundahl's analysts were the best prepared in the Intelligence Community to define future collection requirements.

NPIC had the most experience at looking at Soviet strategic targets, and its photo-interpreters would work with the all-source analysts in CIA and with the newly formed DIA to make the case for more or better space photography to address questions the interpreters could not answer. The all-source agencies came to rely on the expertise and autonomy of the NPIC photo-interpreters to help them understand the art of photo-interpretation and what new photographs they would need.

The interpretation of space photography was not limited to NPIC. Copies of the satellite film were sent to all the service centers. The air force, in particular, the Strategic Air Command (SAC) headquartered in Omaha, Nebraska, had developed its own photo-interpretation capability. SAC needed locational information to support its extensive targeting efforts against the Soviet Union. SAC had the responsibility for building Soviet target packages so it could destroy these targets with its bombers and missiles. But SAC organized the work of its photo-interpreters differently from NPIC, and this difference resulted in different operational and cultural traits.

NPIC's photo-interpreters worked autonomously. They did not have to clear their findings or reporting with any other analytic component. Lundahl had blended his staffing and organized his national center to achieve this end. SAC photo-interpreters, like others in the air force and every other military service, had to have their "calls" approved, either by all-source analysts or targeting officers. Other photo-interpreters, while they also had access to other sources of information and intelligence, were not like NPIC, exclusively focused on the photo-interpretation.

From Neutrality to Consultancy

The NPIC photo-interpreters, whose only mission was to study the photography, were able to derive more information from better photography, more quickly than their military counterparts. NPIC's reporting became a principal tool for the Intelligence Community to determine future collection. With their exclusive focus on the imagery, NPIC photo-interpreters began to advise all-source analysts about what to collect. Much of this ability came as a result of its workforce's greater knowledge of the technical capabilities of the cameras and the satellites, and part came from NPIC's culture of how its analysts pursued their "finds and calls." Because NPIC was designed as a national center, its interpreters were not expected or required to justify any service-based position or program, and their rankings and recommendations were not biased by inter-service rivalries. As a consequence of their experiences at looking at both high and low resolution space photography, NPIC interpreters had become experts in two kinds of work—search and target monitoring.

NPIC's photo-interpreters learned to balance and vary resolution needs with different frequencies of observation, against the varying priorities of different regions, different issues, different times of the year, and different orbits of different satellites. Since the U-2 program started in 1956, the priorities and conflicts for collecting reconnaissance photography had been adjudicated outside NPIC by the Ad Hoc Requirements Committee or ARC. But, even though NPIC did not vote on the committee, NPIC photo-interpreters began to use their technical knowledge and experience to influence the Intelligence Community's collection requirements. As there were a far greater number of requirements for space photography than it was possible to collect, the ability to make a persuasive case for a collection nomination became a valued skill.

Collection management began to become part of NPIC's operating culture. The NPIC Mission Assessment cables, written as soon as the scan of each bucket was finished, became the basis for future mission planning.

Technological Influence

The technologists also consulted NPIC. Art Lundahl's close relationship with camera designers at Itek and Perkin Elmer; the film chemists and processors at Eastman Kodak; photo scientists in the air force, army, navy, and CIA; and satellite manufacturers at GE, Lockheed, and Martin Aircraft shaped and increased his photo-interpreters' knowledge. As director of NPIC, Lundahl visited these factories and laboratories to learn the latest technical developments and the status of ongoing work. He also briefed the cleared scientists, engineers, and managers at their facilities about what NPIC was able to learn as a result of their work. On returning to NPIC, Lundahl told the photo-interpreters about what he had seen on his visits. When the scientists and engineers visited NPIC, the interpreters briefed them on the current intelligence that they obtained from their technology. This symbiotic relationship allowed NPIC's photo-interpreters to better shape collection requirements so imagery was not "wasted" as the result of "unreasonable" or "unachievable" requests. Lundahl's relationship with the manufacturers enabled NPIC's photo-interpreters to directly influence future systems and reinforced the expectation that NPIC interpreters needed to understand the collection technology, its operational and technical limitations, and the criticality of teaching developers from actual examples.

As the photo-interpreters looked at each successive "bucket" of film—a term used to describe the container that held the exposed film at recovery—in the darkened vaults in Building 213, they revised their collection requirements in response to what they had just seen on their light tables. When satellite missions were first flown on a monthly schedule, the photo-interpreters' ability to quickly find, report, and articulate new information needs became critical. From the earliest missions, the need to process large amounts of information rapidly, to identify new changes, and report and reassess quickly were essential and valued at NPIC. But the interpreters' awareness of competition from other imagery analysis organizations affected their interpretation of the film as much as its collection.

Along with the number and technical advancements of the new satellites, the community of photo-interpreters was growing, but it remained small enough to be highly competitive. NPIC interpreters kept aware of what their counterparts at SAC, the Air Force's Technical Analysis Center, and the Naval Intelligence Center in Suitland were reporting. Many NPIC interpreters had previously worked in these organizations. But these military centers often coordinated their analysis with NPIC, because when some military interpreters rotated out to different assignments, they could not keep up or maintain continuity with their targets and issues as well as the NPIC workforce. Another reason for coordination was the high credibility that NPIC had with senior military officers. Frequently, military officers would perform their own good analytic work only to be asked by their superiors, "What does NPIC think?"

Lundahl knew the leaders at each of these interpretation centers, and they often looked to NPIC for technical and contractual assistance in purchasing technology and equipment. As NPIC continued to grow and improve its technical capabilities, coordination among these centers continued. As military photo-interpreters would finish their service obligations, some would be extended offers to come to work at NPIC.

By the end of 1964, the predictable stream of information from space was increasing. It was taking more and more time, even with the additional people hired through 1963 and 1964, to look at and exploit the increasing volume of KH-4a film, as well as the increasing numbers of higher resolution KH-7 photographs. After each mission, the volume of information arriving in Building 213 would build. NPIC coped by working hard and long hours, but more and more effort was required as more and more knowledge had to be managed.

The increasing flow of information caused NPIC to change. In 1965, two different organizations reviewed NPIC. The CIA's Inspector General did one review; a working group from DoD did the other. Each looked at NPIC's capability to manage DoD's departmental requirements and CIA's departmental requirements, in addition to NPIC's existing national mission. Independently, both reviews recommended that DIA and CIA establish independent departmental photo-interpretation organizations to meet their growing needs. The volume of satellite film drove these changes, but the growing volume of information and the need to use the intelligence gleaned from this imagery caused additional changes. Through the Committee on Exploitation Requirements

(COMOR), the collection committee that replaced the ARC, the Intelligence Community agreed to a National Tasking Plan. This plan introduced distinctions in the kinds of intelligence targets, as well as a scheme to distribute work among the photo-interpretation community.

The NTP divided targets for space photography into national and departmental. If a number of agencies in the Intelligence Community agreed that a target was important, it was called national and NPIC took responsibility for looking at it. If a target was considered important by only one agency, it became departmental, and that one agency looked at it. NPIC maintained the responsibility for looking at the photography for all government organizations that lacked their own photo-interpretation capability, like the State Department or the Atomic Energy Commission.

Under the National Tasking Plan, the navy looked at deployed naval forces; the army covered deployed land forces; and the air force covered deployed air forces. But for some select targets, such as Soviet missiles, both NPIC photo-interpreters and SAC photo-interpreters looked at them. After CIA and DIA established their own departmental photo-interpretation organizations, they too looked at Soviet strategic targets. These targets were considered so important that the duplication of effort was deemed necessary. While the NTP was supposed to divide the work, no part of the Intelligence Community wanted to give up a "priority" issue.

NPIC was given one additional responsibility. It became responsible for creating and maintaining a computer database on all national targets. NPIC made this database available to all its customers in the defense department and in the Intelligence Community. During the 145 KH-4 missions between 1960 and 1972, the NPIC database grew to 10,000 targets. Many of these targets were east of the Ural Mountains, the area about which so little had been known in the 1950s and early 1960s. During this interval, all these targets had been located, identified, and characterized. While these external Intelligence Community developments changed NPIC, two internal practices were strengthening its culture.

Photo-interpreters in NPIC dealt with the growing volume of information in two ways—"shoeboxes" and "stories." The shoeboxes were idiosyncratic. Each photo-interpreter kept copies of photos of important targets for reference, or for unknowns and ongoing activity for further review. Many would also keep Polaroid enlargements. Most kept those photos in government-issue wooden boxes designed to hold five by eight inch index cards. These boxes looked like the ones carried by shoeshine boys. But the other, and more important method for holding information was the strong thread that ran through every branch in NPIC—the sharing of "stories" among the analysts.

Because computer memory was so expensive and unreliable, the real database at NPIC for many areas, targets, and issues was held in the memories of the photo-interpreters. From the earliest days in the Steuart Building, photo-interpreters had been constrained in their ability to write things down. Most of their time was spent in the process of interpreting photographs, looking at film on the light tables, scouring other sources of information—which they called collateral—and reporting on current discoveries. All their reporting was hand-written and subsequently typed by the secretaries into cables for dissemination by teletype.

So among themselves, photo-interpreters communicated by telling and retelling the stories of finds and calls on different missions. They used those stories to teach new interpreters or new branch members detailed from the military. So the skills of storytelling, remembering details precisely, and combining the photographs with the narrative of what changed over time became valued. Arthur Lundahl was the most skilled storyteller in NPIC. A great briefer, Lundahl used these skills as much inside NPIC, as he did in the Intelligence Community. In his reminiscences, Lundhal talked about briefing at the White House and then returning to the Steuart Building and telling the interpreters and support people how he used their information and materials, and how much the president and the senior policymakers appreciated these materials.

The value of being a good briefer was also reinforced throughout the entire organization. It was an unwritten expectation for every new photo-interpreter. Along with being able to make finds and calls, each interpreter was also expected to brief their story. When a mission came in, any significant find or call would be briefed to the director. But, before interpreters briefed Mr. Lundahl, they were expected to brief their peers, senior analysts, section chiefs, branch managers, and then their division officers before they would brief the front office.

It was not enough to interpret the photograph correctly. The photo-interpreters were also expected to know the context surrounding the issue they were following, the history of any previous strategic activity in the area, the history of any previous imagery coverage of the area, and how the call or find changed their collective understanding of the intelligence problem. Briefing Mr. Lundahl—who had briefed the president, Congress, and foreign leaders using exactly this kind of information—strongly reinforced this value.

New photo-interpreters were expected to learn the stories from the other analysts, and to "index" or check any of their finds against existing stories, in addition to entering them into a formal database. While the database had the locational information of latitude and longitude, an identifying number, and a target name, it would not have the full record of understanding, the tracking of changes, or the relationship of any particular target to other targets. All this context and operational knowledge was captured in the stories. Even though the flow of information from the space photography increased into a flood, stories continued to be how the interpreters kept up with what they were seeing.

NPIC focused most on the Soviet nuclear and missile forces. Slowly at first, but then steadily, their locations were found, identified, and plotted, and further study yielded comparisons to other activities. Patterns began to emerge, and recognition turned into understanding. Sary Shagan and Plesetsk were related, as were Tyuratam and Semipalatinsk; Kraznoyarsk and Kapustin Yar; and Tomsk, Mozyr, Lida, Pavlograd and Minsk. The same relationships applied to Pervomaysk, Votkinsk, Teykovo, Smolensk and Irkutsk; Anagarsk, and Novosibirsk; Orensburg and Chelyabinsk; and Chita.

The vast number of targets associated with these places started with a photo-interpreter's observation of undetermined activity at a place with no name. Then, over time, one photograph at a time, the interpreters generally characterized and specifically identified the activity. As NPIC discovered more targets–Yoskhar Ola, Tatischevo, Kozelsk, and Vypolzovo–their subordination was discerned and the interpreters related them to others, such as Vladimir. They connected Omsk and Teykovo with Irkutsk, along with Barnaul and Uzhur. Photo-interpreters began to associate which missile systems came from which test centers. With each bucket of film and each new mission, they discovered more and more installations. New bases and new places, and new systems at older bases: Imeni Gastello, Balapan and Leninsk. Sosny and Sary Ozek. Dombarovski, and Postavy all changed slowly from mysteries, to a name, to puzzles, to suspect facilities, and to identified facilities as a result of the careful scrutiny, comparisons, recognition, and analysis done by NPIC's photo-interpreters. As the slow and patient process of identifying, negating, relooking, and chronicling activities continued, the target characterizations turned from possible to probable, and probable to confirmed. And the comprehension of the Soviet strategic order of battle began to take shape.

An important sign of NPIC's success is the fact that most Americans were and are totally unfamiliar with these Russian, Belorussian, Ukrainian, and Kazakh names and places. As NPIC's interpreters and others involved in the Cold War learned, many of these locations held missiles with warheads many times more devastating than the weapons exploded at Hiroshima and Nagasaki. Public ignorance of these place names outside of the Intelligence Community was, in itself, a sort of intelligence success.

From Knowing the Location to Understanding the Operations

By the middle 1960's, NPIC photo-interpreters provided the backbone for the US national estimates on the Soviet strategic forces. During this period, they located this force. As a history of the KH-4 program states, "By March 1964, CORONA had photographed 23 of the 25 Soviet ICBM complexes then in existence; three months later it had photographed all of them." And by 1968, the US Intelligence Community would write: "No new ICBM complexes have been established in the USSR during the past year." But this was not the only work done by NPIC analysts in this decade. After determining the locations of the Soviet strategic forces, they used the higher-resolution satellites to address questions of function and operations. The higher resolution imagery allowed the photo-interpreters to move from locating the targets, to examining the parts of the weapons systems, and this move began the age of comprehension.

The age of comprehension required more search and better resolution. As early as 1963, CIA requested a study of what capabilities future satellites would need to address its intelligence needs. By January 1964, NPIC's photo-interpreters determined that a system would be required that combined the ability of the KH-4 to cover large areas for search, with the better resolution of the KH-7. After considerable wrangling between the air force and CIA, the National Reconnaissance Office was building such a system.

The Parts that Changed the Story

The best example of the work that characterized the age of comprehension was the SS-9 missile silo analysis that NPIC did in the late 1960s. After the KH-7 and KH-8 satellites were operational, NPIC missile analysts, notably Lt. John Merritt, USN, and Lou Kress, studied how the Soviet Union assembled missile silos until John and Lou could anticipate—based on silo components alone—the missile system that would be associated with a silo while it was still under construction. In the late 1960s, these analysts published a detailed report that chronicled the construction sequence and the number and kind of components needed to build these silos. For photo-interpreters, this reporting was a significant step. Up to that time, they were only "allowed" to report what they saw on the mission being currently exploited. Along with the report, the NPIC model shop built an SS-9 silo model. This model was used in more than 120 briefings in the Intelligence Community. In those briefings, the NPIC analysts would assemble the silo model from scratch, as they had seen and measured enough components from satellite imagery to correctly infer how it was assembled.

The model, the report, and the briefings by these two photo-interpreters convinced the Intelligence Community that it could monitor the Soviet strategic missile silos with enough confidence to know if the Soviets were trying to change them. This knowledge contributed to two significant milestones. As well as showing the intelligence and policy community audiences how much NPIC learned about Soviet construction practices and schedules, the briefings also illustrated how well NPIC could monitor physical changes at these facilities. By the late 1960s, the work of NPIC demonstrated that it could then duplicate the missile force monitoring that it had done in Cuba, but across a nation hundreds of times larger than Cuba. The work of the interpreters, along with that of the image scientists who provided the measurements that allowed the construction of the SS-9 model, convinced many in the intelligence and policy communities of the validity of satellite monitoring of future arms control agreements. Among the Intelligence Community analytic managers who became convinced of this in the late 1960s were Howard Stoertz, Bruce Clarke, John Hicks, and Rae Huffstutler, all of whom were working arms control issues for CIA.

This detailed analysis of silo construction, which made arms treaty monitoring possible, was accomplished from the observations and memories of the

NPIC photo-interpreters and the measurements of NPIC photogrammatists. The photo-interpreters lacked the computer tools or a way to query the databases that would enable them to compare information gathered at one location with that gathered at another. Their individual and collective memories of what was seen and when it was seen were the "tools" that they used to perform their preliminary analysis. The NPIC "stories" led the photo-interpreters to do further research and to draw the inferences supported by the measurements and the chronologies that they and others had built.

In the late 1960's, this understanding gained from NPIC reporting provided confidence and information for the early arms control negotiations with the Soviet Union on nuclear testing, anti-ballistic missiles, the composition of the strategic rocket forces, and on the number of associated warheads. The national investment in NPIC had been returned many times over. The analytic support to the arms control treaty initiative on the location and disposition of these fixed Soviet targets was NPIC's purview, and it excelled at it. While NPIC provided equally detailed analysis on the status of Soviet submarine construction, the mobility of missile-launching submarines meant that tracking them was more difficult for the Intelligence Community.

The accuracy and confidence of the NPIC interpreters was alluded to in congressional testimony by Herbert Scoville, the former head of scientific research at CIA, in his testimony to the Arms Control Subcommittee of the Senate Foreign Relations Committee. In April 1970, in one of the earliest unclassified descriptions of NPIC's work, Scoville outlined what the photo-interpreters routinely were capable of observing. "On fixed land-based ICBM's: (These) require extensive launch-site construction in order to provide the necessary hardening to make them resistant to blast from a nuclear explosion. This construction requires many months and therefore ample time is available to permit its detection . . .

Submarine Launched ballistic missiles (SLBMs):

Submarines, which have large numbers of long-range missiles and which can operate for protracted periods at long distances from their home ports, require large and distinctive facilities for their construction . . . After the submarines are launched they require many months for fitting out, during all of which they are subject to observation."

The next generation of photo-satellite, the KH-9, which would turn out to be the last film-based system, would bring an overwhelming amount of information, and NPIC would struggle to handle it. In the planning for this new collection system, NPIC initially estimated that it would need 2,500 photo-interpreters to look at all the film it would provide. This was more than six times the number then at the Center. At the time, Richard Helms, the director of Central Intelligence, did not agree, and he would not approve the additional people. NPIC management had serious concerns about what effect all the additional film would have on its photo-interpreters. New light tables and microscopes would be needed and they were designed for the new format and improved resolution of the new imagery.

Because of the growing sophistication of NPIC's technology and the associated resource demands required by the growing database and the increasing amount of film, CIA re-subordinated NPIC from the Directorate of Intelligence to the Directorate of Science and Technology (S&T) in 1972. Carl Duckett, at that time the director of the S&T, long had been an advocate for the technology that NPIC was increasingly demanding.

The Founder Departs

Art Lundahl, then fifty-nine years old, had become increasingly arthritic over the years from old football injuries. He decided to retire in July 1973. Eight years after his retirement, Mr. Lundahl agreed to tape his reminiscences in an unclassified setting. Beginning in October 1981, over a period of seven months, he recorded his reminiscences with Peter Jessup, a retired Foreign Service officer. These ten audiotapes, now in the Oral History collection in the Butler University Library at Columbia University, contain Lundahl's only personal record. In it, he stated that he would not write a book, and he never did. In these recordings, Lundahl talked about his family, background, education, World War II navy experiences, and how he came to CIA. While these reminiscences are unclassified, Lundahl did discuss how the organization he founded became NPIC, its role in the Cuban missile crisis, and how he saw the photo-interpretation profession developing. Lundahl's narrative illustrated what he accomplished at NPIC and what challenges remained.

In one taping session, Lundahl spoke with tremendous pride about his organization. Specifically, he referred to personnel practices he instituted early at NPIC and, that over time, shaped its culture. One practice that Lundahl observed in World War II, implemented when he founded a civilian navy photo-interpretation center, and brought to CIA was the importance of staffing with younger people. He believed their energy was essential and that they were capable of handling considerable responsibility.

At NPIC, Lundahl started three personnel management practices: lateral mobility, upward mobility, and continuing education. After he selected a new employee, and after the man had proven himself to be a good employee, within the demands of the mission, an employee could gravitate toward the work where he thought that he could make the greatest contribution. Lundahl felt that working on a subject that interested an interpreter would motivate the interpreter. So his employees were allowed to find their niche. In the early days of NPIC and its predecessor organizations, the workforce was small and the amount and difficulty of work were so large that developing multiple skills became an expectation. As Jolien Mierke remembered:

"That was a thrilling time because we were charting new territory. There was plenty of room for creativity, because there were no established rules and regulations. There was just an important job to do, and anybody would do anything that needed doing, for as many hours as required. We didn't have job descriptions back then." After new employees were accepted into that culture, some mobility was allowed. Lundahl recognized that a few people would move out of NPIC, but he thought this approach worked best for the individual and the Center.

Many opportunities presented themselves for photo-interpreters who showed initiative, intelligence, and drive to take on more responsibility. From the inception of PID in 1956, Lundahl supported and encouraged individual growth. Many who started in support positions at NPIC as couriers, personnel officers, clerks, and guards developed into photo and map technicians, as well as photo interpreters and managers. This happened even in the busiest of times. Bill Hanlon was an example. In October 1962, as he was attending photointerpretation training at the Naval Air Intelligence Officers School in Anacostia, Maryland, NPIC detected Soviet offensive missiles in Cuba, and an international crisis was beginning. Hanlon and fifteen other NPIC photo-interpreters in training were called back to work at the Center on evenings and weekends.

NPIC continued its culture of individual growth through an upward mobility program that made training, on-the-job mentoring, and college courses available. Identifying employees with high potential and developing their careers was a point of pride for Mr. Lundahl. He spoke of having personnel discussions with managers about the "high-potentials." Those people were given challenging assignments and managerial responsibilities. Another aspect of developing NPIC officers was the internal training program. Art Lundahl spoke about how if someone needed to learn, either substantive knowledge or academic development, he would be sent to get the training, or college classes would be offered at Building 213 in the evenings or during work hours. Training that could be applied to the large intelligence challenges was especially valued. And when people returned from a training trip or class, they were expected to share the knowledge with their peers. When people assumed managerial positions, NPIC provided managerial and leadership training to help with their new responsibilities. And, if an employee needed to finish a degree to compete more effectively, he or she frequently was given time to take classes.

Lundahl was also proud of the initiative displayed by the NPIC workforce. He spoke of how the NPIC tradition of creating tools and processes to solve its problems had a demonstrable result. CIA, in the 1960s and 1970s, had a cost-saving program where any employee could make a suggestion. These suggestions were studied independently and, if they turned out to save resources, the employee would be rewarded. NPIC employees claimed half of the CIA cost-savings awards. NPIC won these awards so frequently that CIA senior leadership sent a group to NPIC to study how they were so innovative. When other government agencies came to CIA to see how the Agency program was so effective, they were taken to NPIC.

In his reminiscences, Mr. Lundahl wrote about opportunities for minorities at NPIC. He described the Equal Opportunities Panels and how NPIC was determined to, in his words "do a better job on minorities than we felt was being done elsewhere in government." NPIC led CIA in its efforts for minorities. But the NPIC's efforts were predominantly for those in support positions.

Among the photo interpreters, the only African-Americans were in military uniforms. In 1972, the year before Lundahl's retirement, NPIC sent two promising support officers, George Brown and Floyd Short, to the Air Force photo interpretation school, the Defense Sensor Interpretation and Applications Training Program (DSIAP) at Offutt AFB in Omaha, Nebraska. At this time, NPIC had between two hundred and three hundred photo-interpreters, and nearly all were men.

By 1972, NPIC was the CIA office with the largest percentage of African-Americans in its workforce. As the first two floors of Building 213 were mostly support offices, the first impression for new people and visitors to NPIC was often an African-American man or woman.   And, as the African-Americans said about Building 213, "the higher up, the whiter it got." Later in the 1970s, the NPIC upward mobility program was modified to address racial and gender hiring and employment issues. Whether this racial diversity was an outcome of NPIC's location in the District of Columbia, with its large African-American population, or its public transportation system, or an aversion by African-Americans to working in Virginia, from its earliest days the African-American minority population shaped NPIC. As was the case at NPIC, the African-Americans then employed by CIA were predominantly in support positions.

The minority population at NPIC was almost exclusively in lower-graded positions, but recognition of individual contributions, mission pressures, and commitment to producing intelligence, enabled some upward movement. Initially, the treatment of minorities was not equal, but it was perceived to be better at NPIC than in other parts of CIA or the Intelligence Community. This treatment probably was an outgrowth of everyone at Building 213 having to work, eat, commute, and park together in the same bad neighborhood. Building 213's isolation created an environment that many compared to a small town. Pretty quickly, everyone in the building knew who everyone else was, what vault they worked in, whether they brought their lunch or ate in the cafeteria, whether they carpooled or not, whether they took the stairs or the elevator and, most importantly, how well they could learn and do their jobs.

Women are rarely mentioned in the Lundahl tapes, and their acceptance into the analytic ranks was to be delayed until later in the 1970s. Before that time, their efforts at supporting the analysts were recognized. During the history of NPIC, women were hired routinely into secretarial and support positions. As with everyone else at NPIC, those who could work hard under mission pressure were given more responsibility. But, like the rest of CIA, the disparate treatment of women and minorities was part of the NPIC culture until the 1970s.

While Richard Helms had professional disagreements with Mr. Lundahl, he was not inclined to shrink NPIC. That could not be said of his successor, James Schlesinger, who started as DCI in February 1973. Schlesinger, who was DCI for only six months, cut CIA's budget and personnel, and these cuts extended to NPIC. While not many NPIC employees were let go, the issue of having to tell NPIC employees that they were going to be let go weighed heavily on Mr. Lundahl, who personally helped some to find other positions. The reduction-in-force, or RIF, had a large cultural effect in that the NPIC employees who went through the uncertainty before the actual reduction, never again felt the same trust in CIA's senior management, though they did not associate the RIF with Mr. Lundahl.

After Mr. Lundahl's retirement, John Hicks succeeded him as the second director of NPIC. After managing analysts in the Directorate of Intelligence and an overseas assignment, John had been Art Lundahl's executive officer for more than three years. In his earlier CIA work on arms control issues, John Hicks was an avid user of NPIC's reporting. From that experience, he developed a sense that the Intelligence Community needed to understand the work at NPIC in terms unrelated to the technology and to the capabilities of the photography, and he started a change at NPIC that took more than a decade to complete.

Emptying Buckets Would not be Enough

Unlike Art Lundahl, John Hicks did not have lifelong experience in aerial photography and photogrammetry. His prior use of satellite photography was as an aid to strategic weapons analysis. But, Hicks understood that NPIC's consumers needed to grasp more clearly what could and could not be determined from the photography. This awareness, along with his knowledge of the new digital imagery that was under development, led him to recognize that the photo-interpretation tradecraft must change. Hicks needed to change the "type" of work done at NPIC.

With all the world events in the late 1960s and early 1970s, there was plenty of work at Building 213 for all three photo-interpretation organizations. While large parts of the CIA and DIA photo-interpretation organizations were providing operational support to the Vietnam conflict, and CIA's Office of Imagery Analysis (OIA) was beginning its work on Soviet arms control, NPIC focused more and more on the Soviet Union, especially on its strategic forces. The USSR was exporting its communist ideology, as well as military equipment to the Third World, and NPIC tracked Soviet arms transfers to their eventual destinations in Congo, Cuba, Ethiopia, Eritrea, Syria, Egypt, North and South Yemen, Algeria, Libya, and Angola.

The Sino-Soviet military buildup along their mutual border was an issue for which NPIC was the primary source of intelligence, and NPIC used satellite photography to locate and track the respective forces along their shared border. It also covered the border skirmishes between China and India. NPIC followed communist-sponsored conflicts in Angola and the Congo, along with the war between India and East Pakistan. It covered the 1968 and 1973 Arab-Israeli wars. However, inherent delays in the film-return systems limited NPIC's effectiveness, and provided the impetus for future satellite technology changes.

In spring 1973, NPIC created a Special Projects Working Group to think about how to solve these shortcomings. The men on this working group were the first to think about how to prepare for the collection output of a new, near-real-time satellite. This small team started to think how getting imagery every day would change NPIC operations.

While photo-interpretation always had been augmented intelligence from other sources, NPIC began to more frequently combine its interpretation of photography with information from other open and other classified sources in its reporting.

This second era, the era of US comprehension of the Soviet military forces, an era that had started in the late 1960's, accelerated after 1971 when the KH-9 satellites began to fly. This new satellite greatly increased the amount of film and the duration of the missions. The volume of film brought much more work to Building 213. These changes brought two challenges to NPIC. One, the inherent delay in intelligence associated with the buckets of film-return systems became more noticeable as the pace of military deployments accelerated in some regions. This lag time between taking the photograph and interpreting the photograph led to warning failures. Second, in a more promising vein, the increasing volume, reliability, and security of overhead space reconnaissance, along with the proven ability of NPIC interpreters to discern changes and new developments, made additional treaty monitoring possible with the Soviet Union.

Those in the arms control community who were drafting the Strategic Arms Limitation Treaty (SALT) agreements worked closely with NPIC so the agreements could be primarily monitored with satellite photography. The improved resolution of the KH-8 and the large area coverage of the KH-9 validated the earlier NPIC work with the KH-4. The increased level of detail provided by the newer satellites made the United States certain that it would observe any evidence of cheating. These developments inspired the confidence that made negotiating arms control treaties with the Soviet Union possible and ultimately successful.

Inside NPIC, the interpretability of the KH-8 and KH-9 film was so good that some experienced interpreters, familiar with a region or a favorite target, would sometimes try to "crabeye." This was a generally despised practice. It involved experienced interpreters coming in early to watch new interpreters cut the film, checking the coverage plots to see which frame their favorite targets would be on, and asking or intruding to look at a particular target with their 7X magnifier. These experienced analysts often had an inkling, or more than an inkling, that new activity was likely to be found, and they could make a "discovery." In the NPIC culture, the imagery analyst who made the find got to write the report and give the briefings, and build his or her individual reputation. But others who knew that their unscrupulous peers were not doing the arduous work of search did not like or respect this "crab-eyeing," and would sometimes tell them, occasionally in a way that led to the interpreters being physically separated.

But even with increased area coverage and increased resolution, film return satellites still had inherent delays. Receiving the film from space meant that NPIC's customers often had to wait weeks for information. To address that time lag, the NRO had been working on a digital camera that could return imagery multiple times a day from a satellite. Buckets were soon to become much less important.

Well before December 1976, when the near-real-time satellite was launched, the NPIC computer system already had difficulties in coping with the volume of information from the KH-8 and KH-9 film return systems. These difficulties presaged future problems that would grow exponentially when imagery arrived hourly, every day, instead of over intervals of weeks.

The need to more rapidly acquire, process, and make information readily available could not be met by the computer technology of the time. Only a few NPIC employees could enter information into the computer and none were photo-interpreters. The computers lacked the processing speed and memory needed to preserve anything more than a minimum of online information.

As photo-interpretation was starting to transition into imagery analysis, it became more expensive and reliant on technology. The need to improve the communications technology drove the budget upward. Even with the best current technology, the interpreters were writing paper reports on new targets in longhand. These reports, nicknamed "blip sheets," were compiled and keyed into a batch process. But, it took all weekend for the NPIC mainframes to compile and print the work of the previous week, and this lag ensured that the database was perpetually out-of-date. But the cost of NPIC operations was increasing at a time of tight budgets, and this was well before the KH-11 was launched.

John Hicks was among the first to recognize that NPIC's imagery analysts were contributing the preponderance of intelligence information on some issues, and that NPIC would have to add context to its target reporting. His insight meant that NPIC would redefine its work, reporting, and analysis. Hicks's sense that the Intelligence Community needed to understand NPIC's work in terms different from the technology of the photography started a cultural change that would take more than a decade to gain acceptance. Hicks started NPIC 's transition from photo-interpretation to imagery analysis. But, not all of his changes would be well received.

CHAPTER 6

A DIVIDED CENTER

When Art Lundahl retired in July 1973, film from space had become routine instead of rare. In the 153 months since August 1960, when satellite imagery was first returned from space, 155 buckets of useful satellite film had been retrieved successfully. On the first satellite mission in 1960, a bucket held twenty pounds of film; by Lundahl's retirement, a KH-9 bucket held about five hundred pounds of film. The film and its chemical emulsion had become considerably thinner, so even more photographs could be obtained from each pound of the KH-9's film. From 40-foot resolution on the first KH-4 mission in 1960, the resolution had improved to twelve feet by 1963. Starting in 1967, these improvements continued, with the introduction of the KH-8 system, whose resolution was a dramatic improvement over all others. In addition, while the resolution was getting better, missions were getting longer. From the less than one-day mission of the first satellite, by 1973, a single mission duration increased to more than two hundred days. However, space reconnaissance still came with risk. Throughout this period, sixteen missions completely or partially failed. And, two buckets of film were lost and never recovered.

In the late 1960s, when digital technology was judged to have potential, the United States started planning for a digital imaging satellite. Only a small number of NPIC employees were cleared into this special access program. As he became director, Lundahl's former deputy and successor, John Hicks, knew that he would have to prepare NPIC for this new technology. He also knew that he must change how NPIC worked in order to accommodate the new technology. Hicks also recognized that he had to change NPIC's personnel to deal with the social changes occurring at the time. Many of his changes would not be popular or readily accepted, but Hicks began to move NPIC from photo-interpretation to imagery analysis.

Changing the Work and the Reporting

Photo-interpretation had always been augmented with other sources of intelligence. Since its inception, Lundahl's organization used other sources of information, but it never thought that it had enough useful information. Photography was the predominant source of information about most denied areas. More frequently, NPIC began to combine its interpretation of the imagery with information from other open and classified sources, although many all-source analysts in the Intelligence Community objected (and still object) that this "analytic work" was their purview. Other information sources, used to put context onto what was being seen on the imagery, defined the transition from photo-interpretation to imagery analysis. Some interpreters at NPIC had been doing analytic work since its inception, and the SS-9 silo analysis in the late 1960s by John Merritt and Lou Kress exemplified this. But Hicks wanted all NPIC photo-interpreters to do imagery analysis—to combine trained observation with logical thinking about the implications and context of the observation. He wanted this to become the norm rather than the exception.

To change NPIC, the first step that Hicks introduced was standardizing how imagery analysts judged the interpretability of the imagery. Instead of using the mathematics of resolution, which would provide a definition of how good the products of a camera system were, Hicks introduced a scale based on the degree of possible distinctions a trained observer could make from any particular image. As its basis, this interpretation scale would use "known" equipment, components, and objects frequently looked at by NPIC. Where an interpreter located an image on the scale depended on how much more he or she could "know" about the object.

NPIC interpreters and imagery scientists, with Bill Forster and David Gifford in the lead, took the basic correlation between the size of objects and the quality of imagery needed to see them, to create this new interpretability scale in the fall of 1973. Hicks challenged the photo-interpreters to begin using this scale, after the Strategic Arms Limitation Treaty (SALT I) was ratified in 1972. The interpretability scale was refined and published in March 1974, and a variant remains in use today.

The new index to interpretability was called the National Imagery Interpretability Rating Scale (NIIRS), and it would become a way to help NPIC and organizations in the Intelligence Community transition from film-based to digital imagery. It was a unit of measure applicable to both chemical film and digital imagery. As the technology and the proof of concept of digital satellite imagery matured and eventually became operational in 1977, the terminology of digital imagery began to replace the terminology of film-based photography. Hicks anticipated this transition, and he used the scale to remove some of the subjectivity of NPIC's interpretations. Hicks's insistence that the photo-interpreters evaluate the imagery by using commonly observed objects to evaluate the image, caused the community of photo-interpreters to accept these objects as common ways of judging the interpretability of the film.

The scale relied on finding an object of similar size that could be seen on multiple images of increasingly better resolution. Creating examples of the entire scale—1 thru 9—challenged the photo-interpreters, as they customarily did not see imagery good enough to illustrate the top of the scale or NIIRS 9. At this rating, individual parts of a human could be distinguished. This problem was solved when Robert Kohler, a CIA/ OD&E image scientist on the team, received a photo taken by low-flying aircraft over the corridor through East Germany to West Berlin. The photograph that became the NIIRS 9 illustration showed an East German soldier urinating. The scale of interpretation came about for multiple reasons. In 1974, after nearly twenty years of increasing observations, there were fewer new discoveries. The frequency, volume, and interpretability of satellite photographs in 1974 meant that much of the work shifted from discovery, to monitoring and comprehending what was happening at the known targets. The questions coming to NPIC had less to do with finding new facilities and more to do with understanding ongoing activities and changes at known facilities. Increasingly, NPIC was expected to identify subtle changes and to explain how and why these facilities, forces, and strategic targets were changing.

Connecting Targets to Issues

After John Hicks became director, he changed how NPIC wrote the cables that were used to disseminate intelligence. For the first time, NPIC's imagery analysts could address intelligence issues, as well as just reporting on individual targets or locations. This change added perspective and context to the usual target-focused reporting. For analysts at the State Department's Arms Control and Dismantlement Agency, the Arms Control Intelligence Staff at CIA, and the DIA analysts working arms control, it made NPIC cables and reports "easier" to read. The ability to look at and think about categories of targets as a group, and to write about them cumulatively had been the exclusive purview of the CIA, DIA, and State Department all-source analysts.

Previously, NPIC imagery analysts, following the precepts of the National Tasking Plan, were trained to enter information only about individual targets into the database, and, as a result, some in NPIC came to think of the database as the final customer of their interpretation or analysis. Consequently, they were trained to write descriptions of physical changes, but not to relate the changes to differences in a force capability or changes in a weapons system. Hicks wanted to take the "stories" that NPIC had used internally, and make them part of the external reporting. He shifted the reporting from writing extended captions for the photographs, to writing news stories supported by new images.

To help change photo-interpreters into imagery analysts, Hicks brought in a contractor, Al Joseph, to teach a newswriting course to all the NPIC photo-interpreters and their managers. NPIC, with its reliance on stories, was primarily an oral culture. Unlike CIA's Directorate of Intelligence, the quality of an applicant's writing skill was not a critical factor in selecting new imagery analysts. At this time, NPIC was not able to hire many new imagery analysts. It would have to rely on its existing workforce to cope with the volume of and reporting from the KH-9 photography, and for planning for the KH-11 imagery.

Not every NPIC photo-interpreter would make the transition to becoming an imagery analyst, but they would not fail for lack of training. Those who had difficulty picking up the new communications responsibilities were assigned more traditional work, such as search or direct support to other organizations that did not require any writing other than descriptions or annotations on an image. But failing to make the transition to imagery analysis was not career enhancing. Hicks also encouraged imagery analysts to further integrate other sources into NPIC reporting. To aid the imagery analysts with this, the editors and classification control officers provided a quality control function for the imagery analysts' cables and reports.

So, John Hicks consciously pushed NPIC into the transition to imagery analysis. This transition was already underway in CIA's departmental imagery organization, the Directorate of Intelligence's Imagery Analysis Service, which was soon to become the Office of Imagery Analysis. Imagery analysts were now expected to combine their work on the light tables with their own research and raw intelligence from other sources. From 1973 through 1978, this began to happen increasingly. Even though the new digital imagery was not available until 1977, Hicks began to change the terminology and how NPIC workers thought of themselves.

Hicks began to transform NPIC. Initially these differences were most noticeable in the branches working missile, nuclear, and strategic issues related to arms control Issues, followed by branches working research and development, and high current interest topics. The director's focus on narrative news writing, incorporating other intelligence sources, and objectifying the imagery analyst's calls—using the NIIRS scale—changed the work from pure photographic interpretation to a combination of visual interpretation with the intellectual processes of analysis based on visual evidence. On account of the changing output of the intelligence questions related to arms control issues, and the immense input of KH-9 film to look at and report on, Hicks worked at getting more imagery analysts into NPIC.

The External Search

To grow the NPIC workforce, John Hicks engaged three external groups. His first action involved the defense department. From its earliest years, NPIC incorporated a number of positions for members of the uniformed military. In the 1960s, the services filled most or all of these positions. As satellite imagery became more common and the age of discovery was in full swing in the late 1960s, the military was under more pressure to rotate its higher-ranking intelligence officers to support the Vietnam War. The career prestige of a combat tour; the services' focus on supporting tactical intelligence; the shrinking of the military; and the eventual end of the draft in 1972 all increased the number of unfilled military positions at NPIC. As the military officers saw it, commanding a light table at NPIC was less career enhancing than any command in their own service.

Director Hicks made the case to the Defense Intelligence Agency to support NPIC by requesting lower-ranking officers. In light of their own staffing challenges, the armed services were more amenable to his requests. The one unchangeable requirement for Hicks was the CIA polygraph. At that time, CIA asked counter-intelligence questions and "lifestyle" questions that focused on behavior that could make an individual susceptible to blackmail. The polygraph addressed what then was considered socially abhorrent behavior, which at the time included homosexuality. DIA had its own polygraph that also focused on counter-intelligence and lifestyle. One irony at Building 213 was that DIA officers who would fail the CIA polygraph could not be assigned to NPIC. However, if they then successfully passed the DIA polygraph, they could be assigned to the DIA photo-interpretation shop on the fifth-floor of Building 213 instead of the fourth floor that housed the NPIC interpreters. Hicks accepted this reality of the different polygraphs; the result was more eyes looking at the imagery. Hicks also saw another opportunity in selecting junior military officers.

By the early 1970s, the changes in American society brought about by the 1968 Civil Rights Act and the growing women's movement created a demand to diversify the government workforce. Hicks, building on Lundahl's desire for a diverse workforce, recognized that a source for trained minority and women professionals would be the uniformed military, which had integrated earlier and more extensively than CIA. So under his guidance, a larger number of women and minority officers at the end of their service obligations were hired into CIA and DIA to work as civilians at NPIC.

The Internal Look

NPIC complemented its external hiring of minorities and women by developing the existing internal upward mobility program. Each NPIC group identified its high-potential minority candidates, and NPIC put internal and external training programs in place to provide additional development and education. Through these programs, a number of support staff—couriers, graphics artists, editors, librarians, and map officers—became imagery analysts. To develop those willing to put themselves through night school, NPIC sponsored outside academic training at the University of Maryland and other local colleges. For career development, Hicks also introduced a number of rotational assignments in other parts of the Intelligence Community. John Hicks's continued Art Lundahl's workforce development initiatives with the Director's Opportunity Program. Pragmatically, the program was also a way to compensate for the fewer new hires throughout the middle 1970s.

NPIC started sending managers to programs and classes offered by the Center for Creative Leadership in Greensboro, North Carolina. NPIC's senior managers, aware of the isolated culture of NPIC, fully expected that they would have to develop their own future leaders internally. The Center had grown so large that one or two people in the front office could not track all the high potential people who needed to start their managerial and leadership training.

Not all of John Hicks's initiatives were appreciated. Like most leaders who follow a legend, his work was always compared to his predecessor. Some of his personnel initiatives were not popular. One particular reason was his desire to assess individuals in a different way. Just as NPIC for years had relied on the "story" to convey the history of its targets, it also, as is common in oral cultures, used "stories" to convey information about its people.

NPIC's personnel management frequently was based on anecdotes stored in the memories of the managers, and their criteria were often subjective. The informal stories about individuals—the "hall files"—mattered more than their written performance evaluations. Managerial judgments were made without any review, and questioning a manager's assessment was a way to pick up a reputation as a troublemaker. In performance reviews, the informal criteria would matter more than the job descriptions or the work plan. Frequently, the oral record of an employee's performance was a crucial factor in promotion decisions. If an employee had a performance issue, it was called "baggage," and any subsequent improved performance might not matter if a manager was willing to carry that employee's "baggage" to the next career panel. A number of NPIC middle managers resented some of Hicks's personnel initiatives and continued to make personnel decisions based on unwritten criteria. In many NPIC groups, promotions depended on managers advocating for their employees, and favoritism frequently steered the process.

NPIC employees taught this lesson in their own crude adage. Early in their careers most NPIC employees were counseled that "One 'O shit' canceled a hundred (or a thousand) 'Attaboys." The oral nature of performance management was clear, even though its fairness was questionable.

The first generation of leaders brought in by Art Lundhal was starting to retire, and NPIC needed to replace them. John Hicks started an internal NPIC supervisory course to train NPIC managers on how to manage and lead an organization that blended CIA, DIA, and military personnel evaluation systems. With his initiatives on developing the profession of imagery analysis and the NPIC workforce, John Hicks had set in play changes that would reshape NPIC's future. But for all his efforts, the volume of KH-9 imagery increasingly strained practices that had endured since the Steuart Building.

What to Leave in the Bucket

The KH-9, with its improved resolution and collection area, increased the coverage and the frequency of collection enough to make the NPIC database comprehensive. By 1973, the KH-9 would deliver twelve buckets of film annually to NPIC. That translated to a million feet, or slightly more than 189 miles of film. Developed film came to NPIC after processing in plastic containers, called "cans" after their metal ancestors, each holding five hundred feet of film. So each KH-9 bucket would turn into between ninety to one hundred and sixty cans of original film. In turn, these original cans would be duplicated so the branches would have a reference copy, and duplicated again so that analysis of point targets and search imagery could happen individually. When a bucket came to NPIC, it was measured in tons, and it came in large truckloads of film cans.

The imagery analysts' favorite system, the KH-9, covered a contiguous swath of a large area at a resolution that allowed imagery analysts to see and identify most military equipment. Additionally, in 1973, the three KH-8 high-resolution satellites, each with two buckets, would add another 32,000 feet for an annual total of 195 miles of satellite images for 350 imagery analysts to look at.

Depending on how the camera was used, the KH-9 could provide images of different sizes. All the frames were six and a half inches wide, and some were more than ten feet long. Each of these images could cover an area approximately sixteen by three hundred nautical miles, or a total of 4,800 square nautical miles. This is roughly the straight-line distance between Washington

D. C. and Cincinnati, Ohio, and eight miles on either side of the line. The resolution on each of these photographs at nadir was so good that trained interpreters could count individual vehicles and identify what type of vehicle they were looking at. (The exact size of the area covered on each image depended on where the satellite was in its elliptical orbit when the photograph was taken. If the satellite was closer to earth, near perigee, then the photograph would cover less area. When the satellite was farther from earth, near apogee, then it would cover more area.) The KH-9 was a scanning camera. As it scanned an area, the resolution was substantially better at the center of the image frame when the camera was at nadir; rather than at the ends of the frame, where some analysts commented that it was like looking into someone's bathroom window one hundred and fifty miles away.

After the KH-9 film arrived at NPIC, the exploitation process began with long scissors. Using the paper coverage plots for the mission to help identify where the imagery was obtained, the imagery analysts would first look at the locations with the priority questions. Often, there were so many priority questions, that multiple copies of the film were delivered to allow the imagery analysts to look at them simultaneously. This enabled the deployed missile imagery analysts to look at film at the same time as the test range imagery analysts, the nuclear test imagery analysts, and the ground, air, naval, and air defense experts.

While these experts were scouring known targets, the newer, lower-graded imagery analysts were busy with long scissors, cutting and taping photography into rolls of contiguous search areas. Cutting and re-splicing hundreds of rolls of KH-9 film took a good part of the first twenty-four hours. Locating, segmenting, indexing, re-sequencing, and identifying the cloud-free photographs was done on a non-stop, overtime basis. Often, this work took until the second or third day after the mission was received. (By the later KH-9 missions, multiple copies of the film would be delivered, and they would be arranged by search responsibility. Some NPIC branches searched by this code, but some continued to cut up the rolls of film.)

The huge volume of KH-9 imagery meant that rapidly reviewing all incoming film became nearly impossible. So the imagery analysts and their managers devised prioritization techniques.

In the age of discovery, when fewer targets were being identified, monitoring of these "known" targets could be accomplished more quickly and the transition from monitoring to searching could happen earlier in the exploitation process. But, the thousands of targets discovered between 1960 and 1973 meant that the search competed with the increasing amount of target monitoring needed to measure changes at the "known" targets.

The age of comprehension, instrumental in enabling the support to arms control negotiations, meant that with each bucket delivered to Building 213, search would lag even a little further behind. This caused a serious dilemma. The fixed number of imagery analysts, combined with the increased amount of film, covering a larger area in greater detail, meant that each imagery analyst had to assess the risk of not having looked at some film that he or she was responsible for.

The flood of film drove imagery analysts to identify new techniques to manage their work. Those who tried to manage traditional processes more effectively found that they did not work. There were not enough overtime, energy, or imagery analysts available to work the combination of the KH-9 and KH-8 missions as they had worked the KH-4 missions. Those analysts who shifted from managing only the knowledge of individual targets, to assessing the value of an individual target by understanding its relation to the weapons systems or strategic manufacturing processes, were able to create a way of keeping up. The traditional indexing to the "story" was how the imagery analysts compensated for the lack of rapid access to a database or tools to consider the relationship among targets, or to a more rapid reporting mechanism, even for text-only reporting.

Continually, imagery analysts and their managers were calculating the risk of a miss. Some would search areas only if they received information from other sources; some would adopt other schemes like frequency of collection, levels of activity, or accessibility of terrain to decide what to look at. Often this was done with their managers' knowledge and assistance, but not always. These strategies worked, but they also contained the seeds of failure in a few notable cases. The challenge of not looking at all the film as their predecessors had done, weighed on the imagery analysts and the managers. Some branches adapted the technique of assigning more search to junior imagery analysts, and letting senior imagery analysts work the point targets. This gave more opportunity for discovery to junior imagery analysts, but it also increased the chances of a significant "miss" as less experienced imagery analysts sometimes did not know the context of what they were looking at, or they were unable to recognize subtle indicators of change. As a result, some young imagery analysts thrived, while others went through "O, shit" moments that marked their careers.

The photo-interpreters who became successful imagery analysts had learned to "rethink" what they had seen. Instead of focusing exclusively on the physical characteristics of their targets, they learned to look at the equipment that was present, for evidence of changes to the target, the order-of-battle, or force structure. The successful imagery analysts were better able to fit their observations into context. They explained why their observations provided greater evidence for one analytic explanation or story than another. Those interpreters who focused only on the characteristics of equipment or facilities struggled.

Instead of restricting their observations to answer only 'what' and 'where' questions, successful imagery analysts combined their observations from imagery with logical inferences to answer 'how' and 'why' questions. This change in mindset caused them to restrict their observations to those targets that helped them answer key intelligence questions. In this era of comprehension, observing changes in a factory or facility was not enough. It became necessary to explain or relate what any change meant in light of some activity outside that particular installation or how that particular installation fit into the understanding of a more abstract issue such as production rates, or force capability, or arms control, or communication networks, or order of battle. This change from description to explanation altered the NPIC culture. The combination of the KH-9 and John Hicks' changes to NPIC's work accelerated the age of comprehension. Through combining their observations with analysis and other sources of intelligence, it forced photo-interpreters to become imagery analysts, and it prepared NPIC to be one of the first organizations to enter the digital age.

The IA School

The last of Hicks's changes to NPIC was the creation of the National Imagery Analysis Course in 1978. This basic training course was created out of necessity. When the air force couldn't incorporate the information about the new digital KH-11 into its training program, which NPIC had attended for years, NPIC, as well as CIA and DIA needed a new basic training program. NPIC had been using a number of veteran imagery photo-interpreters and managers—Bob Bollen, Jim

Hopkins, Bill Fisher, and Bill Holley—to prepare the new hires before they went to Offutt Air Force Base in Omaha for formal training. Their efforts were formalized into a 21-week program in Building 213 to ensure that the new NPIC imagery analysts had a sufficient foundation in photo-interpretation to be able to work with both film-return and near-real-time systems. NIIRs certification became part of the new curriculum.

As well as the elements of feature recognition and photo-interpretation, the National Imagery Analysis Course taught the new imagery analysts the culture of NPIC. The course taught the identification of all military equipment using the tried and true teaching techniques of flashcards with silhouettes and scale models of the equipment. But the veteran instructors, who had all learned about photo-interpretation in the military in the 1940s and 1950s, had not modified their teaching techniques. So they taught distinctions among types of military equipment without political correctness. In every class, the air instructor would offer to let a student hold his model of the Soviet Antonov-22 aircraft, after which he or she would be told that it was better known by its NATO designator, the COCK. And they helped the new imagery analysts remember the HORMONE, a Soviet light helicopter. "All of you can make a HORMONE. How do you make a HORMONE? Don't pay her." But the curriculum was structured, competitive, and rigorous, and the NIAC became a rite of passage, despite the vulgar teaching. Each class had an honor student and interim grades were routinely sent back to the branch chiefs in the exploitation groups.

The Digital Divide

The KH-8, in orbit since 1965, and the KH-9, in orbit since 1971, had been "dropping" hundreds of thousands of feet of film annually. Throughout this period, NPIC's need to store, array, and communicate all the information from this film could not be satisfied by any available computer technology. And, in 1977, the problems caused by the lack of information technology would become far worse.

NPIC's leadership, long before 1977, recognized the need to automate its data and information. The growing volume of information strained the computer memory, transfer rate, and computational speed of the NPIC's mainframe computer. To some degree, NPIC coped with this shortcoming by relying on the memories, shoeboxes, and stories of its imagery analysts and their managers. The stories saved the system because computer memory and processing power were more expensive and less flexible than the imagery analysts' memories. But this tradition could not be sustained when NPIC would have to operate twenty-four hours a day, seven days a week.

The cost of technology strained the NPIC budget, and NPIC's needs exceeded the state of available technology. By the second year of KH-9 operations, in the early 1970s, the volume of information had everyone's attention at NPIC. Imagery analysts were constantly busy, and they were extremely busy in the first few weeks after a bucket dropped. The process of issuing immediate mission reports continued, and the volume of information in these reports far exceeded that of previous systems.

NPIC's existing technology in Building 213 was not up to the challenge of exploiting, storing, and disseminating the KH-9 intelligence. Until 1975, the mainframe system relied on batch processing. Imagery analysts wrote in longhand, and secretaries typed reports with electric typewriters. But entering information into the database lagged far behind the exploitation process, and the lag was growing. Batch terminals to input the data were first used by some imagery analysts in the early 1970s, but at the time most of the workforce did not adopt their use.

During the 1970s, the imagery analysts and photo-interpreters thought that their time was better spent on light tables than on a keyboard at a computer terminal. Many in NPIC were aware that this process must change, but no one was sure what the changes would entail. The impetus to change their work processes was threefold.

The intellectual impetus came from John Hicks, who knew that if the photo-interpreters were to become imagery analysts, they would have to incorporate more sources of information into their thinking and writing. These sources were most readily available on a computer system that had feeds from DIA, CIA, and NSA. Initially, the workforce used collateral researchers to find information for the imagery analysts. The quality and availability of collateral assistants would become a chokepoint, and an increasing number of imagery analysts became dissatisfied and wanted to do their own research.

The scarcity of time for imagery analysts was the operational impetus for the new process. While the terminals that held information from other agencies were scarce, these imagery analysts would use them when the collateral researchers were unavailable. The analysts wanted more access to information at their desks without the need for "handoffs" and intermediaries.

The technical impetus was driven by their managers who saw how many steps and transfers of information or "handoffs" were necessary to create intelligence from the imagery. The delays between the receipt of film and the release of an intelligence cable or report weighed on them. As they became aware of how much additional information would be coming from the new digital imagery, they wondered how much NPIC would have to accelerate its information flow if it was not to be overcome with film. The small group of managers and imagery analysts cleared into the Special Projects Working group (SPWG) were most aware of this.

As the SPWG learned more about the future near-real-time system in 1973 and 1974, it began to comprehend how inadequate the existing computer support would be. By the middle 1970s, the NPIC mainframes again had been upgraded, but the number of terminals was inadequate. Branches shared one computer terminal for four to eight imagery analysts. Essentially, imagery analysts used the computer terminals for text input only. They modified their work processes to shorten the keyboarding and storage demands by using acronyms, abbreviations, and tri-graphs as much as possible. But the volume of information still strained the NPIC system. All the terminals were hardwired to a local device, called a multiterm, which controlled the communications between the terminals and the mainframe. Imagery analysts came to dread hearing the call to "Reset the Multiterm," as resetting would wipe out any unsaved work for all eight imagery analysts then on that local net.

Each communications line between each piece of equipment had to be encased in conduit to keep information secure. So many thousands of feet of conduit were in the ceilings and along the walls of Building 213, that the imagery analysts joked that after a nuclear blast, they and the concrete would be vaporized, but the conduit would remain standing to preserve the outline of the building.

The Building 213 network slowed noticeably when many imagery analysts were trying to get cables published, or the day's database target entries and remarks entered into the system. Late afternoons, particularly Mondays and Fridays, were notoriously bad. These experiences did not bode well for the future, and the SPWG recognized it. So it began to plan to pull the work of the imagery analysts into the digital age.

As the SPWG began to understand the volume of daily imagery that would come in and the opportunity for near-real-time intelligence, it became more involved in shaping future technology. This new kind of imagery meant that display of an image and analysis of that image would someday be possible on the computer screen. No longer would there be any need to produce hard-copy imagery. Although most imagery analysts had no experience working on computers, much less programming them, some of the more active imagery analysts began to experiment with the computers as a way of viewing and exploiting the new imagery. They began to learn how to program the computers by learning code.

An unexpected challenge for the imagery analysts in the SPWG was moving development beyond what the contractors had done after they had given up trying to understand how the craft of imagery analysis was performed. In an attempt to understand the workflow, the contractors gave the imagery analysts gridded paper—eighty blocks by fifty-five blocks—and told them that they needed to design a separate screen for each step and each decision in the analytic process of selecting an image, and for exploiting either known targets or for looking for new targets.

Drawing the workflow, and defining the information and the format needed to move through each step in the process, consumed about three months of concentrated work. This work was so difficult that it gave Mark Baker, the principal imagery analyst, an ulcer. The new system forced imagery analysts to learn about computers. Although painful, it was the first step in preparing for the analysis of digital photography, and it was the next step in the tradition of NPIC making its own tools.

This exercise also forced the imagery analysts to start thinking about how they were going to manage information on an hourly basis instead of the sporadic monthly, weekly, or daily basis that they had become the norm over the past sixteen years of film-based imagery.

NPIC would no longer be in one place working on one schedule. The imagery analysts and support people working with digital imagery from the new satellite would be at work twenty-four hours a day, seven days a week, in two locations—Building 213 and PEG. Most critical information would come to them when the satellite was traversing the Soviet Union in daylight, which was in the middle of the night on the east coast of the United States. NPIC's practice of sharing "stories," storing information in "shoeboxes," and "indexing" new finds against the story, which had worked well from the Steuart Building until this time, would also have to change.

The cost of the new imaging satellite and its infrastructure, which required an entirely new ground station, made it the object of much congressional attention. The NRO developers may have had a greater sense of the system's possibilities than the imagery analysts. As a result, the satellite program office attempted to have those NPIC imagery analysts working on the near-real-time imagery made subordinate to the NRO. John Hicks successfully made the case to CIA that separating imagery analysts organizationally, only because they worked on different sensors, would damage the craft of imagery analysis. Hicks persuaded CIA leadership that such an arrangement would, in very short order, lead to conflicting, incomplete, or wrong analysis. Although NPIC kept control of the imagery analysis, the NRO's engineers and developers sensed that the new type of sensor would change the nature of space reconnaissance, as well as require much more digital and computer support. Their assessment turned out to be much more accurate than NPIC envisioned. This lack of foresight by NPIC would prove problematic.

While Hicks successfully applied his all-source background to change the nature of the work at the light tables, he did not foresee the inherent possibility that the new sensor could change the amount of intelligence that NPIC could produce on a daily basis. While he recognized that NPIC needed a more robust computer network, he lacked previous experience with managing large-scale developmental or technical projects.

As a consequence, Hicks did not fully recognize the need for better computer support, and his approach to introducing digital analytic tools was evolutionary rather than revolutionary. While his approach might have been limited by the budget, it did not set up the initial NPIC operations at the ground station for success. When Hicks became director in 1973, NPIC had 120 terminals hardwired to a Sperry 494, a computer that NPIC had gotten from NSA. Each imagery analyst's report on an individual target took approximately fifteen minutes to enter, which necessitated lots of batch inputs during nights and weekends after a bucket of film came into NPIC. Imagery analysts had to queue up to use the terminals. When crises hit, or a number of aircraft missions were added, the system was overwhelmed. In recognition of the anticipated daily increase in imagery, this system was upgraded for the digital satellite. A Sperry 1110 was installed and by 1977. It was connected to three hundred Delta Data terminals at Building 213 and the Priority Exploitation Group at the beginning of operations at the new ground station. But from inception this system was overwhelmed.

The Technology Wedge

Before the near-real-time satellite was launched in December 1976, the technology was thought to be sufficient to handle the volume of new information. But the difficulties experienced in coping with the volume from the film return systems alone presaged even worse problems. No one had a real sense of what would be required in the first months when digital imagery started arriving every day, along with photography in buckets every few weeks.

By the late 1970s, the KH-9 and the digital KH-11 had changed NPIC. It had been operating for a few years from two locations, with two kinds of high-resolution satellite imagery, and the two kinds of imaging satellites—chemical-based, film-return, and the digital, near-real-time. Despite the intelligence opportunities provided by the blending of the two complementary technologies, the side effect of the new technology was dividing NPIC's analytic culture, straining the technology, and partitioning a divide among the imagery analysts.

Because the digital imagery file sizes were so large, relative to the computer and communications technology available, images from this new sensor were converted into hard-copy film. While the workstations that could exploit digital imagery existed, they were prohibitively expensive, even by the standards of the NRO budget. So the ground station built a large photo-processing facility to make and sort the images into hard-copy film. This processing started digitally. An image writer converted the digits into a photographic negative and duplicated them into positives that were mechanically cut and sorted for the imagery analysts to exploit. The imagery analysts nicknamed this device the "wacker-stacker." While all of this new technology was being planned, created, operated, and refined at the ground station, NPIC continued to be busier and busier at Building 213.

The original PEG staffing plan to work the new satellite with fewer than one hundred imagery analysts proved successful, but the fast pace of the operation led to some operational decisions about how to collect the new imagery, what work to do immediately, and what to defer until later in the day. This distinction between immediate and the deferred work was known as preliminary exploitation and current exploitation. This distinction was helpful in prioritizing the indications and warning mission. But for the other types of analysis done at PEG—high current interest—the distinction created pressure and conflict with the rest of NPIC.

Despite the frustrations of the new technology and the computer problems, the imagery analysts and their managers at PEG learned two important insights. PEG's imagery analysts began to see quickly the intelligence potential of near-real-time imagery to address a wider range of intelligence problems. After the processes were debugged, the imagery analysts and managers could routinely produce intelligence quickly, in minutes and hours. This recognition would soon transform NPIC.

Training for the new computer system at PEG began right after the initial operation of the KH-11 in January 1976, and testing of the system began in April 1977. The new computer system was turned on in June, but within three weeks database discrepancies arose between the files of the imagery analysts at PEG and the imagery analysts in Building 213. The technology discrepancies compounded a problem created by the PEG managers' ideas about how to operate.

Initially, PEG's managers thought that imagery analysts could be organized by regions of the world, but that concept did not align with a satellite that covered the world nearly hourly in orbits that progressed from East to West. So the imagery analysts were organized by functional specialties: ground forces, air, missile, and navy/nuclear targets all over the world. But PEG managers and imagery analysts began to work in a way that created some internal problems for NPIC. The receipt of imagery before the rest of NPIC, much less the rest of the Intelligence Community, put PEG in an advantageous position. But this advantage sometimes would create unnecessary friction.

The PEG leadership developed a culture around an operating rule that led to unnecessary conflict. They asserted that for the first twenty-four hours, all near-real-time imagery was theirs exclusively to report on. In practice, this meant PEG's imagery analysts published first, whether or not they were the subject matter experts. Because NPIC's imagery analysts who were experts had the same image at Building 213 within twenty-four hours, fierce internal competition and disagreements with the "calls" sometimes developed. This was especially nettlesome to the Building 213 imagery analysts when the intelligence question was one that had to be answered immediately, and they had no input during that twenty-four hour period.

These practices infuriated some imagery analysts. As fiercely competitive leaders led both groups, each group was not above "scoring points" on the other. For those imagery analysts in both locations with a spirit of cooperation, they would ensure that their work included input from imagery analysts from the other group. But the imagery analysts who were driven by a sense of "ownership" would attempt to show up other imagery analysts inside NPIC and outside in the Intelligence Community. The problems inherent in this mode of operating were worsened by the new computer system.

These challenges of the middle 1970s were only the beginning. Even with the planned growth in the number of imagery analysts, the current processes or tools would not enable NPIC to successfully manage this increased volume and pace of data. Les Dirks, who had taken over CIA's Directorate of Science and Technology in 1976, was among the first to recognize this. His recognition of the problem was part of his reason, in 1978, for replacing John Hicks with Rutledge P. "Hap" Hazzard as NPIC director. Hap understood very well the potential of the new technology. But his first challenge was to convince the intelligence committees of Congress to invest a large sum of money in NPIC.

By the time of Hap Hazzard's arrival, the technical and analytic leadership at NPIC understood the problem well. Although the NPIC leadership team was not cohesive, the challenge of digital imagery required them to plan for the future. The new Special Projects Working Group (SPWG) started to define the requirements for a new NPIC computer system that would be needed to double the amount of its computer storage and the number of computer terminals. As is the nature with large government programs, the NPIC modernization program took more than a year to conceive, and its cost had to be spread out over a five-year risky and ambitious schedule. While the program was planned to handle a huge growth in data, the number of imagery analysts over that time would only double.

And, all these technological changes would have to be developed, tested, and installed into a much busier workplace. While the CIA's S&T, NRO's, and NPIC's leadership were defining the requirements for the new system to meet the new challenges, world crises continued. The Vietnamese and the Chinese fought a short border war. The Chinese, now more suspicious of the Soviet Union, kept a large military force along their mutual border. The

Soviet Union had invaded Afghanistan, and Iran was experiencing increasing internal unrest. In addition, the Soviets and the Chinese were developing and deploying more powerful missiles and warheads, and building new generations of aircraft, tanks, artillery, ships, and submarines. Conflict was breaking out throughout the Third World, in Nicaragua, Angola, Morocco, Libya, Sri Lanka, Cambodia, Yemen, and Lebanon. In the Middle East, terrorism by radical Islamic groups continued to develop. And, the US economy was shaken in the late 70s when OPEC raised energy prices, and inflation began to affect everyone's buying power.

Despite the economic travails, NPIC's successes at imagery analysis, and the recognition of its need to succeed persuaded the congressional committees to approve the NPIC Modernization Program or, as it became known, the *Upgrade*. At the time, it was the largest single line item in the CIA's budget. The investment in technology for each imagery analyst was a million dollars. The overall initial estimate of the cost of the program was about a quarter of a billion dollars. NPIC had come a long way from the time when Art Lundahl boasted about spending forty thousand dollars to equip each photo-interpreter. And it had also come a long way from when Art Lundahl knew every NPIC employee by name.

The internal issues simmered through the late 1970s and early 1980s between those NPICers who had served at PEG and those who had only worked in Building 213. Director Hazzard tried to reduce the internal tensions by replacing the first leader at PEG with a respected senior leader from IEG, the analytic group at Building 213, but both group chiefs had a style of managing based on personal loyalty. They relied on subordinates with whom they had long experience, and their definition of long experience included socializing, drinking, and softball.

The combination of two distinctly different operations, the new technology, employee dissatisfaction with personnel practices, and a perception of prejudicial work practices were all in the air when the CIA Inspector General came to NPIC in late 1982.

CHAPTER 7

THE SLAMMER AND UPTOWN

I n November 1982, CIA's inspector general (IG) began to inspect NPIC. The CIA's inspector general reviewed how well offices and programs were being managed; provided suggestions for improvement; identified managerial problems; and conducted independent reviews of business plans, strategies, operational efficiency, customer feedback, employee morale; and any other specific issues requested by senior leadership. IG inspections also discovered unanticipated problems and issues. When employees made specific complaints, the CIA's inspector general investigated the potential wrongdoing, and it also had an auditing function.

By the fall of 1982, NPIC's technical problems looked to be in hand. Hap Hazzard had instituted configuration management, which he had used successfully at the NRO. To diminish the rivalry between the analytic groups, he had moved the PEG senior manager back to Building 213, and transferred an IEG senior manager into PEG. While the director recognized the need for organizational change, unfortunately, he did not fully understand the NPIC culture and how NPIC exerted influence in the Intelligence Community.

As one of the larger CIA offices, the NPIC inspection required several sub-teams comprising one or two inspectors to look at different groups in the Center. The IG operating practice was to interview the group managers, randomly select individuals to interview, and announce the inspection schedule so that any employee who desired could get an anonymous interview. Because NPIC had about a thousand CIA employees and more than two hundred DIA and military employees in 1983, this inspection took longer than most.

In January 1984, the IG presented its not-so-glowing report to R. Evans (Evan) Hineman, the S&T Directorate chief responsible for NPIC. The inspector general also briefed the executive summary of the report to the director of NPIC and his senior group chiefs. The serious findings that required immediate change were specified with a required response and a plan for action that were due in ninety days.

The report found that the NPIC development program, the Upgrade, did not have sufficient oversight. It also criticized NPIC's personnel practices for discriminating against women and minorities. When the IG team talked to the CIA components that supported NPIC, the CIA's Office of Personnel was critical of NPIC's personnel management practices, and the Directorate of Intelligence pointed out that NPIC was not paying sufficient attention to the DI's information needs.

The report criticized NPIC for operating in a way that reduced its effectiveness in both imagery collection and intelligence coordination by not supporting the all-source analysts at CIA and DIA, and by indirectly competing with them by writing uncoordinated analytic products that challenged all-source organizational positions. NPIC's external issues were compounded by the internal rifts that were dividing the imagery analyst groups and by a strong perception of unequal and unfair treatment in different parts of NPIC.

While NPIC had been the Intelligence Community's pre-eminent photo-interpretation organization throughout the 1960s and 1970s, it had developed serious issues by 1983. Some of its issues grew from the conflict between the film-return culture developed over twenty years at Building 213, and the PEG digital culture, which was gradually coming into Building 213 in the early 1980s. As a consequence of the findings in the IG report, some changes were suggested, some changes were directed, and a new director was selected.

The External Issues

Autonomy. From its inception, NPIC was not physically integrated with CIA and, after it became a national center in 1961, it began to emphasize this "separateness." In its most well-known success, the Cuban missile crisis, NPIC's findings contradicted the CIA all-source analysts and the Intelligence Community's national intelligence estimate on Cuba. Since NPIC's reporting on the bomber and missile gaps in the 1950s and early 1960s, the long term search for and identification of targets in the Soviet Union in NPIC's second era—the era of comprehension—had undercut many CIA analytic products and Defense Department program proposals. NPIC always supported the all-source analysts, but, as it began to change from photo-interpretation to imagery analysis, the change resulted in more (sometimes uncoordinated) independent reporting. Some officers in both CIA and DIA thought this independent reporting was not in the NPIC charter or "lane in the road." When NPIC offered reasons for not doing a project proposed by either of these organizations, it worsened its relationships. Frequently, NPIC's reasons, based on a lack of imagery analysts, did not convince either organization.

NPIC staffing remained a combination of CIA and DIA civilian personnel, and active duty military, mostly officers. While most of its support and technical people were CIA officers, NPIC was nearly a self-contained agency, and this enhanced its strong sense of autonomy. Some long-term employees had contact with CIA or DIA only when they were hired, and when they retired. Most dealt with their home agencies only when they were in training classes, needed a physical for foreign travel, took a polygraph to keep their clearances, or travelled to Langley or Arlington Hall for Intelligence Community meetings.

NPIC's "isolated" culture was positive in that the Center focused on its unique mission and tradecraft. But its autonomy fueled a tenacious independence that was not always well received. Much of NPIC's "perspective" grew out of its single focus on the process of photo-interpretation and imagery analysis. For example, the working hours of NPIC's imagery analysts were shaped by the early morning deliveries of hardcopy film from the ground station. While this enabled imagery analysts to get to their information more quickly, and to commute "downtown" before the D.C. rush hour, it also made them reluctant to stay later in the day when either DIA or CIA was coordinating finished intelligence products for policymaker use early the next day. The continuation of the car-pool culture also contributed to this "early in – early out" work schedule. The daily collection meetings, or the daily policymaker production or Intelligence Community coordination meetings often took place later in the day, and NPIC sometimes was either not invited or overlooked.

Autonomy did not help NPIC's standing within the culture of CIA. Proximity to the DCI and the clandestine services was highly valued in this culture, and NPIC had neither. In fact, in CIA, NPIC was looked down upon.

It was not located on the bucolic suburban campus at Langley, but in a run-down D.C. neighborhood on a corner with two liquor stores and a warehouse. At the time, no CIA recruiting brochure contained a photo of Building 213, although it did show a photograph of an imagery analyst at a light table. The Directorate of Intelligence at CIA paid more respect to its own Office of Imagery Analysis, which focused its hiring on academic credentials, as well as experience with interpreting imagery. As a result, some OIA's imagery analysts took on the hauteur that sometimes characterized the Directorate of Intelligence.

The relationship between NPIC and OIA was competitive. Imagery analysis was so important that the Directorate of Intelligence had created its own dedicated support division in 1967. When in 1972, NPIC became part of CIA's Directorate of Science and Technology, this dedicated imagery photo-interpretation division remained in the Directorate of Intelligence becoming the Imagery Analysis Service, and eventually in 1976, the Office of Imagery Analysis (OIA). OIA also provided imagery support to CIA's clandestine organizations, but this always was a smaller effort than its support to CIA's DI all-source analysts. In all three imagery analysis organizations, NPIC, OIA, and DIA's DX-5, imagery analysts competed on priority issues. This competitive practice led to much redundant analysis and many conflicts among the imagery analysts and their respective managers.

Like CIA, the Defense Intelligence Agency had its own imagery analysis organization, called Defense Exploitation (DX), also housed in Building 213. NPIC provided services of common concern to both of these departmental offices. Each of the all-source intelligence agencies wanted to have its own dedicated imagery support elements that could, when it was in the parochial interest of the parent agency, disagree with the autonomous NPIC analysis. Nonetheless, the departmental imagery analysis organizations strengthened NPIC. Each of these smaller organizations also was not in the mainstream of their parent all-source agencies, and neither had the resources of NPIC. Both departmental organizations came to NPIC for systems support, and services of common concern like equipment procurement, software development, some imagery training, photo lab, and publications support. Each of them, in their own way, strengthened NPIC's reputation. While OIA's and DIA's imagery analysts were frequently excellent analysts, they also were not held in the same regard by their parent organizations as the all-source analysts. When disagreements arose between the imagery analysts and the all-source analysts in CIA or DIA, all-source analysts would nearly always get the last word.

NPIC and the Collection Committee

When the U-2 had been new in the late 1950s, the demand for images was far greater than the potentially available number. Art Lundahl had been an advocate for using an independent arbitrator of these competing requirements and keeping NPIC neutral. Initially the Ad Hoc Requirements Committee or ARC adjudicated and ranked these requirements. Lundahl had kept his photo-interpreters away from the collection conflicts, and he insured that his organization would not be a voting member of the committee. But as more satellites began to fly and the competition for their information developed, this arrangement was no longer viable and had to be modified.

In 1960, to make the process more systematic, the ARC had been reorganized into COMOR, Committee on Requirements. In 1967, its name was expanded to COMIREX, the Committee on Imagery Requirements and Exploitation, to reflect that it would now designate which agency or service should exploit the film. This committee had a few roles. Most of its work was managing the collection of the limited number of images that could be taken to meet the vastly greater number of national and military requirements. These requirements often competed against each other geographically. Frequently, in the Soviet Union, missile bases were near air bases, and air defense sites were near to both. The nature of the requirements process meant that the air force, interested in air defense sites, competed against the arms control community, which wanted to look at missile bases more frequently in the same area as the air defense sites. As imagery intelligence grew in importance, the growth in the requested number of images and the frequency of requested observations far outstripped the capacity of the satellites to collect and the analytic organizations to look at them. COMIREX managed the competition for which images were taken and which were not, but after the introduction of the near-real-time sensors in 1976, its processes and managers began to be overwhelmed by the challenges of accelerated collection. Each organization that exploited imagery had its own process for managing the flood of information.

As the competition for imagery collection became more contentious, NPIC began to take on an advisory capability. Because it had no institutional position, NPIC started as a trusted technical advisor about what collection would produce the optimal results. As the capability and capacity of the satellites increased, the Intelligence Community put more collection requirements into COMIREX. As the volume was too much to manage manually, the committee began to use a weighting algorithm. As NPIC used its autonomy to provide advice, the COMIREX used bureaucracy to manage collection conflicts. This process was tolerable until the near-real-time satellites went into orbit. At that time, NPIC, particularly PEG, recognized that it would have to advocate for the collection it needed to meet priority or fleeting national issues. The increasing advocacy of NPIC ran into the COMIREX bureaucracy. NPIC recognized that the bureaucratic application of the collection algorithm cost it fleeting collection opportunities. As a result, the relationship between NPIC and COMIREX worsened.

By the late 1970's, collection requirements were submitted into an automated system, the COMIREX Automated Management System, or CAMS. This system helped the requirements officers rank (prioritize) targets. The system used an algorithm that factored in the priority of the target, its associated intelligence question, the rankings of all requested targets, the target's location, the frequency that imagery analysts wanted to look at a target, and how precisely interpretable an image needed to be to answer the questions being asked.

As the value of imagery grew in the Intelligence Community and in the Defense Department, the process of acquiring imagery over a target became even more contentious. In a bureaucratic reaction, COMIREX became more focused on the process and, as a consequence, its processes became driven by consensus, as much as by priority. Frequently, COMIREX staffers resolved the conflicts by blaming the algorithm. One of the first PEG operations chiefs described COMIREX as a place for those with natural obstructionist tendencies. The difference between how NPIC imagery analysts and how the COMIREX staff defined collection management created a wedge between those two organizations. Imagery analysts, particularly those who had worked at PEG, knew how regular and frequent imagery could change and improve the Intelligence Community's understanding of issues. Unfortunately, COMIREX's collection managers did not quickly recognize the collection flexibility or the opportunities made possible by digital near-real-time imagery. The traditional COMIREX process of relying on the standing collection algorithm was proving to be too rigid to take advantage of the technological capability to change collection more frequently. And, once consensus entered into the discussions, the military services would team with DIA to present a consensus-based case for collecting the departmental priorities that would outweigh the NPIC case based on the national priorities. By 1983, the rift between COMIREX collection managers and the imagery analysts from the various intelligence organizations was becoming poisonous, and it was a prominent factor in the increasingly contentious daily collection planning meetings.

Any community member could veto or stop the nomination of any other member. Sometimes, partisan politics broke out. A simple typographical error could be sufficient for any requirements officer to take a nomination out of contention. While this process did not endear requirements officers to the imagery analysts, the delays introduced into the process did not matter as long as the determination took place before the next launch, and the satellite could achieve the needed resolution to interpret the imagery. But after the near-real-time satellites went operational, when priority collection had to be planned and accomplished within twenty-four hours, this process precluded getting an image quickly or observing fleeting activity.

Missed collection opportunities put COMIREX managers at odds with the NPIC analytic process and its managers. The collection process, as managed by COMIREX, also would let any community member veto any other member's nomination by having the system put the collection into "rework." When priorities were competing in the same geographic area this led to some ineffective and inefficient collection.

Under COMIREX's National Tasking Plan, each departmental imagery organization took responsibility for providing information to its patron service to help develop its programs: the air force took the worst case view on Soviet missiles and aircraft; the navy the worst case on Soviet submarines. NPIC ended up enhancing its reputation by focusing on what it could see and analyze from the film. As it was not subordinate to any one organization, NPIC could take an independent point of view if the imagery analysis supported such a view. The policy community and congressional oversight soon recognized this autonomy as a value and insisted that NPIC's view should be considered in any critical discussions of threats to the United States. But their assessment of NPIC's value was not universal.

Parts of the Intelligence Community thought that CIA was not telling the full story. In particular, when the arms control negotiations began in the late 1960s and early 1970s, a number of skeptics worried about the likelihood of the Soviet Union cheating on the treaties they were negotiating. This group also believed that having CIA, a non-military organization in charge of the imagery satellites, allowed the Agency to slant its reporting in favor of the Soviet Union.

This point of view was captured in 1986 in the opening pages of William Burrows' *Deep Black: Space Espionage and National Security*. Burrows interviewed the retired head of Air Force Intelligence, Major General George Keegan. Keegan believed that the CIA had underreported the extent of Soviet activities so as to facilitate the arms control negotiations between the two countries. But to back up his case Keegan did not cite as evidence weapons or strategic developments. He focused on the identification of basements and building foundations.

Keegan saw fallout shelters being built in the foundations of apartment buildings in major Soviet cities; the foundations of factory buildings held large underground bunker complexes with food, water, and fuel storage. Keegan cited these imagery observations, and Soviet doctrine, as evidence that the Soviet Union had planned an extensive civil defense network with the intention of having its leadership, military infrastructure, and a significant part of its population survive a nuclear attack. Because Soviet civil defense was not allocated to any specific part of the imagery community under the National Tasking Plan, many parts of the community felt free to write about it.

The National Tasking Plan focused on military capabilities, military economics, non-military economics, nuclear energy, and science and technology. The guidance document for the imagery community focused only on the military and strategic capabilities. The only civilian categories in the NTP were related to potential military capabilities, such as nuclear weapons and strategic industries. Measures of social resilience such as civil defense were not considered, as there was too much work and too many targets related to the military capabilities for the imagery analysts to look at. Because there was so little intelligence reporting from Soviet human sources on their intentions or potential responses after a nuclear attack, the understanding of Soviet civil defenses remained a critical, unanswered intelligence gap, but not officially one for the imagery community.

Late in 1976, General Keegan retired from the air force right before the beginning of the Carter administration, almost exactly at the beginning of the use of digital electro-optical imagery. But Keegan's perspective, based as much on opinion and suspicion, as on an in-depth look at the issue, indicated that the Intelligence Community's understanding of Soviet civil defense had not developed much since 1960 when Arthur Lundahl heard Chancellor Konrad Adenauer debrief on this subject. The air force's interest in civil defense also illustrated the uniformed services' tendency to produce intelligence on issues outside of their departmental responsibilities under the National Tasking Plan, especially if they perceived that the reporting would help justify their programs and budget. While the three imagery organizations in Washington usually cooperated, that same cooperation did not extend to individual commands, such as the Strategic Air Command or other service elements, like the naval intelligence organization in Suitland, Maryland. And inside the beltway it certainly was not practiced universally.

Lack of Coordination

The NPIC culture of discovery, which grew out of individual pride and status growing from the original search mission, developed into a meritocracy. Certain imagery analysts were legendary searchers. But, such a culture did not encourage collaborative efforts. As more and more film became available, issues, particularly high priority issues such as the Soviet missile force, were divided among more and more imagery analysts. NPIC's imagery analysts working the Soviet missile force issue were responsible for both area search, and for monitoring the existing targets for any changes. For important issues like the Soviet missile force, OIA and DIA also would look at the same targets to try to either corroborate or contradict NPIC. While competition among imagery analysts was generally healthy, it did not foster a culture of cooperation.

In one instance, one imagery organization believed that some circular objects were evidence of rocket motors related to a certain missile system. This imagery analyst built an elaborate theory about how these circular objects came to be at this particular facility. The theory, if it could be proven, would have forced the Intelligence Community to change how it thought about this weapons system.

The NPIC imagery analyst had a different view. He thought that these circular objects were a pile of discarded tires. He was unsuccessful at convincing his peer of this interpretation. When an image with better interpretability was collected, and the circular objects were confirmed as tires, thoughts of collaboration were not what came to mind among the NPIC imagery analysts or managers. His NPIC peers nicknamed the imagery analyst with the elaborate theory Mr. Firestone.

By the early 1980s, the tension among imagery analysis organizations, while it sharpened the analysis, also made the reporting more contentious. NPIC began taking institutional viewpoints where the interpretations and opinions of the imagery analysts were included and, in some cases, intermingled with their observations, particularly when all-source analysts were not drawing the same interpretations. That development created unnecessary friction with CIA and DIA, each of which claimed that on some issues, NPIC was not interested in supporting their work. Within the Intelligence Community NPIC was accused of taking independent and uncoordinated positions. Yet, the external criticisms were not as damaging as the internal wedges that were splitting the Center.

The Internal Wedges

As NPIC grew from hundreds of people in the 1960s to more than a thousand by 1982, it began to fragment. While all NPIC employees worked in the same place until late 1975, the two directors who followed Art Lundahl lacked his personal engagement with every employee. As the numbers increased, the group chiefs had trouble learning and remembering all their own employees' names. Employees began to identify themselves with one of the two imagery exploitation groups, the support group, the computer group, or the technical development group. It was harder for NPIC employees to relate their individual contributions to the overall work of NPIC.

This fragmentation grew for a number of reasons. After 1976, the two exploitation groups competed analytically, athletically on softball fields, and organizationally, as the junior leaders of these groups developed coteries in support of their respective group leaders. These coteries did not develop in the support groups, in part, because these groups did different types of work, and their local leadership was not as strong. The introduction of complex computer systems to support the increasing volume of information meant that the technology and development groups grew and assumed their own identity separate from the intelligence mission. The same perception developed among the experts who supported the imagery analysts with mensuration, publishing, model making, and reference services.

Bad Administration

Another challenge at NPIC was its management. Some mid-level leaders at the group and division levels were mediocre. In the post-Vietnam era, after budgets and promotion rates were flattened and the size of the Intelligence Community was reduced, the only way to reward people was to create more hierarchy. Unfortunately, each new level of hierarchy slowed the production of intelligence. Some managers who had been technical or substantive experts became managers merely to obtain a promotion. Some were promoted into managerial positions without training or developmental assignments. Frequently, they were not skilled at communicating with the people, at providing feedback, or monitoring or accelerating the production of intelligence. Some managers had been good photo-interpreters, but were not good at managing, leading, or developing imagery analysts.

By the early 1980s, NPIC had at least four levels of management between the imagery analysts and the director: section, branch, division, and group. The top three levels each had deputies and, often, some sections had teams, resulting in a fifth level. These levels slowed and complicated processes and changes. The intelligence production delays mattered because digital near-real-time imagery transformed production timelines. More and more imagery analysts were experiencing faster and faster intelligence cycles than their managers had ever known.

Some managers, imagery analysts, and support officers at Building 213, particularly those with no experience at the near-real-time ground station, did not recognize the potential of the new system to bring overnight intelligence or information. While these managers might have grasped some changes brought about by the accelerated timelines, even as late as 1983, the film-return processes still shaped their thinking. The film return era was still ongoing, but its future was limited.

The Priority Exploitation Group (PEG) developed in a manner that emphasized its differences from the rest of NPIC. Differences in security, opportunity, geography, and culture caused PEG to operate in a way that challenged many NPIC practices and traditions.

Initially, only a handful of NPIC's employees were cleared into the program that created the near-real-time satellite. For security reasons, these few were ordered to keep their knowledge from their NPIC peers. The initial PEG cadre was handpicked, much like Lundahl's initial group at the Steuart Building. They were rightfully proud of being selected, but their peers at Building 213 did not share that pride.

As the KH-11 program became closer to going operational, these individuals would have to go to the new PEG location. They travelled for meetings, training, and tests in an old government bus that closely resembled the buses with wire-mesh-covered windows that transported prisoners from the District of Columbia jail to Lorton Prison in southern Fairfax County, Virginia. The "chicken-wire bus" became the NPIC nickname for the transportation, and the secret location became "the slammer." In its earliest days, NPIC employees who were going to work at PEG could not tell their families where they worked. The initial PEG cadre, when they volunteered, did not know where or how long they would be working, and that shiftwork would be required for this new assignment. Eventually, since they had to work nights, weekends, and holidays apart from their colleagues and families, their shared spirit and humor fueled a jailhouse-like mentality.

Building 213 was also given a nickname. Because the imagery analysts and managers at PEG remained NPIC employees, they relied on Building 213 for training, personnel actions, analytic coordination, and the credit union. As the PEG facilities were new and not in a run-down neighborhood, the PEG personnel would describe visits to the Navy Yard in southeast Washington as going "uptown."

The biggest difference between the "slammer" and "uptown" was the different mindset about the pace of information coming in and going out. Instead of being able to communicate orally or telephonically with the target and issue experts at Building 213, and having access to the story, imagery analysts in the Priority Exploitation Group (PEG) had to rely on the NPIC system and the database during nights and weekends.

Baselines

Whenever an NPIC imagery analyst found a new target, he or she would have to write a description of the target, called a "baseline," so that anyone in the Intelligence Community who did not have access to film could learn what buildings, features, or equipment were there, as well as how the target was arrayed and oriented.

Baselines were organized functionally so that, along with the geographic information, the report contained the imagery analyst's sense of what constituted normal operations at the target. A good baseline would have a normalcy statement that told the reader what routine operations looked like, so that anyone looking at this target could sense quickly whether the amount of equipment or activity being observed was a "normal" number, sequence, or pattern, or if something was out of the ordinary.

Until the arrival of the digital satellite system, writing baselines had been judged less important than keeping a sense of what was the most current activity at a target. Imagery analysts often fell behind searching for new targets, at keeping the reporting of current activity up to date, and at getting through all the exploitation from each mission before the next bucket came into Building 213. As the volume of film increased, many imagery analysts kept more and more stories in their heads, and wrote less. But the volume of information from the near-real-time imaging satellite made the shoebox obsolete, and it made the baseline essential. The quality of the baselines depended on the diligence and professionalism of the imagery analysts, but these qualities were not monitored.

NPIC's managers encouraged their imagery analysts to know the targets and issues. Unfortunately, this encouragement often took two somewhat contradictory forms. Since the "important" targets were also exploited by the departmental imagery analysts in CIA and DIA, some NPIC managers and imagery analysts adopted a competitive and proprietary approach. They focused on getting the call or version of a story out to the Intelligence Community ahead of other imagery analysts—sometimes at the expense of not getting it correct. Beating the OIA or DIA imagery analysts was their measure of success. NPIC was not alone, as many managers in those organizations took the same approach. None wanted to be scooped. This attitude often manifested itself in expressions of "possession." Imagery analysts would refer to "my targets" or "my account," and become irate when other imagery analysts would write on "their targets." Analysts who worked for those managers often did not keep their target baselines current.

The second managerial approach emphasized the imagery analysts' obligation to get information to the community rather than "ownership" of a target. These managers emphasized NPIC's obligation, as the national center, to keep the database and the baseline reporting current as a service of common concern for the entire Intelligence Community. These managers taught imagery analysts that they "owed" information instead of "owning" it. This approach would become more important and challenging when the new satellite came on line in 1977. It required a level of computer and communications support that NPIC struggled to achieve.

After PEG operations began in January 1977, these reporting timelines fueled an increasing number of conflicts between the IEG imagery analysts at Building 213 and the priority group or PEG imagery analysts at the ground station. With their access to near-real-time imagery, PEG's imagery analysts often had a more recent image than the IEG imagery analysts. But a more recent image did not always mean more knowledge or more context. There was no formal communication for the two groups to share what they were about to produce. As a result, on multiple occasions, incomplete, erroneous, or conflicting reporting that "surprised" one of the two groups happened.

The other internal conflict hinged on which group had the "right" to certain targets. The PEG mission was defined as the analysis of, and reporting on all indications and warning and high current interest targets. But of course, analysts who had developed expertise and a reputation reporting on "their" targets of interest over years wanted to continue reporting on those targets when they rotated into PEG. When these imagery analysts would write on a target that they had previously worked on in IEG, these cables would sometimes lead to volatile discussions about who could rightfully report on the target. As each group had a strong leader, the two groups competed to point out each other's analytic shortcomings and inaccuracies. IEG imagery analysts in Building 213 wanted the PEG imagery analysts only to describe their observations, and not to characterize the implications of their finds. PEG imagery analysts at the ground station, many of whom knew as much or more about some of these targets as the IEG imagery analysts at Building 213, believed that, in the first twenty-four hours, they could competently report on these targets.

The crux of the matter was that the two groups did not agree on what comprised current exploitation. PEG managers began to understand the possibilities that near-real-time imagery provided, in particular the potential for rapid reporting and re-tasking the satellite. IEG managers, on the other hand, resented the unexpected internal competition and the loss of autonomy about the pace of their exploitation and reporting. The problem, in characteristic NPIC style, would be put in the first part of a cable that the Intelligence Community would see. These cables would begin with either C-O-R-R-E-C-T-I-O-N, or a first sentence that began "Continuing analysis revealed . . ."

Shift work worsened internal communications. PEG worked two ten and one-half hour shifts. The night shift began its workday at 10 p.m. when the satellite was over the western Pacific Ocean. In order to overlap with the night shift, the day shift came in at 7:30 in the morning. This allowed the night shift to hand off both work in production and the questions to ask the IEG imagery analysts during the day. The overlap was also used to inform the day shift about what had changed in the world since those analysts had gone home the evening before.

The need to cover the world twenty-four hours a day, seven days a week required two teams for a total of four shifts, covering weekdays and weekends. Because of the odd number of days in a week, both teams worked Monday night and Tuesday day in a planned overlap. But, the weekend team would come to work on Friday night or Saturday morning without any awareness of what had happened in the "classified" world since they had gone home on Tuesday.

Of course the teams wrote notes for each other from shift to shift. Often however, what was written was not clear, or something was omitted or not remembered, and at times this resulted in teams dropping knowledge between shifts. To help mitigate these issues, the night shift manager began each day with a formal briefing that described what that day shift had done, what NPIC had published, the anticipated collection for the next day, and what the other agencies in Intelligence Community had produced or requested during the day. If there were any technology issues, they would also be discussed.

But, in the beginning, the day shift did not go to this formal meeting. Instead, individual imagery analysts talked to their peers about what they had seen, but fatigue, a lack of expertise or understanding all affected the quality of the communication or this "pass to." In the early days, despite the best intentions, the lack of a formal meeting led to a number of misunderstandings.

The final internal conflict had to do with the division chiefs who ran each shift. Division managers had been chosen for their experience at crisis reporting, ability to recognize which observations warranted immediate reporting, ability to edit intelligence writing, and judgment in managing the analytic operation without guidance on nights, holidays, and weekends. Proud and competitive veterans of many intelligence crises, all were familiar and comfortable with making autonomous decisions. Some took delight in contradicting decisions made by their counterparts on the other shift, or on the other side of the week. So, at times, imagery analysts on one side of the week used one set of terms and target names, and their peers on the other side of the week used different terms and target names. None of this improved the analysis or the reporting. And, it was not appreciated by the Intelligence Community that tried to track events. Nor was it appreciated by any of NPIC's managers or imagery analysts. And yet, it went on.

It took some time for the PEG managers to institute common practices on both ends of the week and to schedule morning shift change meetings that allowed a more formal pass-to. While they were gradually improving the seven-day/twenty-four-hour operation, they did seize upon one real advantage of having imagery analysts at the satellite ground station, proximity to the collection function.

Collection—Must be Present to Win

Until 1977, the limited supply of film carried by the satellites, and the inherent delay in obtaining photography from space, no matter how important the issue, drove the process for obtaining imagery collection. Collection planning was part of the launch schedule, as it had been since 1960. This deliberative process led to a focus on standing collection, or routine scheduling. The targets to be collected on a particular issue came to be called decks, as the imagery analysts thought of the collection algorithm as an automatic shuffler from which no one could predict what would be the next picture taken. And clouds were always a problem.

Every day, clouds cover about one half of the world. Some parts of the world are nearly always cloud covered, especially the Andean ridge in South

America, or parts of sub-Saharan Africa. The limited scientific predictability of weather forecasting, though much improved with the introduction of weather satellites in 1962, still limited the effectiveness of taking pictures from space. Clouds sometimes get in the way of the best laid plans. Nonetheless, from early on, imagery analysts learned to take a quick look at cloud-covered images, because, from time to time, many a target and many a find were seen through a hole in the clouds. But imagery analysts have little good to say about cloud-covered imagery, except at the end of a long night shift.

Once the near-real-time satellite began to collect in 1977, clouds remained an issue, but imagery analysts and managers recognized that they could obtain imagery far more rapidly than before. So they started to focus their attention on ad hoc collection nominations instead of the standing collection deck. NPIC imagery analysts recognized ahead of the COMIREX staff, that making rapid changes to the standing deck could allow PEG to capture fleeting events if the collection could be modified rapidly.

Until this time, NPIC had only put limited resources into collection management, and it paid requirements officers significantly less than the imagery analysts. But the possibilities of the KH-11 caused PEG managers to dedicate requirements officers around the clock. This happened in the first year, and it succeeded in meeting the PEG need for immediate collection support. However, because ad-hoc collection was thought to "interrupt" standing collection, the COMIREX staff did not always receive immediate collection requests favorably. COMIREX staff measured success as "keeping the average up for all requested collection," while NPIC imagery analysts measured success as locating a new activity or target, answering a question about what was happening at a critical location, or bringing new information to a fleeting priority issue. PEG responded to its collection challenges by training a number of intelligent and assertive requirements officers, and by sending them to the COMIREX meetings where they built reputations for making the strongest cases for that day's collection. Even so, collection remained bureaucratic.

Production Challenges

The early PEG concept of intelligence production was based on wet film and analog processes. But, when a briefing board took eight hours to produce, the support people quickly changed their processes. The ground station had invested in a relatively new technology, a custom-built classified fax machine, called the WashFax. This hardwired system sent primitive copies of images, with only slightly reduced resolution, to the DCI's Operations Center at CIA, to the DIA imagery analysts in the Pentagon's Joint Chiefs of Staff watch center, to the State Department, and to the White House Situation Room. This early fax machine was about two-feet wide, six-feet long, and four-feet high. Though slow, it performed well. Each transmission took about five minutes per page to ingest, and about fifteen to twenty minutes to arrive at its destination. This technology was the first significant change in how NPIC communicated visually, but this change was initially made only at PEG.

The WashFax led to the creation of the mini-board, an eight-by-ten annotated image with a single page of accompanying text. The graphics shop worked at cutting its production timelines, and soon could routinely turn mini-boards out in an hour. Most of them were still sent around Washington, D.C. in courier bags, but the senior-most customers received them from the WashFax.

Previously, NPIC had made large twenty- by twenty-four-inch briefing boards that had been hand-carried and driven to customer locations in large, locked courier bags. These large format briefing boards allowed even the most "non-visual" senior official to "see" what the analysts wanted to show. The new, smaller format mini-boards, however, forced the recipients to trust the imagery analysts' interpretations, as the picture could not be enlarged enough for easy interpretation by those who were not imagery analysts. While NPIC still created larger format boards, they were made only rarely for special occasions, for example, when President Reagan used them as background for his television talk about the Nicaraguan and Libyan military buildups, or when senior-level visitors visited Building 213. The mini board and fax dissemination technology did not migrate from PEG to Building 213 until 1981.

The accelerated production of images changed the mindset of the PEG imagery analysts and managers. For the first time, photographic intelligence could be created for customers in a few hours after collection, while at Building 213 the near-real-time imagery came a few hours later or the next day. It still took days or weeks to get the most recent imagery from film return satellites.

This difference in production schedules created a divide between those imagery analysts and managers who felt that products would be large and take days to produce, and the PEG imagery analysts and managers who learned to produce cables in an hour and annotated images with text in the next hour. The imagery analysts, managers, and support people in Building 213 would never be regarded in the same way by those who rotated back from PEG. As a result, production improvements from this point on were driven as much by PEG as by the larger graphics, photo lab, and print operations in Building 213.

PEG drove the need for faster and better computer support. With a daily download of imagery, the need became evident, especially in the early days. The thinking at Building 213 was that operations would work around the computer. At PEG, the computers drove the operations. PEG imagery analysts, who had to exploit an increasing stack of images, relied on the computers much more than any imagery analyst at Building 213 to let them know what targets collected, the reason for collection, and the target history. Unfortunately, in the first year at PEG, the computers would fail frequently. So, early in its operation, PEG managers learned the value of a backup system. The early backup system was pencils and yellow legal pads. Afterwards, when the computers came back up, the support people would re-key the analysis and readouts into the system. But the daily operations never ceased. To keep the system operational as much as possible, the need for computer and support redundancies had to be addressed. As a result, at night and on weekends, support staffing was increased substantially.

The Increasing Volume of Imagery-derived Information

Despite the new mainframes and terminals, the pace and volume of imagery delivered by the KH-11 overloaded the computer system. The rapidity of daily collection meant that the amount of imagery-derived intelligence also grew exponentially. For the first time, it became possible to track changes in denied areas that previously had to be inferred. Now changes were being seen, understood, and reported as they happened. The imagery analysts at PEG began the transition from the era of comprehension to the era of tracking.

This new capability allowed imagery analysts to discern indicators of future activity, and to provide more detailed warning on ships leaving port or on military vehicles leaving garrisons. This was particularly true in the first few months of 1977 when the Soviet Union and China did not know about the capabilities of this new satellite.

This period of rapid and significant gains in imagery-derived intelligence ended unexpectedly. After William Kampiles, a 22-year-old CIA watch officer, sold a copy of the KH-11 operations manual to the Russians in February 1978, imagery analysts noticed that what they had started to see over the past year inexplicably had gone away. Only after Kampiles was arrested that summer did the imagery analysts begin to learn what he had shared with the Soviet Union. Not until the Intelligence Community finished the damage assessment did the imagery analysts learn why they had stopped seeing certain activities. An indication of the intelligence lost through this treason was the 40-year sentence that Kampiles received, though his sentence was reduced, and he was paroled in 1996 after serving eighteen years.

The operational and cultural impact of PEG on NPIC and the imagery intelligence business developed over three to five years. Because of technology limitations and technical failures, the first year at PEG had periods of inactivity but, by 1978, the processes were workable, the technology more reliable, and the peer pressure to make accurate calls was palpable and firmly in place. The collective impact of these changes grew into points of friction that later emerged in the inspector general's report.

The quality of the database work done by the imagery analysts developed into an open and sometimes hostile debate about analytic knowledge. When all NPIC imagery analysts were in the same building, at the same time, the content of the database did not matter as much. After PEG began to operate, the different approaches to what imagery analysts should know, how they should work, and what they should capture in writing developed into two strong cultures, led by two strong leaders, but it devolved into a divisive concept of operations. And, finally, the social pressures of the time began to impinge on NPIC in ways that the leadership did not effectively manage.

Analytic Breadth Versus Analytic Depth

The baseline issue introduced more friction about analytic focus into the debate between the two analytic groups. Some imagery analysts in IEG at Building 213 worked at attaining a depth of expertise on a few targets and building a deep understanding of an issue. These imagery analysts often gravitated to a functional or process-based specialty such as nuclear testing, strategic industries, or missile R&D. Other imagery analysts, more comfortable working with larger numbers of targets and search, worked regionally deployed forces or, in the Third World, worked entire countries with all their military equipment, in every order of battle.

In PEG, imagery analysts were expected to develop a breath of knowledge rapidly, rather than deep expertise on one issue or area. When they were made responsible for all worldwide targets of a certain type, some imagery analysts learned rapidly and adapted very well. Others, more comfortable with studying fewer targets in depth, had challenges with the unrelenting pace driven by the constantly imaging satellite. The number of targets for which they were responsible also was an issue. PEG's managers valued fast and flexible learners. IEG managers valued thorough and deliberate learners. For the first time in NPIC, imagery analysts were being measured differently, and each group began to devalue imagery analysts in the other group. While not constant or systemic, it did not help morale or operations. This divide started to come to a head in 1980, when the initial cadre of imagery analysts who had gone to PEG in 1976 and 1977 started to return to IEG at Building 213. These returnees needed to be backfilled at PEG.

The call for replacement imagery analysts did not go smoothly. About two-thirds of the initial PEG staff wanted to return. But the call for volunteers in IEG did not produce enough replacements. Not all IEG imagery analysts thought that going to PEG would be career enhancing. Most had developed expertise in a regional or functional account, and they thought that leaving "their" account for two years would hurt their careers. In addition, not all IEG managers thought a tour in PEG worthwhile.

There was also a social and family cost as the imagery analysts at PEG worked nights, weekends, and holidays. Because they worked weekdays only about a third of the time, it limited their opportunity to stay in touch with their Intelligence Community peers who were also working the same areas of expertise. The tension between the "expertise" of the IEG imagery analysts and the "experience" of the PEG imagery analysts had already led to coalitions on both sides. The leaders of these groups, air force and CIA officers respectively, had not worked together to diminish the different points of view. In fact, their competitiveness at work and on the softball field intensified the internal competition between the two analytic organizations.

This competition produced strong internal friction, compounded by perceived favoritism and "in-crowd" management styles. Both organizations believed that the path to career success lay in being thought highly of by the respective group chiefs. Imagery analysts would describe other imagery analysts unflatteringly as one of "Mike's boys," or "Gordy's boys."

When a ground forces imagery analyst who had developed himself into an expert on the Iraqi military refused to go to PEG, it infuriated director Hazzard and the group chiefs. This imagery analyst, who had done excellent reporting during the Iran-Iraq war, felt that he could make the most contribution by staying on day work and working from the Navy Yard. He also lived near West Virginia and carpooled about seventy miles to work. His managers thought otherwise and began to pressure him to go to PEG. Because of his analytic reputation, he was able to rapidly find a new job in OIA, CIA's imagery analysis office, where he continued his work on Middle Eastern ground forces for many years.

This imagery analyst's departure caused the director to write a notice to all NPIC imagery analysts. In his employee notice he described the value to the NPIC mission of service at PEG, and he stated that the assignment would not adversely affect any imagery analysts' careers. But he added a sentence that no imagery analyst forgot. The director stated that "any imagery analyst who refused to go to PEG would be considered 'excess baggage' by the NPIC career service and declared surplus to the needs of the service." The threat of being fired got the imagery analysts' attention.

The director's military approach to staffing did not sit well with the imagery analysts. Also, OIA's imagery analysts, looking at NPIC from outside, viewed this policy as a characteristic lack of respect for analytic expertise on the part of the NPIC's leadership, and it widened the rift between the two organizations. In 1982, OIA would raise this policy with the CIA's inspector general.

The director's memo had the desired effect, and nearly all the imagery analysts directly assigned chose to go to PEG rather than protest. Yet the cultural differences persisted between IEG and PEG. This divide in how each group valued imagery evolved from the group leadership. From the early days at PEG in 1976, camaraderie there developed quickly. The first group chief, C. Michael Poell, an air force lieutenant colonel, built a handpicked, loyal, and hardworking leadership team that played as hard as it worked. PEG's chief and the chief of IEG started an annual softball game, in addition to the NPIC softball league in which each group already fielded teams. These group chiefs, with their emphasis on personal loyalty and shared experiences, created strong bonds on the respective management teams. These very bonds, which helped to forge strong teams, also served to repel those who did not share experiences with the teams outside the workplace. With two analytic groups developing this way, an obvious leadership move presented itself. By 1980, the two group chiefs were swapped.

But the strong bonds that characterized these management teams were perceived as a result of their being nearly exclusively white males. By this time, there were twenty to twenty-five African-American imagery analysts in NPIC. While their overall number had increased since 1972, they remained under-represented in the senior imagery analyst and managerial ranks, and in 1982 only one held a branch chief position.

In addition, NPIC had a small number of female imagery analysts, about the same number as the African-Americans. Like the African-American imagery analysts, the first women imagery analysts at NPIC mostly wore military uniforms. The civilian DIA and CIA women were a lonely few. A number of female imagery analysts had become analysts through the CIA intern program and the NPIC upward mobility program—Arlene Leatham, Patsy Jarvis, Monica Gaughan, and Brenda Wynn. A few started as interns or students—Lynne Wilder, Mary Ellen Keene, and Paulette Deitz. But none of the women in the analytic group were in any leadership position above a first-line supervisor. For the imagery analysis managers in the early 1980s, developing the careers of women and African-American imagery analysts was not a priority.

The operational, social, personnel, and policy fissures at NPIC were growing, and their documentation in the Inspector General's report became the catalyst for selecting a new director.

Art Lundahl late in his time as Director of NPIC.
(Photo: Courtesy of NGA)

Art and Mary Lundahl (left) at ASP reception in 1954.

(Photo: Courtesy of ASPRS)

(Photo: Courtesy of ASPRS)

Art Lundahl speaking at 1955 ASP conference. He was President of the ASP at this time and very busy designing and building the organization that would look at the U-2 Photography.

Steuart building
(Photo: Courtesy of NGA)

(Photo: Courtesy of NGA)

7-X tube magnifier, one of the principal photo-interpretation
tools for the aircraft and KH-4 search mission.

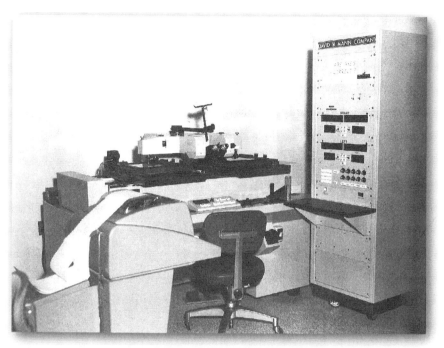

(Photo: Courtesy of NGA)

A Mann Comparator used for making precise measurements from film. A Mann comparator was used to confirm the photo-interpreter's measurements of the Soviet missiles in Cuba.

An early Richards tiltable light table with hand cranks.

(Photo: Courtesy of NGA)

Building 213 (Before addition)

(Photo: Courtesy of NGA)

John Hicks, the second director of NPIC.

(Photo: Courtesy of NGA)

A Sperry Univac 494 on which target reports were batch processed at night and on weekends.

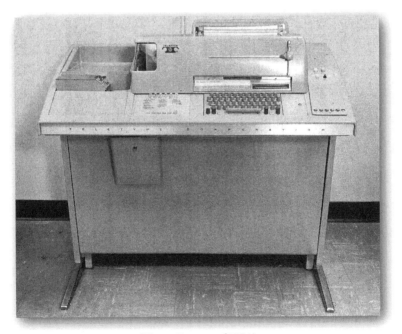

A teletype machine on which the early cables were formatted and released.

(Photo: Courtesy of NGA)
Film cans

(Photo: Courtesy of NGA)

A 1540 AIL light table with a Zoom 500 stereoscope. The dark-toned round objects at each end are film motors used to more quickly find an image on long rolls of KH-8 and KH-9 imagery.

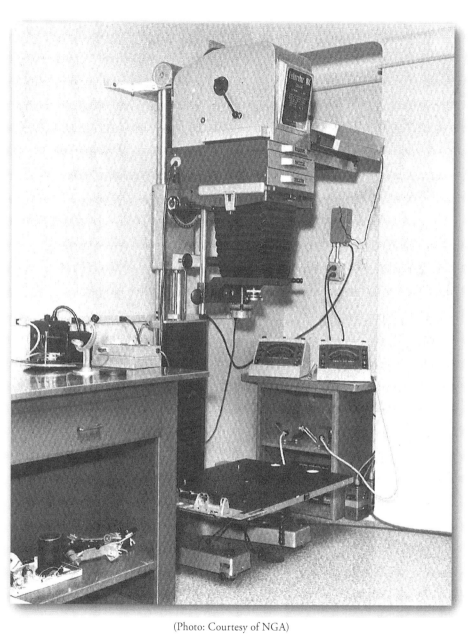

(Photo: Courtesy of NGA)

Durst enlarger: A photo lab workhorse for many routine magnifications.

A Beacon Precision Enlarger for higher magnification and large format work
(Photo: Courtesy of NGA)

(Photo: Courtesy of NGA)

R. P. (Hap) Hazzard, the third director of NPIC.

Figure 2-1. IA Workstation

-11

(Photo: Courtesy of NGA)

An imagery analyst workstation before the upgrade.

R. M. (Rae) Huffstutler, the fourth director of NPIC.

(Photo: Courtesy of NGA)

UNCLASSIFIED
APPROVED FOR PUBLIC RELEASE
DECLASSIFIED BY DNI
13 JANUARY 2012

TCS-28207/82
MISSION 1217-4
OPS 1613
TYPHOON CLASS SUBMARINE
AT SEVERODVINSK
80X   10 OCT 8

KH-9 Panoramic Camera Image of Typhoon Class Submarine at Severodvinsk, Former Soviet Union, 10 October 1982

(Photo: Courtesy of NRO Center for the Study of National Reconnaissance)

A declassified KH-9 image, magnified 80X, of a Typhoon SSBN from 1982.

Photo: George Chernilevsky

SS-20 Transporter-erector-launcher (TEL) with missile canister on display in Kiev.

Building 213 after the addition.

(Photo: Courtesy of NGA)

Rae Huffstutler and Art Lundahl on stage January 1987.

(Photo: Courtesy of NGA)

CHAPTER 8

RAE HUFFSTUTLER—THE FIRST TO GROW THE LEADERS

Robert Macrae (Rae) Huffstutler came to NPIC in February 1984 from the Soviet office of CIA's Directorate of Intelligence. Rae was a slender athletic man with blue eyes and a high forehead. A career CIA analyst and manager, he held his undergraduate and master's degrees in economics from Berkeley, and he had spent his junior year in Switzerland at the University of Geneva.

The previous NPIC director, Hap Hazzard, had been an army general. He had an officer's bearing, but the conversational style of an Alabama farmer. While knowledgeable about missiles, satellite program management, missile technology, and its military uses, he was not an intelligence analyst. When imagery analysts briefed him on a current find or issue, they were not questioned about tradecraft or how their findings affected US policy, intelligence, or diplomatic outcomes. Often, imagery analysts would come back wondering if Hap understood what they told him because their briefing had set him off on an old story from his army days or back in rural Alabama. The imagery analysts' perspective changed the day Rae arrived.

Rae Huffstutler had experienced changing the culture of an organization. In his most recent service at CIA's Office of Soviet Analysis (SOVA), one of the largest offices in CIA, he had been part of its move in the late 1970s to an area several miles away from the CIA campus. Though this move was a result of the office becoming CIA's largest analytic office, the SOVA analysts did not view the move positively. It created much organizational turmoil and increased the difficulty of coordinating with other DI offices on the CIA campus. Throughout its time away from the CIA campus at Langley, SOVA's morale suffered. Rae had firsthand knowledge how the lack of awareness of an organization's cultural values could affect its operations and morale.

Evan Hineman, head of the Directorate of Science and Technology, selected Rae Huffstutler to come to NPIC. Both had worked together on Soviet strategic issues in the Office of Weapons Intelligence, including the development of Soviet strategic weapons systems. This experience gave Rae familiarity with the new technologies but, more importantly, it gave him a sense of what he did not know about them. While he understood the potential of the new technology, as well as its frailty, he also understood the need to trust his technical managers and specialists. While Rae lacked a program management background, he had regularly worked with technical program managers, and he had long experience at using technology to assess Soviet strategic weapons.

Rae brought these lessons and an intelligence analyst's approach to NPIC. In his initial meetings with NPIC's managers, the analytic approach came out very clearly. In his first weeks, he made a point of visiting the meetings held by each group and its leadership. He met with each group's managers in the Blue Room—one of the sixth-floor conference rooms in the director's area. Rae spoke to each of these groups about intelligence challenges, and how he planned to help NPIC overcome those challenges. He had a clearly organized plan written in longhand on a yellow legal pad. He spoke clearly, in an organized manner and, as customary among Directorate of Intelligence leaders, with a sprinkling of arcane vocabulary. Some of the NPIC managers who heard him later asked each other what "feckless" meant.

His message was clear. He mentioned that NPIC had issues to be resolved. He spoke of the differing approaches to promotions and career development, and of how he would create a single approach to career management for NPIC. He recognized the need to grow the Center and to develop its leadership and imagery analysts to face a looming Soviet intelligence challenge. He also spoke of NPIC's technical challenges with a large modernization program that was having difficulties.

At the time, the Soviet Union was developing its mobile missile force. Many NPIC imagery analysts knew about these missiles in 1984. But, in his first talk, and many times afterwards, Rae referred to them as strategic relocatable targets. These missiles, specifically the SS-20 medium-range ballistic missile (MRBM), were a great concern to the Intelligence Community. While NPIC led the community in finding and characterizing fixed targets, mobile, strategic weapons challenged NPIC in a number of ways. Rae's general term for this kind of weapon would force NPIC to recognize that its expertise at dealing with fixed targets would become insufficient to warn and track the weapons that most threatened United States allies in Western Europe. The new director challenged NPIC to develop its expertise in re-locatable targets and to learn to track them.

Since the late 1970s, NPIC had followed the development and deployment of these weapons. One branch was dedicated to following the SS-20 weapons system. This weapon was a medium-range, solid-fueled, mobile missile on a six-axle truck that also served as its launcher. It was threatening for a number of reasons. While each truck carried only one missile, that missile had three independently targetable nuclear warheads. Its attributes complicated any possible defensive measures. Because the SS-20 was mobile, locating and targeting its base did not automatically mean the weapons would be destroyed. Additionally, unlike the missiles it replaced, it was solid-fueled. This meant that the missile was ready to fire as soon as it was in position and programmed, which was a matter of minutes. Unlike liquid-fueled missiles, it did not require hours to set up, arm, aim, and fuel.

This missile deployment coincided with one of the more dangerous periods of the Cold War. While in 1979 the United States and the Soviet Union had negotiated a treaty on silo-based missiles—the Strategic Arms Limitations Treaty (SALT) II—Congress had not ratified it. NPIC's efforts through its ages of discovery and comprehension made treaty monitoring possible, but when the treaty was not ratified, the Soviet response was to begin to deploy the SS-20 MRBMs. While deployment of this missile posed no greater threat to the continental United States, it put every part Western Europe at more risk.

The US response to the SS-20 deployment surprised the Soviets in two ways. One response was a US deployment decision. In November 1983, the United States and NATO began to deploy the Pershing IRBM into West Germany, after basing nuclear-armed ground launched cruise missiles in England and on the continent starting in July 1982. The second surprise was a future weapons program. In March 1983, President Reagan announced that the United States would begin to fund and develop a space-based interceptor, named the "Star Wars" missile defense system. These announcements put more pressure on the Intelligence Community in general, and NPIC in particular, to find all the new SS-20 bases. The greater challenge would be to track each missile launcher at every existing base.

Rae Huffstutler had long experience in working arms control issues. For many years he had supported arms control negotiations and participated in the prolonged Intelligence Community disagreements that accompanied the production of the National Intelligence Estimates on the Soviet Union and on the discoveries of its new weapons systems. These debates frequently polarized the Intelligence Community, with agencies and bureaus taking dramatically opposing positions. As with all National Intelligence Estimates, CIA had to reconcile all opposing points of view.

Rae knew how the Intelligence Community, specifically the arms control community, used NPIC reporting to inform its discussions and negotiations. He brought a clear understanding of the need for NPIC to provide direct, daily support to all the negotiations and to engage with the arms control staffs in the monitoring discussions that involved the use of National Technical Means. His understanding of the value of imagery analysis in the arms control process, along with the political agendas among the agencies in the Intelligence Community led him to assert that NPIC could earn a "seat at the table," if it focused on its imagery analysis. Rae was going to "re-make" NPIC's efforts on strategic re-locatable targets and specifically, the SS-20s.

The mobility of the SS-20 meant that discovering its bases and comprehending its capabilities and range would not be enough. NPIC would be called on to learn to track this mobile force. Tracking the SS-20 force required changes in exploitation, in collection management, and in NPIC's reporting. Success would require changing the internal coordination between PEG and IEG, changing the external tasking of other intelligence sources, and creating a database that was topical rather target-based. And finally, the imagery analysis and reporting would have to be done much faster.

From his many years of all-source analytic experience with Soviet military issues, Rae understood how the all-source analysts relied on imagery, and where NPIC could make real contributions to build relationships with these all-source analytic offices and with the National Intelligence Council. His knowledge of the players, their backgrounds, and the strengths and weaknesses enabled him to prepare NPIC for analytic challenges that only he was aware of when he arrived. His political acumen would be invaluable in garnering political support for NPIC. With the trust of Evan Hineman, Bob Gates, and William Casey, he made decisive moves quickly, and his understanding of the issues enabled him to anticipate Intelligence Community and Department of Defense reactions before they happened.

From his first meetings, Rae wanted every NPIC manager to recognize how much NPIC would have to change to analyze and track this challenging intelligence issue. Success would mean integrating new technology, which the NPIC modernization program was supposed to deliver. Success also would require streamlined exploitation, collection, reporting, and managerial processes. More importantly, the director said that success would require many new imagery analysts.

Rae's short talk contained the seeds of future changes. Some changes were needed, some were planned, some were fortuitous, and some were surprises. But Rae started with two clear messages: first, he was there with a plan; second, every manager at NPIC had a large part to play, and he had high expectations of them.

One change was related to space photography. The age of the film-return satellite was nearly over. The technological wonders created to support space photography had pushed the industry to invent a number of advanced technologies that were no longer needed. The mechanical and chemical improvements in space and aerial photography over the past twenty-five years, while very impressive, were like a steam locomotive—beautiful, powerful, mechanically intricate, even majestic, but slow and inefficient in comparison to the digital imagery that moved electronically from space to the ground station, and then to NPIC in trucks. Film-based technology had been essential to NPIC's past success, but some imagery analysts and managers failed to see how other new technical developments, namely digital imagery, would transform their work. Although the need for a digital infrastructure had been identified before he arrived at NPIC, Rae inherited a large and troubled modernization program. Rae saw that NPIC did not have a plan for how to work in this new technological environment. He also saw that imagery analysis would need a different style of leadership. To replace retiring pioneers from the 1950s and 1960s, he saw that he would need new senior leaders. He also saw that he would need to develop new types of imagery analyst and support personnel to analyze strategic re-locatable targets.

The recruiting push started a trickle of new imagery analysts into Building 213. These new imagery analysts who had been part of the applicant surge through 1982 and 1983 were starting to report for duty. Inexperienced in imagery analysis for the most part, they differed in other ways as well. As most were recruited from college campuses, they had more formal education on average than previous new hires. After Rae came in February 1984, he eliminated NPIC's traditional military-based hiring test for imagery analysts. Huffstutler had supervised a number of outstanding female military analysts in CIA, and he knew that none of them could have passed the NPIC test. This change, and the end of the draft in the late 1970s contributed to an unforeseen outcome in that more women than men were selected for entry-level imagery analysis positions.

Most new imagery analysts, men and women, had little or no military experience. This created tension between the new hires and some older managers who had developed their management and interpersonal skills while in uniform. But many of the new people were ambitious, and many of them had used computers and analytic tools in college. Their energy and experiences would serve NPIC well in the next few years.

CHAPTER 9

THE THIRD TYPHOON

Rae quickly entered the world of the imagery analysts with phone calls. When the new director liked a cable or report, he phoned the imagery analyst directly on the secure line. Initially, the calls created some unexpected responses. Among some veteran analysts, skeptical after experiencing some NPIC practical jokes, Rae initially was not believed. At least once, the director had to call back after he was hung up on. With newer imagery analysts, some naiveté showed when one asked, "And who do you work for?" The director persisted, and the news about his calls quickly spread throughout the building. One branch chief, Frank Douglas, gathered his imagery analysts together and told them: "If you get a call from a guy named Rae, talk to him. He's the director."

To make NPIC imagery analysts more aware of the importance of their work, Huffstutler let them know individually. He expressed his appreciation directly to the imagery analysts, but their managers also learned quickly that the new director read all the cables and reports released the day before. For most imagery analysts, direct communication from the front office was a new experience. The last director who engaged NPIC employees as directly was Art Lundahl. Rae's calls quickly taught imagery analysts that their work mattered. But the calls generally had two parts and two messages for them.

The general message was always praise for a find, for putting pieces of a story together, for making sense of a new observation, or for adding to the Intelligence Community's understanding of an issue. But, ever the intelligence analyst, Rae would ask questions. Sometimes he would ask about the use or availability of information from other intelligence agencies; sometimes he would ask about future imagery collection; or sometimes he would ask about the views or opinions of other intelligence agencies, or what the policy community thought of the report. But always there were questions.

The two-part message, praise and question, left imagery analysts no doubt that the new director paid attention to their analysis and reporting. His message also created the expectation that analysts would have to anticipate what the next steps or questions might be. Rae's calls got the attention of every imagery analyst and analytic manager. The experience, grade, status, internal or external reputation of the imagery analyst did not matter to the him. He wanted the workforce to know that their new director cared about imagery analysis. To make his point, he inserted himself into a controversy that grew out of an NPIC cable issued shortly before he came to NPIC.

In the late 1970s and early 1980's, the Soviet Union began to build and deploy the Typhoon-class submarine, the world's largest ballistic missile submarine. As its characteristics were not well understood, it was of great concern to the Intelligence Community. In particular, the US had two intelligence questions: how fast were the Soviets building Typhoons and how quickly could they deploy them into the fleet?

Since the U-2 era in 1957, NPIC and other intelligence organizations had tracked the growth and deployment of the Soviet Navy. In particular, the United States had focused on the ships and submarines capable of carrying nuclear missiles. The Typhoon-class submarine, first deployed in 1981, was a weapons platform with significant firepower that caused great concern for the United States and the West. Learning how long it took for this kind of submarine to join the fleet was important. By 1983, only two Typhoons were in the Soviet fleet, and their production rate and deployment time were unknown. Observing the "fitting out," the process of finishing a ship or boat after its launch was important, as it would tell the Intelligence Community when a new boat would join the fleet. But the United States did not know how long it took to build a Typhoon. With only two Typhoons in the fleet, the status of the third was a critical intelligence question.

NPIC had been diligently watching Severodvinsk, a major shipyard in the western Soviet Union for years. In late December 1983, while many Americans were watching *A Christmas Story*, a movie about a boy named 'Ralphie' who wished to get a Red Rider BB Gun, a senior NPIC imagery analyst who had been watching Severodvinsk published an intelligence cable. In it, he stated that the Soviet Union was about to launch another Typhoon ballistic-missile submarine. Although based on careful imagery analysis tradecraft, and close scrutiny of the target over time, this cable was not well received. Much of the Intelligence Community disagreed with the call. CIA, DIA, and navy's all-source analysts had taken institutional positions that the next Typhoon could not be launched sooner than the summer of 1984. The all-source community was not pleased that NPIC had taken a different position, and the Intelligence Community's meetings on this issue grew more heated. The entire all-source community criticized the NPIC cable.

Unfortunately, the US Intelligence Community was not going to learn any more for some time. The Russian winter set in. Throughout January, the imagery analysts and collection officers fought the weather, and the satellites took many pictures of clouds. With each day, uncertainty increased about the accuracy of the call, more photos of clouds were taken, and uncertainty continued into February when Rae arrived as the new director of NPIC. The new director requested a briefing about the potential Typhoon launch and about the Intelligence Community's responses.

The NPIC imagery analyst, a retired chief petty officer, was now a DIA civilian at NPIC, and one of the most respected Soviet submarine analysts. While his knowledge of his targets and the issue was very good, his demeanor was not. He behaved churlishly on some days and unpleasantly on others. Once, when he learned that a new NPIC imagery analyst was a reservist, he publically said, "I'd rather have a sister in a whorehouse than a brother in the reserves." (The new imagery analyst, in response, asked Charlie how his sister was doing.) He took great pride in his work, and he resented having anyone review his calls or his writing. When a new editor made the security error of mentioning a target name during an unclassified phone conversation, he hung up instantly, stomped into the edit shop, yelling, "WHICH ONE OF YOU STUPID BITCHES MENTIONED SEVERODVINSK OVER THE BLACK LINE?"

This senior imagery analyst was very proud of his writing style, which he self-labeled *Charliegrams*. For those readers expert in Soviet submarine construction, these cables were comprehensible, but to generalist readers they were full of naval jargon. As with much writing by experts, the cable also was full of technical terminology. When NPIC editors tried to change this imagery analyst's writing in published reports, he often would resist nearly all changes on the grounds that the editor was insufficiently knowledgeable and probably insufficiently intelligent to learn his subject. But the senior analyst could not make that case with the new director. Because of the contentiousness of the argument in the Intelligence Community about the December 1983 cable, Rae asked for a briefing from the imagery analyst who wrote the cable. The new director intended to review the imagery analysis tradecraft, the evidence, and the reporting that led to this call.

After the February briefing, Rae decided that NPIC would issue another cable with the December information. But, the second cable would be different. When the director reviewed the December cable, he found a chronology of previous database entries interspersed with analytic comments. All of the evidence for the "call" was in the cable, but the facts were not clearly organized, and they were not separated from the imagery analyst's judgments and extraneous information. It was not clear to a reader, which statements were a result of the imagery analyst's observations, and which were his judgments. The February cable had no more recent information than the December cable, as Severodvinsk remained covered by clouds, so the NPIC prediction still could not be proven or disproven. But the February cable was differently organized.

In his review and revision, Rae changed the format by putting the case for the third submarine in the beginning of the cable, and following this assertion with the chronology of the shipyard's activities. After the chronology of evidence, from which extraneous detail was deleted, the director told the imagery analyst to insert a heading at the end of the cable to indicate that what followed were analytic comments on the implications of the observations.

More importantly, Rae struck the phrase "NPIC believes" from the report to meet the community's criticism of NPIC for taking an institutional position. By doing so, the record of observations could stand on its own. This second change mollified the other Intelligence Community organizations that believed that NPIC did not comply with the same coordination constraints as they had.

The director also reorganized the cable to separate the evidence for the submarine launch from all the other data in the cable. These changes tightened up the cable and improved its readability. While this rewritten cable remained contentious, it could not be criticized, unlike the December cable, on the basis of its writing, logic, or organizational position.

While other all-source analytic organizations continued to assert that NPIC was wrong about the imminent Typhoon launch, the director's revisions addressed their perception that NPIC was competing with them. The director's insistence on clarifying what NPIC said, as well as his backing of the imagery analyst's call resulted in some important internal and external effects.

Inside NPIC, the director's actions showed the imagery analysts that if their tradecraft was sound, he would back them when their work was publically questioned or criticized in the Intelligence Community, even if his former CIA office was one of the many Intelligence Community offices that objected to NPIC's work. To the Intelligence Community, the new cable showed that NPIC would continue to use empirical information as the basis for its analysis. While this debate over the submarine continued, so did the Russian winter, and the clouds continually covered Severodvinsk through the beginning of April 1984. Throughout this time, Rae continued to back the imagery analyst's call.

Rae's actions showed NPIC managers that they could expect his support when their work passed his scrutiny. It also showed the imagery analysts that he would look critically at what they saw, and what they thought, and how they reported their intelligence discoveries. His backing came with the insistence that they communicate well, and when they had not done so, he would point it out to them and their managers.

And there was an additional side effect for the support people, in particular the editors. Their work came to be more valued internally, as they could help imagery-analysis managers meet the director's standards.

When in April 1984 the clouds finally broke over Severodvinsk, as the NPIC imagery analyst had predicted five months earlier, the third Typhoon was visible. The Intelligence Community was forced to recognize the accuracy of NPIC's analysis that had been derived solely from imagery. For this reporting and analysis, the senior imagery analyst received a DIA Exceptional Civilian Service Medal later in that year.

Almost immediately, Rae Huffstutler began to use this story, a great predictive success for NPIC, to teach senior imagery analysts and imagery analysis managers how taking an institutional position raised unnecessary, unproductive, and unhelpful scrutiny. He pointed out that if NPIC stuck to the record of its imagery analysis, and expressed confidence in its tradecraft, without stating an institutional position, it could avoid unnecessary coordination delays with the all-source organizations. He also had shown his workforce that he would back his analysts. By focusing on imagery analysis, NPIC could make its case autonomously and effectively. Rae would conclude by stating that this kind of imagery analysis and communicative effort was what it took to earn and keep a "seat at the table" in the Intelligence Community. But it took a new director, with a long background in all-source analysis, to bring that message to NPIC. The new director would repeat this story many times to audiences of imagery analysts to reinforce his desire for NPIC to become more influential.

After seizing on this early opportunity to influence the NPIC workforce, and correctly assessing that the imagery-based analytic prediction would be proven true, Huffstutler challenged NPIC to focus on two types of Soviet targets where NPIC needed to invest more effort.

Not all of Rae's observations were complimentary. From long experience at Soviet military analysis, he had known and used NPIC reporting and analysis, and he knew NPIC's strengths and weaknesses. In his previous position, as chief of the Office of Soviet Analysis in CIA's Directorate of Intelligence, he had relied on NPIC reporting and imagery analysis to do current all-source reporting, to shape and buttress Soviet estimates, and to provide supporting information and analysis for the monitoring work necessary to negotiate arms control treaties with the USSR. He had witnessed the ages of discovery and comprehension and had seen NPIC's contributions and the growth in imagery analysis capabilities.

Since the early 1980s, NPIC had produced a series of reports on the organizational structure of foreign militaries. This discipline is known as order-of-battle analysis, and some NPIC imagery analysts were very good at it. While NPIC excelled at imagery-derived work, it was starting to devote more resources to command and control analysis. In its simplest form, command and control analysis deals with identifying which military units give orders to subordinate units, and which military units take orders from superior units. At its essence, this analysis relies upon signals and communications traffic, which was done at NSA. In short, while NPIC could contribute, this line of analysis could not happen independently of NSA, and NPIC did not have the resources to invest to make a significant contribution to this kind of analysis. Rae thought that this work was not playing to NPIC's strength.

At the time, signals intelligence (SIGINT) from NSA and human intelligence (HUMINT) from CIA were compartmented. The dissemination of these types of information was restricted. Only a limited number of analysts outside of these organizations had access to those compartments. The same had once been true about access to the imagery and the resulting intelligence, but, starting in the late 1960s, it was disseminated more widely throughout the Defense Department. The need for imagery by other intelligence agencies, as well as the operational arms of the military services and commands, as well as the military planners and mapmakers pushed the Intelligence Community to disseminate imagery much faster than the other types of intelligence.

But imagery, if used as the primary source for command and control reporting, could only, at best, discover part of the story. The new director, cleared into far more compartmented information than anyone in NPIC, including the division chief attempting this order-of-battle analysis, knew this analytic effort would be feckless.

Initially, the director suggested that this command-and-control analysis be discontinued, but the division chief was resistant and headstrong. So Rae ordered that this type of imagery analysis be stopped. While the director very much encouraged research, he was a shrewd calculator of the potential return on the analytic investment. The division chief was reassigned to another region, and the director, while not mentioning him by name, would talk at employee and management offsites about this analytic resource decision as a teaching point about analytic focus at NPIC.

Rae chose a meeting of imagery analysts in the NPIC auditorium to clarify his desire for a different kind of imagery-based analysis and reporting. He brought onstage a Basic Imagery Interpretation Report (BIIR) that NPIC had just published. As part of his talk about imagery analysis and reporting that NPIC needed to do, he held out this recently published report, which was essentially a single facility description in a format designed by COMIREX. He then began to take it apart. In addition to criticizing the format and analytic content, the director opened the fold-out's pages and pointed out that the report would not even fit into most file drawers in any government desk. He also pointed out that the writing met the needs of imagery analysts but not the needs of the all-source analysts and arms control specialists who were the audience for the reporting. Finally, he pointed out that description was not analysis. At the end of his talk, everyone in the auditorium understood his intent. NPIC never published another target BIIR on a Soviet installation.

After Rae identified an issue that he thought NPIC ought to cease work on, as well as the kind of reporting he wanted, he again repeated his message about strategic re-locatable targets. The Typhoon was a strategic re-locatable target, and the US Navy had devoted a great amount of its Cold War resources and efforts to tracking Soviet submarines. But the Soviet land-based mobile missiles, in particular the solid-fueled SS-20 MRBM, presented an equal and similarly difficult land-based tracking challenge for those attempting to hold them at risk. That challenge complicated the work of the Intelligence Community, and NPIC in particular.

It would be up to NPIC to have the imagery analysts, exploitation technology, processes, knowledge, and leadership to bring into being the new era of tracking. If NPIC was to track strategic re-locatable targets, it would have to develop and change quickly, and developing and changing NPIC was the new director's priority.

CHAPTER 10

THE IMPRESARIO OF PORT DEPOSIT

Well before Rae Huffstutler arrived, nearly everyone at NPIC knew that it needed more imagery analysts. Ronald Reagan had been elected president in 1980 and promised to make America great again and to roll back communism, but because of a freeze on government hiring NPIC gained only one imagery analyst in 1981. Through 1982, the growth in the number of imagery analysts was not significantly larger. The hiring rate, in fact, was so low that a small staff in the IEG front office handled all interviewing and hiring decisions. Essentially, the new NPIC hires were barely covering retirements and attrition.

Part of the attrition came about because CIA and DIA had long recognized that NPIC was a very good farm team for future all-source or military analysts. These agencies paid all-source analysts better than NPIC paid imagery analysts, and neither CIA nor DIA routinely had shift work as part of their assignments. Both agencies observed NPIC imagery analysts in Intelligence Community working groups and meetings, and they easily could see who would be a good fit for their organizations. At the time, DIA's all-source analysts were in Arlington Hall Station and CIA's Directorate of Intelligence was in Langley. Although DIA's facilities in Arlington were old, both agencies had far better amenities, access, and ambiance than Building 213. Mid-grade NPIC imagery analysts with proven skills were those most frequently recruited. Although each of the other agencies had been under hiring constraints, both were successful at attracting NPIC imagery analysts.

Rae knew, as did his predecessor Hap Hazzard, that NPIC needed new imagery analysts to cope with the volume of future imagery. Although NPIC was planning for more imagery from new and improved sensors and satellites to arrive in 1984, not until the hiring freeze was lifted in October 1981 could imagery analysts be brought on board. As it took most of a year for successful applicants to be interviewed, investigated, polygraphed, and hired, the hiring pace could not meet the need. When William Casey became the director of Central Intelligence in 1981, CIA greatly increased its hiring, but it focused primarily on hiring case officers for human intelligence operations. It would take time for those in the CIA hiring pipeline to reach Building 213.

Rae he knew how badly he needed new imagery analysts. But he also knew on arriving in February 1984 that he had to justify NPIC's need for more imagery analysts to his CIA leadership. Making this case mattered because the CIA's Science and Technology Directorate comprised mostly engineers, program managers, and scientists. NPIC, and the Foreign Broadcast Information Service, the organization that monitored foreign media, never were fully "integrated" into this directorate, which never really assimilated imagery analysis as one of its mainstream missions. Developing new technology and managing projects were more highly valued by the S&T Directorate.

Rae had to make the case that he had taken all possible internal measures before he could credibly request additional personnel. Making this case took most of 1984 and part of 1985. Inside NPIC, he worked with his group chiefs to eliminate levels of management, and he contracted out some NPIC support work to free up positions that he converted to imagery analyst positions. So, even before the new positions were approved, Rae gambled and directed NPIC to recruit, interview, select, and hire new imagery analysts. He took this anticipatory step, as he knew from experience that it took nearly a year to hire and clear an imagery analyst. And, at that time only one candidate out of nine or ten interviews would be cleared and hired. Rae knew that if he wanted to increase the number of imagery analysts, he could not lose the time before the positions or billets would become available.

The number of interviews to find prospective imagery analysts was large, and NPIC handled it with an effective bottom-up process. Aware that the centralized hiring was overwhelmed, the exploitation group in Building 213 distributed hiring authority to the exploitation division chiefs. While the division chiefs kept the final decision authority, they delegated the applicant review, interview, and selection recommendations to a group of about ten branch chiefs and senior imagery analysts. These first-line managers and senior imagery analysts read thousands of resumes, selected and interviewed applicants, and stayed in touch with the candidates throughout the lengthy clearance process. Among themselves, this group introduced formal and informal measures of accountability. One procedural measure was that the interviewers had to sign each recommendation for those they chose to hire.

The selections were tracked and the interviewers' judgments about applicants were "noted." Those who hired imagery analysts who struggled were watched more closely. A few consecutive bad hiring decisions would result in the interviewer being replaced. Some managers introduced a more effective quality control process to ensure good hiring practices. One division chief, Ron Snyder, called new interviewers into his office: "If any of you recommend an asshole, I'm going to move that asshole to your team in your branch."

Through 1982 and 1983, the trickle of new imagery analysts grew into a steady stream. By 1984, the exploitation vaults were starting to get filled. This group of new analysts differed from previous new hires mostly in that they lacked previous military experience, which meant that they had much more to learn initially. They were eager, energetic, intelligent, and a large number were intelligent young women. Some of these new imagery analysts were hired through CIA and some were hired through DIA.

When new people arrived at NPIC, there were a number of formal and informal orientations. Formally, new employees were generally assigned a mentor, usually an imagery analyst who had been in the building for a while, but who was junior enough to remember what new employees needed to know or what they would struggle with. Many branches had routine activities designed for or assigned to inexperienced employees. Some branches had the new analysts study "reference" rolls of imagery with the best images of types of targets or equipment. Other branches traditionally assigned "traditional" work to new employees, such as filing film or cutting apart frames from the rolls of film when a bucket came in. Cutting film taught imagery analysts very quickly about the volume of work involved in search and how important it was considered in their branch. In some branches, KH-9 buckets would take more than a day simply to cut apart the frames and to re-sequence the photographs so that the individual imagery analysts would have their areas of responsibility grouped on the same roll of film.

Film filing was not sporadic. The daily arrival of imagery from the ground station enabled new analysts to learn the targets and areas of interest for their branch, and how each branch stored information. Some filed by date, some by geography, some by priority, some by issue, some by military unit structure, and some by work assignment. The new imagery analysts had to figure out the branch system, and the quicker the better. Their approach to the mundane task of film filing also gave the branch, and the branch chief an early indicator of the new imagery analyst's chances of fitting in and succeeding.

Film filing was onerous, but important. New imagery analysts would just say it sucked. It had to be done every day, accurately, and well, and it had no immediate reward. But all imagery analysts did it, and the new analysts' willingness to pitch in and not complain was observed and noted. And those new analysts who had a new idea about how to file the film were listened to skeptically.

Along with the formal orientations, a number of informal practices existed to let new employees know their roles. While new imagery analysts and employees were welcomed, acceptance was neither immediate nor assured. One new editor, on his first day, was greeted with "O great, another f---ing Irishman." A new army officer on his first day was told, "Here's some film. Take it back to your light table and don't bother me with any stupid questions." Female imagery analysts were not spared. On being sent to a senior imagery analyst, to have a call about a piece of electronics equipment reviewed, one was greeted by, "Where did you get that skirt? It looks like you shot and skinned a sofa."

Many new employees were tested with practical jokes. Some were told to hold up their badges to the ceiling camera before opening the vault doors; some were told to shout their name and badge number down the burn bag chute before putting the bags into the chute; and some were sent to the IEG supply room for cloud eraser or left-handed film scissors.

Once imagery analysts were past their first few weeks, the pranks became more subtle. The "old timers" would reverse the direction of the film motors so when the new imagery analysts turned on their light tables after lunch, dozens of feet of film would spool onto the floor. If an imagery analyst had a hard night and was dozing at his/her scope, he might get a helpful suggestion to splash water on his face. While he was doing that, black marker would be put on the rubber eyecups on his microscope so he would later be walking around with a "raccoon look." But once new imagery analysts had time and proved themselves, the tricks generally stopped.

While identifying changes from imagery was difficult, much strange and unusual behavior was tolerated from those who could do the difficult work of finding new targets on search and of making calls. Some lacked basic hygiene and social skills. Some dressed nattily, and some came to work to wear out old clothes. Surprisingly, some were colorblind, which did not matter in a darkened room with black and white film, but it did matter when they left the building to give a briefing. Some never spoke unless spoken to. Some never shut up. They often found themselves seated behind columns or stacks of film cans. Some overtly stared at women, all women. Some would not look at women, and some covertly stared at women. Some were drunks, lechers, braggarts, barracks lawyers, fools, politicians, clowns, and naifs. Contributing to the mission brought acceptance, but acceptance sometimes came with a nickname.

A loud, overweight branch chief was the Round Mound of Sound. The imagery analyst who never turned right was Lefty. The Prince of Darkness wore only black clothes. The Cool Fool had no common sense, which he proved by picking up a guard's loaded rifle. One who missed many softball games was No Show. A branch chief who spoke very slowly was The Human Rain Delay. But those who could not make finds and calls generally were not nicknamed. The organization and the imagery analysts both easily recognized when someone could not read out the film. They generally did not last in the branches, as the peer pressure to perform was constant and fierce.

In some cases, new imagery analysts discovered soon after graduating from the basic imagery analysis school (the NIAC) that, while they could do the work, the microscope or the light source caused severe headaches or vision problems. These people generally were reassigned to support positions in requirements, or in the edit shop where they did not need to use a microscope. Many went on to rewarding careers. But some, who were reassigned away from the analytic groups, left NPIC quickly after not being able to perform as analysts.

Hiring bright, young people, a number that grew into the hundreds by 1986, provided NPIC much needed energy, which the new director used to propel change. This group was very amenable to the NPIC cultural tradition of giving new people important work, and many of them, early in their careers, started making significant finds and critical intelligence calls. They were willing to work hard for long hours, and they adapted to the competitive environment and the peer pressure. Some new imagery analysts received a frightening amount of responsibility early on, and some were mentored by imagery analysts who had been at NPIC for only two years. Some had to make calls and stand up to senior imagery analysts very soon after graduating the NIAC, and they were able to prove their calls to be right and the senior imagery analyst wrong.

One of the best accounts of how NPIC was regarded came from a former air force imagery analyst assigned to the Strategic Air Command. "I started out as an imagery analyst with a focus on Libya, Egypt, Israel, . . . It wasn't long before I started to develop into a good analyst. I made a few good imagery finds and found out that whatever I did, before I could produce a finished report, my findings had to be verified by NPIC. . . the 'authority on imagery analysis.' This reputation carried over to my next assignment in 1982 with the 544th SIW (SAC, Offutt AFB) where I was a supervisor of the Middle East Branch. No matter what we did relative to imagery analysis findings, we had to verify with NPIC. If there was a difference of opinion on your findings vs. NPIC, SAC always took the side of NPIC."

Despite the long-standing traditions of NPIC, new imagery analysts would also question practitioners and practices if they thought them arcane, obscure, or just plain stupid. Their questioning, while not endearing, would prove useful in learning and coping with the new computer technology, which challenged them far less than it did some of their managers and mentors. They were also undaunted by the volume of imagery, shift work, the need to define new processes, or to focus collection.

They also were irreverent. A senior military officer managing a DIA all-source component visited an NPIC branch working African issues in 1985. Although the branch walked him through its analysis, he dismissed its findings and told the NPIC imagery analysts that they were only "bean counters." He told them that he would have some reservists come into the DIA spaces on the weekend so that "real" analysts could review their work. This did not impress the imagery analysts and, when the officer returned the next day, the NPIC imagery analysts he met the day before all had new nameplates on their desks: Green Bean, String Bean, and Butter Bean.

The new director focused the energies of the imagery analysts, and one of his most effective ways to create focus was outside the workplace. As a way of accelerating change, Rae introduced a different form of offsite meeting to NPIC. Through one structured conversation, repeated multiple times with groups at every offsite, Rae created an environment where every NPIC employee, even new employees, could voice his or her opinion, ask questions, and take on a leadership role, for a short time. They would also see the new director's leadership in action over the course of dozens of offsites at Port Deposit, Maryland.

Rae held his first leadership offsite in the spring of 1984. About every four weeks throughout his tenure, he would hold these meetings, nearly all at the Donaldson Brown Conference Center run by the University of Maryland. This center occupies a large, Georgian-style house, on a farm on a cliff on the north bank of the Susquehanna River overlooking I-95.

On the northern river bank at the cliff bottom was the small town of Port Deposit. The town was sustained by a gravel dredging operation that had given the town its name, and NPIC applied the town's name to these offsites. At this isolated location, nearly every NPIC visitor enjoyed the farm-grown food. Next to the "home," a former stable had been converted into bedrooms. The conference center could hold about sixty visitors, and it became the theater for a series of leadership performances. Rae used Port Deposit offsites as his stage where NPIC employees got to see, rehearse, and perform as leaders. They also were able to see Rae demonstrate his leadership, clarify the roles of NPIC leaders and managers, and get the employees to understand and play their roles in the NPIC he envisioned.

Rae brought many groups to Port Deposit, and their composition varied. Sometimes they would include only first-line managers from throughout NPIC; other times, division chiefs. Some meetings were "vertical cuts" with selected employees and managers from each level of the organization. But bringing together people from all NPIC groups accomplished a number of the director's purposes.

These meetings all shared the same agenda. Jack Elberti, Rae's executive officer and later chief of the Exploitation Support Group, would facilitate the offsite. Jack was Rae's trusted advisor, and his intelligence, long managerial experience, good judgment, and deep knowledge of NPIC were a great help to Rae when he came to Building 213.

The participants would start at 10 a.m. Jack formed them into groups of seven or eight and sent each group with an easel to different rooms. Their task was always to answer the following questions: What was going well at NPIC? What was going badly at NPIC? What was going on in NPIC that should be stopped, and what was not present that should be started? On the first day, the groups generally worked on these questions between 10 a.m. and 4 p.m.

Rae and the group chiefs arrived between 4 p.m. and 5 p.m. Along with all of the attendees, they would listen to the first group make its presentation on the questions. The participants sometimes joked that they worked hard all day solving the Center's problems, only to have the group chiefs arrive in time for the beer. After dinner, the director made a few comments to the whole group about current Intelligence Community issues and issues for NPIC that he saw on the horizon. This would be followed by questions in open session, and then everyone was free from about 7:30 p.m. on.

The evening was unscheduled. The location was sufficiently remote that most people stayed at the farm. The little store on Bainbridge Road did a thriving business in beer and cigarettes. After dinner, when everyone was sitting around talking about work, imagery analysts would gain an understanding of the various technical or support issues, and the support people would learn the story behind a particular intelligence find or NPIC's role in a policy or operational outcome. Often, over drinks, the stories of NPIC past, or the story behind the intelligence story, would be told to newer employees. Port Deposit had facilities for cards, TV, shuffleboard, billiards, darts, and volleyball. Some brought the new board game, Trivial Pursuit, to these meetings. The joggers, walkers, and birdwatchers had a large farm to explore.

The second day began with group presentations from about 8:15 until about 10:30 a.m. After a break, the director and the group chiefs would respond to the small group's questions, issues, suggestions, and proposals. This would go on until lunchtime. After lunch, the director summarized the actions to be tracked from the offsite, and he would talk about his priorities for NPIC. Nearly always, he talked about the new personnel management system and the Supervisor's Handbook. He also addressed the looming issue of strategic re-locatable targets, and new technology—either the "Upgrade" or the National Exploitation Laboratory. Sometimes he would announce plans in work, future meetings, or travel he would be undertaking on behalf of NPIC.

These offsites were powerful at accomplishing a number of organizational goals. First was improving communications. Anyone could ask the new director questions. Rae used Port Deposit to remove the organizational filters between him and the employees. The second goal was linking the work of every group at NPIC to the impact that NPIC was having in the Intelligence Community through its warning efforts; support to all-source analysis; arms control; reporting on regional conflicts; and its strategic research and development. The director showed the external impact of the imagery analysis to those who had only been focused on internal NPIC's processes. And, the director announced what he was going to do, which gave the employees the sense of being in the know before events transpired.

The structure of the Port Deposit conversations meant that no work-related issue was off-limits. If employees thought that a program or issue was in trouble, they could raise their concerns without fear of attribution or retribution. Rae invited everybody's opinions and ideas. The last question for each group—what should be stopped and what needed to start—gave every participant the opportunity to shape NPIC's future. Many of the small groups did just that. This new approach to conversations with NPIC employees worked. It caused issues to be surfaced, and the employees saw leadership responses and responsibility for change assigned to the group chiefs. There was also the public solicitation for participation on the part of every employee, and every participant's relationship to the Center's mission and challenges was publicly reinforced.

Port Deposit also used blended groups to create the healthy peer pressure that Lundahl initiated in his initial staffing in the Steuart Building. The mixture of NPIC employees from analysis, support, and technical groups created a healthy competition as to which group could make the best presentation and the best recommendations. Employees would meet NPIC people who they didn't work with. Mutual respect was one outgrowth of these blended groups, as well as employee networking.

Rae used these meetings to show NPIC employees how he was leading, and how he was advocating for NPIC in the Intelligence Community. The director demonstrated his receptivity to innovation and new ideas presented in an accountable way. For the group chiefs, who formerly operated with far less visibility and accountability, Port Deposit was not always a comfortable stage, but the successful leaders soon adapted. Every employee, whether as a small-group spokesperson, note taker, questioner, or group member had to take an active part. And, from participating in these small group discussions, many NPIC employees had their first experience and encounter with leadership.

Issues raised at Port Deposit were dealt with back at NPIC. Among the issues were cultural differences between experienced imagery analysts and new hires who frequently lacked military experience; the large number of new female employees; racial diversity; advancement opportunities at NPIC; the redefinition of NPIC's role in the Intelligence Community; plans for future systems and new technology; and valuable feedback on new technology, processes, and changes in the Center. Differences between CIA and DIA promotion schedules, which led to perceived disadvantages, were surfaced at Port Deposit, and consequently, the time-in-grade guidelines for lower graded GS-7 to GS-10 CIA imagery analysts were changed to address this inequity.

At nearly every offsite, Rae talked about how he was assessing employees. Everyone present heard the criteria he used to judge and rank employees. They also heard how their managers were supposed to communicate the process to them, along with their role and their managers' roles in the process. Finally, they heard a clear explanation of how they were competitively ranked, and the implications of their rankings.

The Port Deposit sessions engendered new ideas for reporting intelligence discoveries, new training courses, new technologies and applications, new methodologies, and new reporting formats. The NPIC Employee Handbook was one of these changes. The sessions helped restore the NPIC esprit de corps. At Port Deposit, supervisory counseling and NPIC orientation programs had their genesis. Employees returned from these offsites and changed how they worked in response to the discussions.

The director worked very hard at Port Deposit. For each group presentation, Rae sat in the front row in the large living room with the entire group. He took lengthy notes on a yellow legal pad. At times he would ask clarifying questions or request details for better understanding. But for more than an entire day, each month for four years, he sat and listened to NPIC's employees. As he listened to all the presentations, five or six for each session, repetitive for him, but new to each group of employees, he summoned the energy to listen attentively, and then to channel and direct the energy of the employees.

Often, after the small group presentations, he had to work with the group chiefs to get a more complete picture. As can be imagined, many concerns were common to multiple groups, but Rae always received them politely and respectfully, even after hearing dozens of times about the parking lots, the long line at the cafeteria salad bar, the shuttle busses to headquarters, soggy potato chips at the sandwich station, the dust and inconvenience of the METRO construction, or crime on M Street. At Port Deposit, Rae Huffstutler demonstrated repeatedly that listening was as important to NPIC leadership, as was the vision of the analysts at Building 213 and the ground station.

But not all was serious. In the evenings, the employees could drink beer with senior managers and listen to stories not usually told in the workplace. At one offsite, two young female employees pulled off the successful operation of short sheeting the director's bed. During one senior leadership session scheduled immediately after a session with new employees, one group chief decided that the yellow bikini panties he discovered in his room really belonged in another group chief's rear pants pocket where he usually kept his handkerchief.

After listening to the groups' reports, the director would assign a group chief to work issues that had been raised and to provide feedback to all employees. These meetings also provided the director with opportunities to announce, elaborate, or repeat his vision to a different group, to describe changes in work at the Center, to challenge and request help from employees with issues he was working, and to present perspectives from the Intelligence Community that had not been made available to NPIC employees since the time of Art Lundahl. The director's talks were so motivating that employees spoke of driving back to work after the offsite instead of going home.

Port Deposit became special. The smaller group settings and the facility itself enabled the director to combine his vision with the NPIC culture. Ideas were sparked, actions were generated, and experiments envisioned and sketched out. NPIC's business processes, technology, people management, and mission were all analyzed, dissected, tinkered with, scoured, and thought about. Employees could see their group chiefs in action, sometimes effectively, sometimes not, but always on stage.

NPIC employees were also on stage when they made their presentations or asked questions. They also would hear the director's reports about mission successes, community influence, and engagement with senior leadership in the intelligence and policy communities. They also could hear Rae's proposals to change NPIC personnel management practices, to move the focus of imagery analysis from targets to issues, to drive collection management, and to share in his vision for the Center. For the first time, many NPIC employees saw leadership practices at Port Deposit that they would later try to emulate. Everyone at Port Deposit was expected to think about NPIC, and their thinking was taken seriously. These meetings generated many new ideas, many personal renewals, and thoughtful initiatives that improved NPIC.

Rae Huffstutler's decision to bring employees away from NPIC to examine and change the Center achieved success far out of proportion to the expense. His investment in time, particularly his time away from the everyday urgency was not trivial. For each of the four years that he was director of NPIC, Rae spent twenty-four to thirty days a year at Port Deposit. Each month, for two or three days, he turned NPIC over to his deputy, either Colonel Lucero or Colonel Watson. Many times, he would have to take calls from them in the evenings. Even when crises arose, he viewed these offsites as a necessary investment to focus all the employees to share and help shape his direction for NPIC, to take the pulse of the Center, and to give all NPIC employees the opportunity to share in the leadership of NPIC. At least ten percent of the director's time was spent in this effort, but it produced both short-term returns at NPIC and long term returns in the Intelligence Community. The NPIC meetings at Port Deposit improved and developed employee morale, business processes, policies, operations, training, and culture. In the small groups at Port Deposit, many future Intelligence Community leaders first spoke outside their branches and first acted publicly as leaders. Others witnessed effective executive behavior for the first time, and took what they heard back at NPIC. And, later in their careers, many in Rae Huffstutler's Port Deposit audiences found their own stages and developed into senior leaders in their own right.

CHAPTER 11

MANAGING BY THE BOOK

From his first talk in spring 1984, Rae made clear that one of his priorities was installing an NPIC-wide system of reviewing, evaluating, and promoting NPIC employees. Many of the issues in the 1983 Inspector General report had their basis in opaque and sometimes biased personnel practices.

In his early talks to the group managers, the director spoke repeatedly of two new NPIC employees, hired on the same day, doing the same work, but in two different groups. Two years later they were being paid different salaries, but with no good explanation. Characteristically, Rae never mentioned by name the offending groups or their chiefs. Many NPIC imagery analysts had developed the perception that it mattered more to their career if you either had the "right" boss, or played on the "right" softball teams rather than if you were skilled at imagery analysis. There was a sense that for some managers playing softball for the Flyers mattered more than day-to-day performance.

Even serious imagery analysts who played for the Flyers could find themselves in the group staff meeting well prepared to brief a new intelligence find, only to be asked by the group chief how many hits they got the previous night before being told they should start the brief. While intended as a joke, the question communicated clearly what some senior managers really cared about, and it sent a clear message to those who did not play softball or golf in the NPIC tournament. Even those who played felt that this behavior demeaned their analytic efforts. Some senior managers developed groups of followers. Many imagery analysts and other managers referred to their junior managers as their "boys," though generally not to their faces. Whether this perception of cliquish management was real or not, the new director set about changing it.

Rae's approach was systematic. He did not introduce a cleverly named initiative or a communications campaign. Instead, Rae modified existing personnel practices and used them to shape expectations for the NPIC workforce. As the director, he took responsibility for constantly explaining what the personnel system should do for all NPIC employees. He also created pressure from the top on NPIC's middle managers to match the bottom-up pressure of the new employees. Between his expectations as director, and the expectations of the new employees at the bottom of the organization, the supervisors and managers were forced to start paying attention.

Huffstutler started first with some top-down changes. He reduced the levels of analytic management. He insisted on only three levels of supervision between any imagery analyst and the director. Up to then, there had been four or sometimes five levels. Reducing the levels of management created a number of important effects.

As the number of required approvals diminished, intelligence production accelerated. Analysts were able to produce more intelligence, more quickly. Most of the displaced managers became senior imagery analysts, and this group began to mentor the new imagery analysts. Fewer levels of managers reduced the amount of horizontal distortion in the communications between the director and the Center's employees. Having fewer first-line supervisors forced senior managers to increase their span of control or influence. The decision to reduce the number of first-line managers also served notice to group chiefs that they would have to identify and do something about their least effective managers. Some acted willingly, and some begrudgingly, but all the groups did what the director wanted.

Reducing NPIC's managerial overhead accomplished another goal. It demonstrated to CIA that NPIC made internal changes to increase the number of working imagery analysts. And, it demonstrated to the exploitation group chiefs that the director was going to shape their organizations to meet his priorities, not necessarily theirs. With these early decisions, the director started to change how NPIC was led and how it would be managed.

The director's next step was to introduce identical performance standards for all NPIC managers. Many groups and divisions resisted by trying to insist on their uniqueness and offering reasons why this proposal would impair their operations. But, with the help of Jan Petersen, an able CIA personnel officer on rotation to NPIC, who had worked with Rae in SOVA, the director pushed this change throughout the organization.

At every level—branch, division, and group—Rae evaluated all NPIC managers on how well they performed five duties that reflected his management style and leadership principles. The five duties were:

> Supervisory Skills: supervises the _____ Branch/Division/ Group (T/O-XX); organizes, plans, achieves goals.
> Personnel Management Skills: trains employees; rewards excellence, confronts weak performance, gives candid appraisals.
> Technical Skills: understands and applies knowledge in area of expertise.
> Leadership Skills: communicates, persuades, and deals effectively with colleagues.
> Corporate Skills: coordinates branch/division/group activities with appropriate components and views branch/division/group interests from corporate perspective.

Rae used the first and last duties to relate the work of every component and manager to the corporate perspective of the Center. His use of identical criteria for judging managers provided a way to align each individual manager's behavior to the changes and organization that Rae wanted. It also sent a clear signal, particularly to feuding analytic groups, that internal cooperation and coordination were mandatory and would be measured. In clear terms, Rae redefined all managerial evaluations so as to emphasize the similarity of purpose for all of NPIC 's managers.

For the first time, every manager was evaluated on how well he or she performed in light of the common NPIC mission. Rae used managerial evaluations as a way to reconnect every component to the overall NPIC mission. In its early years, when NPIC had been smaller and in one location, the common mission and goals did not need emphasis. But, by 1985, Rae needed to restore an eroded mission focus. The middle three managerial duties outlined what Rae expected from everyone on the NPIC leadership team.

Personnel Management Skills. The new NPIC evaluation system introduced a different responsibility. Teaching became an explicit managerial responsibility. Many NPIC supervisors operated from a command and control model, which they had learned in the military. Rae perceived that this model was not helping NPIC deal with increasingly complex intelligence problems, the increasingly large amounts of information, or the growing number of new employees without military experience. Many new imagery analysts and managers felt and endured the ineffectiveness of command and control as a means of motivation. The new imagery analysts needed a different kind of management, and Rae sensed their need. The old style of managing would not prepare NPIC employees or NPIC analytic managers to deal with increasingly complex intelligence issues and digital technology.

Technical Skills. This duty made explicit a cultural trait practiced since Art Lundahl's time. From everyone's first day, the clear expectation in Building 213 was that each new NPIC employee had to prove him or herself by answering or helping answer intelligence questions. From his or her first day in NPIC, every employee felt pressure to become better at his or her occupation. Rae explicitly incorporated the strong tradition of NPIC tradecraft and craftsmanship into his management.

Leadership Skills. The interesting aspect of this managerial duty was the internal focus. From the inspector general's report, Rae knew that he had to reduce the internal conflict and increase cooperation among his leadership team. Cooperation and coordination among the groups was a serious challenge, and Rae started addressing this issue on his arrival. By connecting this internal coordination challenge with the most aspirational of the supervisory duties, Rae clearly let all managers know that it was his priority, and he challenged the leadership team he was building.

The common supervisory evaluation was an effective way for the director to exert downward pressure on middle managers. Standardizing the evaluation applied the director's expectations to all NPIC managers. For the ambitious managers, they saw that the quicker they changed, the better it would be. Other managers changed as the peer pressure increased. However, pressure from above and employee pressure from below could address only some of the behaviors that the director wanted to change. While Rae used the formal personnel review process as one organizational lever, he also incorporated the traditional NPIC cultural norms. For good reporting he would call the imagery analyst directly. And for other important and less glamorous work, particularly for the challenging work of search, he introduced an informal award.

To recognize imagery analysts for this critical task, the graphics shop designed an award the director could give to celebrate the good "finds." Shirley Hogan, a talented freehand artist, created the Eagle Eye award, a cartoon version of the eagle from the NPIC seal. Rae wrote a short note about the particular discovery on the drawing, walked down to the analyst's branch, and presented it to the imagery analyst in front of his or her peers.

"Eagle Eyes" quickly became prized workspace decorations. They were also given out for particularly significant or difficult intelligence finds at known targets. This informal award, with no money attached, excited both those who earned it, and those who did not. Over a period of time, the best imagery analysts had a number of these awards at their desks, and the few imagery analysts who earned five "Eagle Eyes" were given the Order of the Eagle in recognition of their accomplishments. The director instituted a similar award, "The Feather in Your Cap," for support and technical personnel who made significant contributions to the imagery analysis. Support people prized these awards as much as the imagery analysts prized their "Eagle Eyes."

Reshaping personnel management took much of Rae's time in his first year. One personnel issue in particular took a number of years to change, but NPIC imagery analysts considered it critical. This was increasing their pay.

In the early 1980s, CIA and DIA were trying to increase their hiring. Part of the increase was related to the national security initiatives of the Reagan administration, and part was compensation for the post-Vietnam War personnel cuts that had weakened the Intelligence Community. While starting salaries for imagery analysts were generally similar across the agencies—GS-7 for potential imagery analysts with a four-year degree or equivalent experience and GS-9 for those with a masters—a wide disparity in promotion opportunities existed among the different imagery analysis components. For both NPIC and DIA, in the early 1980s, imagery analysts were GS-12s at the journeyman level, but for the Office of Imagery Analysis, the journeyman level was a GS-12 and 13 and, there were even four GS-14 senior imagery analysts in OIA.

Each leader of the imagery organizations—NPIC, OIA, and DIA/DX-5—had struggled to raise salaries for senior imagery analysts and journeymen for a number of years. Strong cases were made to the personnel departments in CIA and DIA but, as it turned out, the change came about as a consequence of a visit by DCI Bill Casey to OIA at Building 213. The leader of that organization, Wayne Strand, a former OIA imagery analyst, informed the DCI that his imagery analysts often accompanied operations officers in the field, but their pay was not comparable. After the visit, Casey decided to raise the pay grade at OIA. As NPIC was also under CIA administrative control, Casey's decision meant that CIA should also pay NPIC's imagery analysts equally with their OIA counterparts. But NPIC was at least five times larger than OIA. This meant that changing the journeyman pay ceiling in NPIC would have to be implemented over a number of years. But this was only part of the pay disparity issue that faced NPIC.

Rae Huffstutler, who had all his previous experience in CIA's Directorate of Intelligence, noticed the disparity in managerial pay. NPIC's division chiefs, with divisions of one hundred and twenty imagery analysts or so, were GS-15s, while DI office chiefs, managing similar numbers of all-source analysts were four pay grades higher (SIS-4s). If Rae was to develop the leadership necessary to grow and sustain NPIC, he needed more senior executives. When Rae arrived in 1984, only six NPIC officers were senior executives.

With the help of the director of Science and Technology, Evan Hineman, Rae was able to get an administrative upgrade that meant he would have the points for the expanded leadership and workforce that he would need when the new satellite systems came on line. But, the director knew that additional positions alone would not suffice. He knew that he would have to provide reassignments and rotational assignments to increase the capabilities of his GS-15 officers to allow them to gain the experience and acumen to compete successfully for senior executive positions.

After he had been at NPIC for about six months, Rae started to reassign senior personnel. He had seen his leadership team and their subordinates, and he had formed his personal impressions. In that time, he had excellent help from his executive officer, Jack Elberti, a respected NPIC senior manager. Jack provided Rae with the context and history for many of the situations and individual behaviors that the new director faced. By mid-1985, Rae had introduced the new process of competitive evaluation rankings, and had seen the early results of that process with his GS-15 population and the junior executives. He also had used a time-honored organizational test—the task force—to see potential executives perform.

NPIC and CIA had long used task forces. When some operational change or senior leadership initiative came about, an ad hoc group would be formed. Rae used these task forces to evaluate how well high-performing individuals worked outside their customary responsibilities. Some of these task forces dealt with technical issues; some were on Director Casey's initiatives; and some were commissioned by the Directorate of Science and Technology. One division chief, Nancy Bone, was detailed to CIA Director Casey as part of a group that wrote a credo for CIA; another, Niles Riddle, was sent off to evaluate new sensor technologies; and a third, Cal Freeland, was detailed to work on a portable system to transmit images remotely to hostage response teams.

In all of these cases, the individuals performed well and were recognized by being selected for positions of greater responsibility. Individuals from other DS&T offices were also sent to NPIC for analogous broadening experiences. Rae considered these task forces important development opportunities to complement excellent daily performance. In his criteria for management selections, an individual's ability to cope with the new and to deal with change mattered.

By 1985, Rae knew where NPIC was and was not working effectively. His early impressions had been shaped by witnessing personnel management issues, technical problems with the upgrade, operational tension between the two exploitation groups, and the mission challenge between the growing volume of film and the limited number of imagery analysts. In the fall of 1985, the director decided to reorganize the Center, and he announced the reorganization and personnel changes in December. The new structure was more akin to the NPIC of the late 1970s. The Technical Support Group was divided into an Exploitation Support Group (ESG) and an Operations and Engineering Group (OEG), a move that gave the computer network its own organization for operations and maintenance while moving intelligence production support into its own group. For the analytic groups, he left the names and structure alone, but he changed the reporting responsibilities to allow the Imagery Exploitation Group and the Priority Exploitation Group to focus on discrete missions. The re-alignments in IEG and creation of the Customer Service and Support Center were intended to develop its strategic mission and priorities, while the mission changes at PEG were intended to focus its imagery analysis effort on indications and warning, current intelligence, and crisis support.

Throughout NPIC, he also eliminated many staff positions, and the outcome of this change created twenty-two more analytic positions. With additional scrutiny on NPIC, the director had to show how NPIC was addressing its own shortcomings before he could expect any relief or new positions from the Directorate of Science and Technology.

Computer programmer positions in the Operations Support Group, which maintained the computers and communications equipment, were converted to contractors. The remaining government positions were then converted into new imagery analysts. This transition would enable the NPIC workforce to remain more current with the rapidly changing technology.

The Exploitation Support Group cut back the effort given to Services of Common Concern, where NPIC supported other components of the Intelligence Community. And the development group, DPG, still challenged by the size and scope of the modernization effort, found its leadership team under the director's scrutiny.

The director also made some leadership changes. Ted Clark became the new executive officer. Jack Elberti moved from executive officer to become the new chief of the Exploitation Support Group, and Steve Clark became his deputy. Tom Appleberry went into the Operations Engineering Group with Walt Shafer as his deputy. The dissemination division was aligned into the Support Group, and its personnel were transitioned from NPIC into the Directorate of Administration. These organizational changes over the next two years added seventy-five desperately needed new imagery analyst positions.

This reorganization addressed critical structural issues and gave NPIC employees and managers a clear sense of the director's priorities. But the new organizations retained much of the same senior leadership, particularly in the analytic groups. These leaders would work under a different set of expectations in 1986. And they would be judged differently.

Spotting Future Talent

While Rae used common managerial and supervisory duties to develop potential talent, the variety of skills, trades, and knowledge needed to staff and develop NPIC meant that he needed another way to inform his workforce about their individual potential and what it would take to succeed at NPIC.

By virtue of its heritage and highly classified mission, the NPIC workforce was a smaller version of CIA. NPIC had its own mathematicians to help imagery analysts measure objects on the images. It had physicists and experts in orbital mechanics to help computer programmers write programs to locate exactly where on earth and from what angle the imagery analysts were looking. It had world-class experts on military equipment, nuclear weapons, military R&D, electronics, every order of battle, ships, and railroads. It had regional experts for every continent, many of them for the Soviet Union and China. It had graphics artists, compositors, photographers, and photo lab specialists. It had librarians, researchers, editors, artists, cartographers, pressmen, and even a barber. It had its own couriers and guards, optics shop, model shop, machine shop, cafeteria, gym, credit union branch, and four libraries—one each for books, maps, aerial photography, and ground photography. Geologists, geographers, and videographers worked there. In its own school, NPIC had teachers to teach imagery analysis; it had a small staff to handle its budget, foreign liaison, classification and distribution, and planning. It had a development group, an engineering group, two support groups, and two exploitation groups. Its employees came from CIA, DIA, the uniformed military services—mostly officers—and contractors. While it needed all these different skill sets, NPIC never needed its own lawyer.

This broad array of skills, crafts, trades, and education served NPIC well and created a culture of problem solving and innovation. This broad diversity of experiences resulted in each NPIC group assessing potential differently. The director recognized the need to develop future leaders as well as to fix the "broken" personnel practices. He designed a system to evaluate and develop the current NPIC workforce as well as the new hires. Rae knew that NPIC would be changing. He knew that NPIC would have to deal with new satellite systems and harder intelligence challenges every day.

Rae Huffstutler changed how NPIC evaluated people. At the time in CIA and NPIC, personnel evaluation was a two-part process. The first part was the Personnel Assessment Report or (PAR), a one-to-seven (seven being the best) rating system with a narrative about the specific evidence behind the numeric scores. The narrative described the job, the scope of responsibility, and the experience of the individual. The second section of the PAR described the individual's performance; it too required examples that justified the scoring. This final section was supposed to describe individual strengths and weaknesses, and what actions the employee should take to improve his or her competitive standing. Such actions might be training courses, future assignments, or improving some aspect of an individual's performance. These actions could be designed to improve present performance or to prepare for a position of greater responsibility.

The PAR fed the second part of the assessment that evaluated the employee's potential. Rae used this second part of the assessment process to meet the younger NPIC employees' expectations that they would be told what it would take to succeed. Through this process, called the Competitive Evaluation Rating, Rae began to shape junior employees into future leaders.

The personnel system for competitive evaluations incorporated every employee's Personal Assessment Rating. After discussions with the employee, supervisors used the PAR to prepare for the Competitive Evaluation ranking meeting, a meeting that considered the potential of employees at a given grade. Until Rae Huffstutler's arrival, these meetings had been secretive with little feedback. Rae changed the process to insist that the factors and ratings be standardized, distributed, and publicized to every employee in the Center. For employees from grades GS-7 to GS-14, group chiefs led these meetings. For the GS-15s, the grade below that of a senior executive, Rae himself led the process.

Under Rae's system, all NPIC employees were reviewed against four standard factors: *Performance, Expertise, Personal Traits,* and *Potential. Performance* had four separately scored factors: Productivity; Initiative/Innovation/Creativity; Judgment; and Self-Expression.

Expertise was evaluated as either managerial or non-managerial. *Personal Traits* were judgments of an individual's interpersonal relations. *Potential* was an estimate of future growth capability. Each of the seven criteria was evaluated on a one to nine scale, with four being the acceptable norm. Written descriptors for were provided for the even number values. These descriptors were keyed to explicit skills, traits, or attitudes.

For instance, in order to be scored eight or nine in Productivity, a manager had to certify that an individual "Completes assignments with unusual perception in advance of deadlines and looks for additional tasks." To attain a high score, along with demonstrable high production, the anticipatory mindset was necessary. For a high score in Self-expression, excellent briefing skills were not sufficient. Employees also needed excellent writing skills. To score well in Managerial Expertise, managers had to show that they had developed their subordinates. With Interpersonal Relations, for an individual to score well, rapport, empathy, and leadership would have to be shown. The final criteria, *Potential*, was an assessment of an individual's ability to develop, grow, and advance into assignments of greater responsibility.

After the employees had been ranked, they were grouped into four categories. Category I employees were the exceptional employees who demonstrated the necessary traits of performance, production, and potential to be rapidly promoted ahead of their peers.

Category II included above-average employees who were doing quite well, and who merited watching and developing. Category III grouped good employees, making valuable contributions, but who might have reached their potential or who would take longer to reach their potential. In his Port Deposit talks, Rae pointed out that every NPIC employee, including himself, would eventually develop into a Category III employee.

The final group had personnel and performance problems. This group—labeled Category (or Cat) IV—was to be given specialized, individual work plans. Individuals in this group would be evaluated more frequently. Essentially, this group was on probation and getting special managerial attention. If their problems or performance issues were not corrected over two years, the CIA or DIA process to separate these employees would begin. NPIC fired government employees, though not many of them, from each of its groups.

Although this competitive review process existed at NPIC and elsewhere in CIA, Rae made two important changes. He standardized the process and made it transparent. To make his changes take effect, he publicized and published the schedule, the participants, the criteria, and the process. Initially, the director witnessed and reviewed how NPIC's group chiefs managed this process. Through his first year, he attended many group panels, particularly in the three months when GS-12s, -13s, and -14s were reviewed. As the Center had six groups, he was unable to make all eighteen panels but, by consulting with the respective personnel division and EEO representatives who attended each one, he reviewed the results of every career panel.

Midway through his first year, with the revised CER process established, the director had a sense of how well the group chiefs knew and led their people. Those managers who tried to use the old, opaque practices had identified themselves to the director and isolated themselves from their peers. At every Port Deposit offsite, the director publicized the CER process. He distributed examples of the review sheets for every employee, and explained the process in the *Update*, NPIC's newsletter, as well as in the recently published Supervisors and Employee manuals. Rae used the CER and the personnel evaluations to create the slow and steady upward pressure of expectation from newer employees.

The director focused personnel discussions strictly on the CER criteria. The standardization of the process had a few effects. With the increased transparency instituted by Rae, the evaluation processes became less secretive and fairer. Issues raised in the IG inspection—favoritism by some group chiefs, bias against minorities and women, a lack of understanding of the personnel management system by the employees, and capricious behavior by managers—were all spotlighted. In many cases the better managers and supervisors made personnel discussions far more transparent and useful for their employees. For those who did not, the additional review and openness made those past practices, which had caused suspicion, much more difficult to sustain.

Some managers tried to game the system. A few IEG division managers reverse-engineered a numerical key so that they could rank individuals without going through the CER process. But this attempt to rig the ranking could not be sustained during the discussions among all the IEG divisions. And, their branch chiefs also complained. The disparity among the rankings ended up becoming the basis for the discussion, and the input from that one division generally varied from the final rankings arrived at in the group panel.

Rae made NPIC personnel management a written rather than an oral process. With the *NPIC Supervisor's Handbook of Personnel Policies and Procedures*, and later the *NPIC Employee's Handbook*, he published the CER process, criteria, and annual schedule. Rae himself wrote the first draft of the supervisor's handbook at home, and Nancy Bone, head of the Graphics and Publications Division in the Exploitation Support Group, led the team that edited and published it in 1985. Tom Jarvis led the team that produced the *NPIC Employee's Handbook* in the following year. One addition that Rae suggested to the employee's handbook was a short history of NPIC that Tom wrote.

Managers could still follow the old NPIC oral tradition, but they had a more difficult time bringing old information or 'baggage" into the career panels. The personnel officers on rotational assignment from CIA monitored the process, and the other voting members would not risk their own rankings by agreeing to a ranking based on old information. Also, the newer and younger employees were not shy about asking for CER feedback. They could tell quickly if their feedback and experience tracked with the printed evaluation process that the director was repeatedly briefing at Port Deposit and throughout NPIC.

About this time, Rae commissioned a classified history of NPIC. In the late 1960s, Urban Linehan had written a classified history about the early years of the Center through the U-2 program. But little attention had been paid to capturing history since the departure of Art Lundahl. The director sensed the need to preserve NPIC's unique culture and accomplishments as only a few of the pioneers and early members remained. Rae brought back Dino Brugioni, a retired IEG division chief, to write this history.

Although sensitive to NPIC's history and culture, Rae used the CER process in both subtle and prominent ways to drive change at the Center. The common terminology provided all NPIC managers a standard way to assess an individual's performance even if they didn't fully understand the nuances of his or her unique profession. It took considerable reading and discovery for managers of one profession, like editors or computer programmers, to learn how to judge photo lab, printing, or photogrammatic experts, but the revised CER process forced the managers to have a structured conversation based on the written criteria, and to make competitive cases for their own rankings and the rankings of others relative to their own employees.

The process worked well to identify the best imagery analysts, support personnel, technical personnel, and supervisors. From this group, the inventive, the leaders, the extremely capable, and the visionaries came to the fore, and their talents were applied against the Center's challenges. The open evaluation process rewarded performance, and it provided a basis for making distinctions among the employees.

Not everyone thrived. The CER, which had its basis in performance above all other criteria, reinforced the critical NPIC cultural values of expertise, performance, and communications. It was a great improvement over the old system, but it was still not perfect. One branch chief, nicknamed the "Strutter," used to tell his employees, "I'm a CAT I. If you want to be one, you should imitate me."

The CER process openly identified promising individuals and allowed for spotting, developing, and managing talent. For many new hires, the process let them know where they stood, and if NPIC management saw any future leadership potential as an outcome of their performance. The feedback conversations that grew out of the competitive evaluation process channeled the competitiveness of the new hires into line with NPIC's challenges. These evaluations resulted in some selections into growth positions or test assignments. As a side effect, the new CER process revealed a number of candidates, particularly among the surge of new hires, who under previous personnel practices might not been identified as having potential. In the analytic groups, the new system's openness greatly diminished perceptions of favoritism or "coterie" management.

Of course, weak managers did not explain the new evaluation process. When their employees would ask for CER feedback, they would get dismissive explanations such as, "Well that's how we see you." What the weak managers did not account for was the talk among the imagery analysts who quickly identified the weak managers; the openness about managers' performance at Port Deposit offsites; and the message sent by those who "voted with their feet" when they sought work in other branches. Many weaker supervisors did not recognize the building pressure of expectations among the younger workforce.

With its reliance on competitive rankings and external assignments, the director's personnel selection process did not sit well with all the group chiefs, particularly those who had been grooming acolytes. Rae reached below many of the deputy group chiefs to select a number of junior division chiefs for senior positions. He did this on the basis of their performance at managing change and competing against their colleagues. He did not make these decisions in a vacuum, but only after consultation with his chief of personnel, his deputy, and executive officer. In his first year, he replaced his executive officer and both exploitation group chiefs. Rae used the CER process to make other selections; some in response to events associated with the Upgrade, and others based on his observation of trends mentioned in the IG report. But the important parts of his pattern of selection were his establishment of performance expectations, and his specific expectation that managers take responsibility for communication, employee development, and performance.

By 1986, the first influx of new hires had begun to establish their professional reputations, and the CER process had identified those with the most potential. The large influx of new imagery analysts in the middle 1980s and the growth in the number of imagery analysts meant that some new supervisors would be needed. This organizational development provided the opportunity for the new chiefs of IEG and PEG to reach below some of the senior imagery analysts and former section chiefs to choose talented GS-12 employees and to choose the best as first-line supervisors. This group, whose performance and ranking in the CER process had made them stand out, had earned an opportunity to help influence NPIC.

The selection of the new branch chiefs was not universally applauded. Many imagery analysts who had been stuck for years at GS-12 heartily resented these "baby branch chiefs" who were quickly selected to GS-14 positions even though some of them were brand new GS-12 and 13s. Some saw these selections as the same old favoritism with new names and a new group chief. While some acrimony and resentment were expressed, the group and division chiefs supported the new front-line managers. The newer employees wanted first-line managers who would give useful feedback on what they had to do to become competitive. They did not judge the new managers as inadequate simply because they lacked as much experience as some of their peers.

The other change Rae made was opening up rotational assignments, much like those Art Lundahl once sponsored. The difficult issue of finding imagery analysts who wanted to work shiftwork, nights, weekends, and holidays at PEG for two years remained, but the new exploitation group chiefs worked together to ensure that PEG was fully staffed. Nonetheless, branch and division chiefs were sometimes reluctant to lose additional good imagery analysts to service at PEG. Often they discouraged, openly or subtly, lateral movement between branches or divisions.

To retain good, younger employees and to keep controlling supervisors from clamping down on new employees, the director introduced the NPIC rotational program. Under this program any employee could apply for internal rotations without the immediate supervisors' permission. If the gaining organization would agree to pay the salary of the NPIC employee, this process also could be used for external rotations. This program worked effectively. Only a small percentage of NPIC employees chose to participate. Some of those interested in rotational assignments would be tripped up by the requirement that only those with satisfactory performance were eligible, and others who tried to use their potential departure as a negotiating lever found that their plan was not very effective. In the few instances of legitimate conflicts, this rotational process worked to the advantage of both the individual and the Center. The upward pressure of employee expectations removed much of the branch chiefs' ability to restrict employee movement, especially imagery analysts.

Rae changed NPIC personnel management by clarifying and publicizing existing processes. NPIC employees, CIA, DIA, and military, were no more talented than their peers in other imagery analysis organizations or other Intelligence Community offices. But the young intelligence officers at NPIC, through the CER processes, were told what they were doing well, where they needed to improve, and what it took to succeed. Many of the young officers took the feedback and began to develop their careers. The healthy pressure of fair competition created an environment that allowed many to thrive

While the director was able to use the downward pressure of communications and clear written guidance, and the upward pressure of expectations to shape future leaders, NPIC's technical challenges would not be so easy to fix.

CHAPTER 12

EVERY UPGRADE IS A SETBACK

B y late 1984, NPIC's computer system upgrade was in trouble. Intended to help imagery analysts manage the increasing volume of near-real-time imagery, it was far behind schedule, did not function as promised, cost far more than anticipated, and presented a large problem for the director.

The NPIC Modernization Program—the formal name for the Upgrade—was ambitious, perhaps too ambitious. It was intended to bring information electronically to the imagery analysts' desks and light tables. Through the Improved NPIC System, the new computer network that was part of the modernization program, NPIC was attempting to become one of the first organizations to build an entirely digital workflow. It achieved only a small part of this goal. While Rae Huffstutler never really got his hands completely around the Upgrade, he did bring in a brilliant program manager to rescue it. Although the Upgrade experience taught Rae a hard lesson about the limits of new technology, he used the experience to create a new organization inside NPIC for research, development, and technology insertion.

The Background

Technological challenges and shortcomings were not new to NPIC. Development of the NPIC upgrade program began in the early 1980s, after the first digital satellite overwhelmed the existing infrastructure in 1977. While this long delay may not seem logical, it reflects a political and cultural reality in the Intelligence Community. It was easier to get funding for new sensors or satellites, because they could be tied to current intelligence challenges.

Nearly all the attention and resources were focused on the technology related to the new sensor, the satellite, and its internal communications. But similar attention, funding, and resources were not dedicated to the "back end" of the intelligence cycle—the exploitation and dissemination pieces of TPED—the tasking, processing, exploitation and dissemination.

The NRO's investment in new technology and program management far outstripped NPIC and other imagery analysis components in the Intelligence Community. The NRO, funded separately and far better than NPIC, did consult with these organizations on the requirements for the sensor and the satellite, but it focused more on building satellites than on building tools for imagery analysts. The first electro-optical satellite was so computer intensive that existing computers and networks in the analytic community were no match for the flow of its data.

When the first softcopy imagery analysis workstations were built, their infrastructure was wired point to point, and the custom-made workstations were so expensive—more than one half a million dollars each—that only a handful existed at the ground station and at building 213. So all the imagery, after it was turned into hard-copy film, was put into lockable steel bins called 'hoagies' and trucked multiple times to Building 213, CIA headquarters, and the Pentagon every day.

In the early 1980s, NPIC's imagery analysts were expected to be conversant in photography, military intelligence, geography, and current events, but not computer technology. Experts in other NPIC groups met their technology needs. In hiring imagery analysts, technical skills were not a factor. The computers for the imagery analysts were all mainframes, with their own government and contract hardware and software specialists. Image scientists and programmers worked on standalone systems in the Technical Support Group to write the specialized and esoteric software needed for mensuration and plotting imagery collection.

Hard-copy film was the medium the imagery analysts worked in, wrote on, filed, stacked, and moved around. Next to every analyst's desk, were two burn bags, one for film, which actually was destroyed by burning and a separate one for paper, which was mulched. Film was everywhere in the vaults, stored as "flats" in cabinets, in accordion folders, in desk drawers, spooled in rolls, in file folders, on or under imagery analyst's desks, and in boxes on the floor. Wood and fiberboard racks lined the vault's walls along the internal hallways. These racks held plastic film cans with labels on their lids indicating the mission dates. The first floor of Building 213 had a large film vault with older film. Even older film, back to the first U-2 mission in 1956, was stored offsite in a secure, bombproof, concrete vault that held one record copy of each aircraft and satellite mission. NPIC used so much film that it recycled duplicate copies of old film for its silver halide content. In the 1980s, as a result of this recovery process it returned more than seventy thousand dollars annually to the US Treasury.

When imagery analysts needed multiple copies of images, the photo lab on the second floor would make them, along with enlargements, and any "special" work. The NPIC Photo Lab had the first Beacon Precision Enlarger, a custom-built, room-sized photographic enlarger that could magnify part of an image as many as 153 times, and print it on thirty-inch by forty-inch paper. For much of the work that did not require as much enlargement or precision, the Durst enlarger was the workhorse.

Some imagery analysts kept lots of film at their desks, others only a little. From branch to branch, informal storage methods differed; thousands of copies of images were stored in thousands of target folders. To make their own quick enlargements, imagery analysts used Polaroid cameras attached to microscopes, and later thermal printers attached to the video monitors on the light tables. Working among all this plastic film and photographic paper led to a macabre recognition. If Building 213 ever caught fire, toxic fumes from burning film would likely kill most of the NPIC employees (but not the roaches) before they had any chance to escape.

Branch target folders had the best quality (or most interpretable) image of any facility, area, or piece of equipment that imagery analysts had looked at. Previous NPIC reports or cables also would be in the same folder, as well as related intelligence from other agencies. For every target in the NPIC database, a folder existed and, if the target was important enough to be looked at overnight, another folder for the same target would be kept at the ground station. The process for making target folders varied by branch, issue, and imagery analyst. Of necessity, more rigor was in the target folder process at the Priority Exploitation Group where all the imagery analysts shared target folders.

But at Building 213, individual imagery analysts filed information in individual ways. Each imagery analyst still had his or her own stash of images, still called "shoeboxes," although cardboard folders were mostly used to hold KH-8, KH-9, and KH-11 images. The organizing and filing system for branch information was in the heads of the managers and imagery analysts. In well-run branches, peer pressure and managerial oversight would ensure a good filing system. But in some branches, imagery analysts filed images by individual preference, rather than systematically.

Some senior analysts would only file "their" targets and would leave the remainder to the junior analysts. In these branches, film filing was usually made the work of the new person, while it was shared in the well-run branches. Everyday imagery analysts had to file their own film by hand. Whenever a branch grew or shrank, or reorganized so that an account was moved to another branch, the filing system had to be redone. When most imagery came from film return satellites, these filing systems were sufficient. But after the introduction of the near-real-time systems in 1977, the volume of film and information began to mount, and the hardcopy storage and all these "unique" filing systems became unmanageable.

Intended to alleviate the information access and storage problem, the Upgrade was designed to provide electronic files to give imagery analysts an on-line collection history for every target, and a chronology the reporting, and other classified information on the targets. It did not succeed at reliably meeting these basic needs until the late 1980s. Until significant improvements were made to the system, and the computer technology became much cheaper, hard-copy imagery remained the most efficient storage medium, and the memories of the imagery analysts were the best databases available. The technical challenges of storing global information in a readily accessible way were also compounded by the cost of computer memory. At that time, the entire capacity of NPIC's computer storage was measured in megabits. In 1984, sixteen kilobits of storage, enough for about five or six pages of text, cost eight thousand dollars.

Handoffs

In this hardcopy environment, creating intelligence from looking at film involved many steps, people, workarounds, and transformations. At NPIC they were called handoffs. At its basis, imagery analysis is deriving information visually, converting it into words and, if the observed change is important enough, storing it in a database and/or sending it to the Intelligence Community. The handoffs involved in this process had been carried forward from 1960 when satellite film began to arrive in buckets. And, while developments through the 1960s and 1970s meant that more buckets of film arrived more often, these same handoffs continued, so the speed of the imagery analysis was not significantly increased. The film, and the information derived from the film, continued to be stored every which way. Throughout those years, electronic storage was so expensive, both online and offline, that only text could be stored on a mainframe computer, and in as abbreviated a form as possible. While that had to suffice for NPIC, it was wholly inadequate as a method of communicating information and intelligence from NPIC to the Intelligence Community.

When NPIC's imagery analysts captured new information, this information had to be converted into a format "acceptable" for a "cable" to be transmitted electronically to the Intelligence Community. After 1977, this process was performed through the mainframe system using Delta Data green-screen terminals and a light pen. The light pens were tethered to the Delta Datas, and they were used to "highlight" and fill-in brackets on the screen. In Building 213, the imagery analysts shared these terminals communally, as there were not enough for all the imagery analysts. Imagery analysts wrote their draft reports either in longhand, or they typed them into the NDS. They were reviewed in turn by a senior imagery analyst, a section chief, a branch chief, and sometimes the branch chief's deputy. Generally the branch chief had release or approval authority. A collateral researcher formatted the cable before its release. When intelligence was considered contentious or sensitive, a division chief or his deputy also reviewed the cable. It then went to the edit shop where an editor and compositor looked at the format and grammar before it was released for dissemination throughout the Intelligence Community.

If the product included a photo and a simple map, then a visual information specialist and the photo lab would be involved, as well as the couriers from the registry. Because of the extra steps and handoffs, this format generally was reserved only for important intelligence that had to be produced as quickly as possible. These products were called mini-boards. The analog technology of that time meant that including photos with text took much more duplication work in the photo lab. These products could not be digitally transmitted, and secure couriers delivered them around the Intelligence Community.

When imagery analysts wanted to produce a more detailed or complex intelligence report, even more people and steps were needed. If their work involved measuring an object or area, imagery scientists were called in. If a drawing needed to be made, the visual information specialists were required and, if the work was to be published in hard copy, compositors, editors, and the technicians from photo lab and print shop were involved.

Some innovations came about because of the limitations of the handoffs. While writing on either gray thermal paper or green and white striped tractor paper was sufficient for the imagery analysts' needs, the secretaries' need to produce memos drove the Center to purchase an early word processing system from Wang Laboratories. Use of the Wang spread from the secretaries, to imagery analysts, and then to the managers. While keyboarding was not a valued skill among older managers who needed secretaries, the new imagery analysts were familiar with typing and computers. NPIC continued working with Wang Laboratories to develop a system that provided an early, networked e-mail, word processing, and database capability. Eventually, an interface with the NPIC Data System (NDS) was designed. At PEG, the Wang system was modified to serve as a backup system for the NDS, and it was used regularly.

NERC-M and the New SPWG

In the late 1970s, when the volume of the KH-9 photography was beginning to swamp the imagery analysts, senior NPIC leadership, though aware of the cumbersome production processes, did not have a plan for improving them. As far back as the summer of 1975, John Hicks raised the issue of the quality of the information infrastructure with Les Dirks, then head of CIA's Directorate of Science and Technology. While Hicks was steeped in the utility and technology of the older KH-8 and KH-9 film-return systems for discovery and understanding, he did not envision how the new near-real-time technology would change the imagery analysis profession. He did know from the NPIC imagery analysts' experience with the KH-9 that NPIC needed a new system to exploit imagery in Building 213. After January 1977, the KH-11 was declared operational and the imagery analysis technology lagged farther behind. In early 1978, General Hazzard commissioned a study of the Center's preparedness for the future satellites, and the results were not good.

By 1979, the budget for new technology was less than a tenth of what the new director knew he needed. Hap Hazzard knew that more resources would be required to get the needed workstations and computer infrastructure to allow imagery analysts to gain intelligence more rapidly. The existing computer infrastructure allowed only a limited number of NPIC imagery analysts to access the computer at the peak times, and the functionality was limited to mensuration and to an interface with the older system that provided information to NPIC from the other agencies in the Intelligence Community.

General Hazzard brought a program management background into NPIC. Externally, he took on the responsibility of making the case to obtain the needed funding from Congress. He brought in Fred Evans from CIA/ODE to lead the Upgrade, and he commissioned a study by four individuals—Ted Clark, Niles Riddel, Jim Wason, and Charles Keenan. This was a re-creation of the Special Projects Working Group. This new group, which combined imagery analytic experience from IEG at Building 213 and from PEG at the ground station, along with computer and support expertise, worked most of a year, and in March 1980, they issued a technology plan for NPIC.

The imagery analysts needed technology to bring them the necessary historical, geographic, and reference information about every image, the targets on it, and its location on the earth. Imagery analysts also needed intelligence from other agencies at their desks. To improve the analysis of imagery, the new system would have to improve mensuration capabilities, accelerate the information transfer to the imagery analysts, improve imagery enhancement capabilities, along with providing the technology to improve reporting and communications, as well as handling a planned three hundred percent increase in the daily volume of imagery.

The study also outlined the need to develop a second-generation of soft-copy workstations so imagery analysts could look at digital imagery without losing any of its detail. The design and delivery of these workstations were anticipated to take at least a decade. These computer workstations would have to be custom built, and much of this software and hardware would have to be designed and invented. This upgrade was also intended to reduce the daily operating expense of transferring digits into hard-copy film. For new mainframe computers and other planned technology to fit, Building 213 would need an addition. And NPIC would require a lot more money.

But General Hazzard had a plan. He personally prepared and delivered a series of briefings for the congressional intelligence and appropriations committees. While his briefing style appeared homespun and folksy, in reality, he tailored each briefing to the interests and background of the individual members. At that time, a large number of southern congressmen and senators sat on the intelligence committees. Hap was able to persuade this group very effectively, often with stories about fishing and down home in Birmingham, Alabama. Additionally, his McLean, Virginia next-door neighbor and back-yard drinking companion was the director of the Congressional Budget Office. When Hap had finished briefing the congressional committees, he had gotten enough to make the NPIC Modernization Program, the formal name for the upgrade, the largest line item in the CIA's S&T budget, at about a quarter of a billion dollars. But on account of the immense cost, the upgrade funding had to be stretched over ten years. This caused the planned development to take longer than anyone wanted.

Inside Building 213, Hap made other changes. He understood that NPIC would have to track fiscal, technological, and physical modifications in a far more organized fashion than had existed. In 1980, he set up a Configuration Management Secretariat to track the various schedules with their dependencies and sub-schedules for the technological developments and deliveries. It would also track the construction of the addition to Building 213, which was needed to store all of the new computers. He personally chaired the new Configuration Control Board that established an operational baseline and tracked changes to NPIC technology and systems. This board comprised all the NPIC group chiefs, as well as the budget staff and the secretariat.

By late 1981, the tracking and scheduling processes were underway, contractors had been selected, and in July 1982 the Upgrade effort was organized into the Development Program Group (DPG). Fred Evans, who had come from OD&E, became the group chief, but on account of the size and scope of the Upgrade, he also was given the title of the associate deputy director of NPIC.

The secretariat created an NPIC concept of operations for the new technology, along with a facilities baseline document. The facilities baseline document meant that, for the first time, NPIC would track the location of all its equipment. Until then, imagery analysts could move a light table and their files, and that was about all the effort it would take to grow or shrink a branch. But with a computer terminal coming for each imagery analyst, the NPIC computer network would constrain imagery analysts to a specific place. By 1982, congressional funding had been secured and the contracting process was started. In July 1982, DPG selected a team of a few younger imagery analysts and managers and put them into a group where they would not have any day-to-day analytic responsibilities. Instead, their work was to revise the existing workflow and to design formats so that the new system could handle the increase in analytic work and reporting. Once these formats were created, they would be sent to the programmers and the contractors who were to code and build the Improved NPIC System (INS).

In the late 1970s and early 1980s, all NPIC cable writing was done in upper case text, with eighty characters per line, and stored in the computer in that form. Some punctuation was not permissible, as it had been already used for computer software coding instructions. The group did painstaking work with the reporting formats. They had the advantage of the earlier work done by Mark Baker and others for the PEG startup. But the challenges that had stumped the programmers and contractors in 1976 and 1977 continued to frustrate their efforts in 1980 and 1981. Some earlier work could be brought forward, but an immense amount had to be redone from scratch.

The small group had to figure out the format for database entries, or descriptions of a single place or target on the earth. They had to design the format for a baseline report, the initial report on a location or facility. They had to anticipate what features or changes the Intelligence Community would care about. Along with the descriptive writing, they had to design formats for the daily cables that were used for varying priorities; as well as summary cables that covered activity over a designated period of time; and order-of-battle cables so analysts could list all the observed equipment at a facility. There were also formats for different types of aircraft missions, search reports, and satellite film-return missions.

Capturing text at that time required scarce computer memory. As a result, many words in the most common imagery analyst reports were reduced to trinomes, three-letter acronyms or abbreviations. NPIC at the time measured its computer memory in the number of words stored, and it could store only three million words of memory in its mainframes. (This is approximately ninety megabytes with uncompressed files, or one-sixth the text capacity of a single CD-ROM) The most common trinomes for imagery analysts were a NRC or a NAC, which meant no reportable change or no apparent change at a target. Other trinomes and binomes indicated if a target was occupied, operational, cloud covered, or clear.

The small group created a document known as the NERC-M (National Exploitation and Control Manual), which eventually ran to hundreds of pages. It was an interface control document, which meant it contained mandatory design specifications for the contractors. While mundane, this documentation was essential to force contractors to understand and attempt to meet the imagery analysts' needs. The NPIC cables had to meet Defense Department and Intelligence Community formats for their external communications systems. These systems used limited bandwidth and transmission capability. In the early 1980s, some of these were still teletype systems, the more modern of which printed on green and white tractor feed paper.

Nonetheless, in contrast to the world that imagery analysts lived in, some development contractor briefings would talk about "paperless work environments," and how the new system was going to simplify and accelerate imagery analysis. These briefings did not go over well with either skeptical imagery analysts or their managers who, with straight faces, would ask if the fourth floor men's room was the prototype for the paperless environment.

During the Cold War, satellite imagery was so compartmented and controlled that it could not take advantage of technological changes happening in the outside world. Every computer terminal and piece of hardware at NPIC continued to be "tempested," that is, encased in a metallic conduit to guard against electronic emissions. The software was all controlled and designed from scratch.

These security constraints made systems development prohibitively expensive, which made incorporating new technology much more difficult. As the technology required at NPIC had never been built before, the development program made costly mistakes. Although the beginning of the personal computer revolution was taking place, it took many years before commercially available software could be incorporated into NPIC's architecture. NPIC purchased early Apple Lisa and Macintosh computers for graphics work, but these were standalone systems. NPIC also used an expensive proprietary system, Genigraphics, for making color viewgraphs.

While its text-only limitations might seem primitive today, the NERC-M served NPIC well in keeping the contractors focused, and it continued for many, many years to be the basis for much integration and systems work. Although the rapid growth in visual and photographic formats came into commercial computer technology later in the 1980s, in spite of the work done on the NERC-M, there were no classified formats or easy ways to get images into NPIC's computers. And all other information formats brought exorbitant storage demands.

The initial work done by the SPWG with the NERC-M was ground breaking, but little known by many of the imagery analysts. That gap was not discovered until the first readiness testing for the new system. The challenges that the NERC-M presented to the programmers were not fully clear until the early factory acceptance tests. But, by that time, the need to deliver was paramount if the schedule was to be kept.

From 1982 through 1984, the early INS deliveries were fiascos. The system kept crashing, and the evaluations failed as individual workstations or terminals were not available for the imagery analysts to test software. Instead of working on a terminal, imagery analysts were shown photocopies or viewgraphs that envisioned the sequence of computer actions and screen flows. For the processes to be tested, no explanations were available. Not enough people knew how the new system was supposed to perform, what to expect, or what each test was trying to measure. Factory support was lacking. The segment testing was behind schedule, backing up schedules for other segments, and creating doubt among the imagery analysts that the developers had a plan or could succeed.

Yet, the early development reports and briefings carried an entirely different message. They glossed over the problems, and declared success by redefining the criteria to what they had been able to achieve. The developers' desire to accentuate the positive did not go over well with the imagery analysts who had no confidence in the process, the developers, or the system.

The leadership of the development group (DPG) worsened the situation. They wanted to celebrate the achievement of having a delivery, so they distributed coffee mugs to celebrate their efforts. While the developers and contractors were celebrating, the imagery analysts were hanging homemade posters in their branches that said: "I survived the INS upgrade." But what really irked the imagery analysts and their managers was the retrospective DPG briefing that tried to blame some of the failed delivery on the ignorance of the imagery analysts. The diminished trust between the two groups complicated the task of getting imagery analysts' participation in the future development process.

At the time, DPG had the largest budget in NPIC. In General Hazzard's briefings, he would mention that the Center was planning to spend about a million dollars for each imagery analyst. While this number impressed the imagery analysts and other audiences, it also made them skeptical about how well the money would be spent. The greatest challenge for the Upgrade would be to prove its worth to the imagery analysts.

To mirror the imagery analysis workflow, the Upgrade was organized into segments. The Data Control segment gave the imagery analysts information about the image that would be coming to them for analysis. It told them when the image was taken, and where on the earth the image was. This segment took information from the ground station system and passed it to the imagery analysts' workstations. When imagery analysts wrote descriptions of what was on the image, or when they wanted to read what had been seen at a target previously, or if they wanted to note that it was cloud-covered, this information would be contained in one of the massive files in this segment.

If imagery analysts wanted information from other intelligence sources, it would be contained in the Collateral Information segment. This segment held another set of large electronic files with information from other agencies. To help imagery analysts search the database, it also had a series of structured queries.

The third segment was Exploitation and Reporting. It was intended to take the imagery analysts' written drafts, integrate their text with images and maps, and convert the report into the formats required for electronic publishing. This segment was intended to keep all the information in a digital format until it reached the print shop or photo lab.

A fourth segment created new software models to allow the imagery analysts to accurately measure objects at their workstation. A fifth segment brought improved secure communications to and from Building 213.

DPG quickly developed its own jargon to overlay the configuration management terminology that it had imported from the NRO. Its people and briefings began to refer to segments and upgrades, installs, patches, and builds. Each file or piece of software that digitized some analog process was given an acronym. Many imagery analysts at the time noted that outside NPIC some of these acronyms had different meanings, such as the Precision Mensuration System (PMS) and the Analyst Integrated Display Station (AIDS).

The three main segments: Collateral Information, Data Control, and Exploitation and Reporting were intended to connect serially to support the exploitation, imagery analysis, and reporting processes. Connecting the segments was the responsibility of a separate contractor who functioned as a system integrator. This plan was supposed to make sure that the developers and designers worked in concert to meet the demands of performance, cost, and schedule. However, each segment was so large and technically sophisticated that it had its own prime contractor with a number of sub-contractors. They were so large it made "working in concert" nearly impossible. Many people in DPG were spending lots of time flying to various contractor facilities for design reviews or factory acceptance tests. Eventually, more than a thousand contractors were involved in the Upgrade.

The segments made some progress with the available technology. But the progress made in individual segments could not be integrated. As each segment grew, the integration challenges and the cost grew disproportionately, and the schedule and performance declined. Because of the scale of the program, it was regularly briefed to Congress. Although the early slips had occurred during General Hazzard's time, much of that early work was only focused on defining the requirements. The consequences of the slipped deliveries were not yet visible. When Rae Huffstutler came to NPIC in 1984, the program was already eighteen months behind schedule, and some individual segments were even further behind.

Initially, Rae trusted DPG leadership, and his initial briefings and reports to congressional oversight were optimistic. However, as difficulties mounted, and the schedule continued to slip, he began to be concerned about the program's chances for success and his credibility with the congressional oversight committees. The DPG leadership remained optimistic and continued to press the contractors, but at a critical point, the contactors began to ask for additional funding to meet the requirements, and they delivered far less than promised. The requests for additional funding and the diminished deliveries forced a confrontation over the next big milestone. Fred Evans, the head of DPG, gambled his position on its success. When the 1985 delivery functioned much worse than expected and cost far more than estimated, Rae had no option but to accept Fred's resignation. Rae was left to report to the congressional oversight committees that his previous reports were overly optimistic and that NPIC needed more funding.

After the resignation of Fred Evans, Rae worked with Evan Hineman, director of CIA's Directorate of Science and Technology to find a replacement. Hineman was instrumental in selecting and persuading Dennis Fitzgerald from

CIA's Office of Development and Engineering to come to NPIC to straighten out the Upgrade. Dennis had earned two masters degrees from Johns Hopkins University, one in mathematics and one in physics. He had experience in running large satellite development programs; his new challenge would be to turn around an earth-bound program that was in serious trouble.

Dennis inherited a number of problems—technical problems that manifested themselves in the delivery but not in the testing; schedule problems that compounded as a result of the failed delivery; budget problems as the upgrade needed more funding; internal credibility problems in that few NPIC imagery analysts believed that the Upgrade would ever help with the mission and, finally, external perception problems in that NPIC had yet to prove to the S&T, the Intelligence Community, and congressional oversight that it could manage a large technical program.

Dennis made quite a first impression. Rae's meeting style was more gentlemanly than the OD&E culture that Dennis came from. When Dennis announced that the Upgrade was feasible only if the NPIC leadership team had balls enough to act, it sent a different signal.

One of Dennis's first decisions was to commission a program review by an independent contractor that had delivered many large and technically complex programs and installations. This group took a few months to review the deliveries, the accomplishments, the deficiencies, and the remaining challenges. In the interim, work was ongoing with the contractors working off the liens and the discrepancies. But there was one difference.

In Fitzgerald's first meeting with the contractors, one contract officer brought up the award fee for a particular stage of a development in one segment. Dennis set the tone by saying forcefully that would be the last mention of any award fee for any segment until the performance and schedule were restored. Although contract information was supposed to be confidential, this news traveled throughout the Center. Dennis's management style and his judgments on the Upgrade were clearly different. With this meeting, NPIC's began to manage the Upgrade effectively.

When the independent review panel finished, the results were mixed. They found the Upgrade to be conceptually feasible, but with serious technical and cost challenges. The panel believed that additional money and time would solve these challenges. But the independent panel also recommended that one segment, Exploitation and Reporting (ER), be severely reduced in scope. The delivery of the standalone components was allowed, but the plan to install connectivity between the analytic group and the production support group was scrapped. So improvements would be delivered in the publications and mensuration systems, but Dennis Fitzgerald cut the ER segment. Its funding was used to offset the increased costs of the other segments. Once the program was scaled down, DPG reviewed its processes for developing and testing technology. Some personnel changes took place, and more importantly, DPG also made a number of process changes.

Imagery analysts were brought earlier into the process to test and review each segment. An increased number of junior imagery analysts, along with the developers, participated in the testing. Imagery analysts began to travel to the factories. From a cultural standpoint, the analysts' involvement diminished their animosity toward the developers. Often, relatively junior imagery analysts took on this responsibility, as the computer technology did not intimidate many of them. Nor did they especially care what the contractors thought of their judgments.

The previous "paper screen reviews" were replaced by scenarios where imagery analysts got to evaluate from the keyboard, using a real computer. For the first time, programmers, developers, and imagery analysts began to talk face-to-face. Design reviews became more rigorous, and the factory "beat and bash" tests were made more strenuous. Also, contractors were beginning to come to Building 213 to "live with the imagery analysts" for extended stays. The new term the imagery analysts taught the developers was "workaround," or a process that partially compensated for inadequate software.

The remaining two segments, Collateral Information (CI) and Data and Control (DC) were also scaled back. Some planned improvements were delayed a number of years. The visual depictions of the daily coverage were scaled back, as were the kind and number of applications intended to simplify the daily work of the imagery analysts. Storing and retrieving the large amount of textual data remained a daunting challenge. The NPIC imagery analysts worked using their traditional oral process of indexing finds to the "story," and the upgrade tools did not help this process.

Slowly, the Upgrade started to change the work of the imagery analysts. The older and unreliable Delta Data terminals with their light pens began to be phased out. As the Unix-based Sun terminals were installed, network reliability began to improve. The word processing capabilities of the standalone

Wang administrative network began to be supplemented and replaced by software packages installed on the new Sun Analyst Integrated Display Stations. As each delivery was installed and eventually debugged or experimented with by the imagery analysts, either the functionality improved, or the imagery analysts developed workarounds, or both.

While the Upgrade attempted to address various types of information, it focused primarily on text. Because of storage, bandwidth, and processing limitations at the time, NPIC's softcopy imagery was still restricted to two custom-built IDEX 1A standalone workstations in a special room on the fourth floor, and to the four workstations at PEG. But by 1987, at least a hundred more imagery analysts were competing to use these workstations at Building 213.

Despite the few technological gains for the imagery analysts, the DPG technologists were still promising that the imagery analysts would get automated graphical display tools and statistical tools, as well as help with strategic re-locatable targets, and a digital process for requesting imagery from their workstations. However, individual imagery analysts and individual developers were doing much of the development of these tools, instead of DPG.

The National Exploitation Lab

Rae Huffstutler saw opportunity in the Upgrade's budget and technical problems. As the national center, he thought it was NPIC's responsibility to provide another service of common concern to all Intelligence Community and military components doing imagery analysis. For years, the two other imagery analysis offices, CIA's Office of Imagery Analysis, and DIA's DX-5— both tenants in Building 213—partnered with NPIC in technology and infrastructure investments. Yet, when it came to softcopy exploitation, all three organizations had independent and costly initiatives to fund development of different workstations. As a result, Rae envisioned that the Center would have to take a different role in regard to research and development activities. His experiences trying to lead the NPIC Upgrade, a the large development program with a three to five year formal requirements definition process, convinced the director that the Intelligence Community needed another way to introduce new technology. The computer industry had started to change so quickly that the deliveries of the Upgrade, envisioned to be modern, were obsolete before arrival. And, softcopy workstations remained so expensive that it would be years before the government could benefit from the commercial computing revolution.

Rae commissioned a study group on establishing a laboratory that could develop and assess technology designed to support imagery analysis. After the recent experience where NPIC had to get technology help from the S&T with the Upgrade, the director knew that NPIC and the rest of the Intelligence Community needed another approach to technology insertion. This decision reflected Rae's awareness that some of the analytic tools promised in the Upgrade would not be delivered.

While better computer tools were coming into the marketplace, the challenges of the strategic re-locatable targets and the volume of information needed to provide intelligence on this issue meant that the NPIC's acquisition process had to change. Technology changes once driven and funded by the classified world were now accelerating in the commercial world, at a rate that would require constant monitoring. NPIC needed to monitor the new technology marketplace and to develop faster processes to insert new desktop tools into imagery analysis. Rae saw this before other community leaders.

Establishing the National Exploitation Laboratory required political support from CIA's Directorate of Science and Technology. The study group assessed NPIC's future needs, and those of other Intelligence Community and military imagery centers. The study group received the approval of the S&T, and in 1987 the National Exploitation Laboratory (NEL) was established. It also received staffing and funding from the air force at its start.

The NEL focused on areas of interest to imagery analysts. It drew its initial government staff from a mix of imagery scientists, former imagery analysts, and technologists. It brought in contract scientists and mathematicians to augment its staff. With a research budget funded by the DoD and CIA, it began experimental studies and technology assessments in renovated space on the third floor of Building 213. Walt Shafer was selected as the first NEL director, and he led a number of initiatives that focused on the imagery analysts' requirements.

Imagery analysts had a long tradition of adapting technology developed by the NRO to meet their intelligence needs. But that process was neither timely nor repeatable, and the learning had to be shared informally. The NEL provided an environment where the imagery analysts' expertise could be inserted more consistently and evenly into the various development processes. But the

NEL work was not restricted to development and assessment. It also began to research the imagery analytic processes of search that had been developed over the past twenty years. Rae intended the NEL to function as a classified version of the Underwriters Laboratory to independently and impartially validate products for the imagery analysis community. Among their early studies was a significant effort to develop sensor capabilities, which required the imagery analysts' perspectives on which sensors would provide the most information against selected intelligence questions.

Among the most important work of the NEL was determining the technology needed to exploit imagery in softcopy (electronically on a computer screen). This effort involved studying workstations, software packages, electronic monitor display assessments, ergonomic studies, illumination experiments, memory, and hardcopy storage devices. Much of this research resulted in the creation of strategies by which NPIC, or other IC components, could insert commercial computer developments into the classified environment.

NPIC had a number of existing activities addressing these challenges. The exploitation support group and the imagery analysis groups had small staffs to look at new technologies. But these efforts were always ancillary to an operational mission, and consequently their results and learning did not always have the needed effect or reach a wide enough audience.

From inception, the NEL undertook research with operational implications in mind. The use of statisticians and operations researchers in imagery analysis began in the NEL, on Elaine Gifford's initiative, and subsequently moved into the Imagery Exploitation Group. This move enabled the operations researchers to refine their methodologies against real world intelligence issues. On the SS-20 issue, statisticians were brought in to support the imagery analysts. The statisticians made contributions that led to improved analysis and better collection, and their successes on this issue led to their emplacement into the Exploitation Group. The statisticians were also used to analyze and validate the information gained from the first joint NPIC and community database audit.

The influx of junior imagery analysts who went to the NEL on rotational assignments accelerated its operational effectiveness. Their experiences with the Upgrade and the workarounds required to make it functional, helped shape the developers' insights and provided recent operational context for their research. In particular, they worked hard on developing the requirements for the digital light table and on digital tools for exploitation. Their strong sense of community with their peers also motivated them to keep the developmental work relevant to the needs of imagery analysts.

One other NEL effort was its futures program. This brought together sensor developers, imagery analysts, technologists, and scientists to work on a number of scenarios. These scenarios combined the pragmatism of the imagery analysts with the imagination of the developers in a structured effort to address future intelligence challenges. While these scenarios frequently did not have predictive value, they did focus the participants on future challenges, and they did result in some prescient attention to challenges that later emerged. But, while the NEL was considering the future, the NPIC analytic groups had to respond to current surprises in the world and in outer space.

CHAPTER 13

VERIFY THEN TRUST— THE SS-20 SEARCH

I n the spring of 1986, NPIC's requirements officers were far busier than usual. Since the previous winter they had been busy planning area collection for the last KH-9 film-return mission to answer two important questions: how many SS-20 bases were in the Soviet Union and were any new SS-20 bases under construction? The answers to these two questions mattered more that spring because of the January "surprise."

Late in 1985, Mikhail Gorbachev offered to put all Soviet missiles under a treaty with the West. His initiative surprised the arms control experts as well as his own military. Gorbachev's specific offer to eliminate all SS-20s intrigued Western intelligence services. Because of its mobility, the SS-20 was the most difficult Soviet missile system to track and target, and the West was skeptical about the sincerity of the Soviet's proposal. Why would any nation negotiate the removal of one of its most capable and threatening weapons systems? NPIC analysts, who knew better than most the difficulty of tracking the SS-20 units, were among the most skeptical.

To provide the imagery that would answer both questions about the SS-20 force, the requirements officers were building collection nominations for the areas that the imagery analysts most wanted to see. Because of their knowledge about the capability and capacity of the satellite's camera system, the requirements officers plotted the number, size, and sequence of the needed photographs. With film-return systems, the most critical areas were planned to be collected early in the mission, so if the returned film from the first bucket was cloud-covered or of poor quality, the same areas could be re-collected on the same mission and returned in subsequent buckets. With four buckets, the KH-9 would provide three re-tasking opportunities. The NPIC collection effort entailed plotting tens of thousands of separate potential images. It involved factoring how near or far the satellite would be from the earth at a particular time, how much film remained on the satellite, how high the NIIRS (or how good the resolution of an individual image needed to be), how large an area needed to be imaged, and the likelihood of cloud cover at the time of collection. More images were planned than could be photographed, as collection managers would not know which areas would be cloud-covered, or if a previous failure to collect useable imagery would override other planned collection opportunities.

Gorbachev's surprise proposal intensified all this work. The previous KH-9 mission had deorbited early in October 1984 because of system problems, and NPIC was acutely aware that for nearly two years, parts of the Soviet Union had not been searched comprehensively. NPIC built a plan for this last KH-9 mission to search as much of the Soviet Union as possible. This effort took most of January through March, with NPIC requirements officers, in coordination with the NPIC Arms Control Staff, and many imagery analysts spending many nights, weekends, and holidays writing collection nominations.

The arms control community wanted to be certain that it knew the total number of SS-20 bases, and if any new bases were under construction. Over the previous seven years, NPIC had developed a sense of where the SS-20 could operate effectively, making it confident that the imagery analysts had discovered the locations of all SS-20 bases. The operating areas for these bases covered about sixty percent of the Soviet Union—about 5,200,000 square miles. That is 122 times larger than Cuba, or slightly more than the area of the United States, India, and Pakistan combined.

The requirements officers were plotting the area rectangles to photograph as much terrain as efficiently and quickly as possible. They had to plot the corner coordinates for each image, make sure that the coverage aligned with the adjacent collection, and then prioritize the collection in light of the intervals since these areas were last collected. Unfortunately, an event in April 1986 was to make all their work useless.

The End of an Era. This launch failure caused shock among the younger workforce at NPIC, as, during the early 1980s, the NRO had enjoyed a long string of successful launches. These analysts had not experienced the loss of a reconnaissance mission. The NPIC veterans recalled the string of launch failures in the early days of the KH-4 program, and the 1964 series of KH-7 failures. But for the younger imagery analysts, this was their first experience.

One unanticipated benefit, however, did emerge. The lack of new information actually eased the need to rapidly train the new imagery analysts. Those who had graduated from the basic imagery analysis training in the past eighteen months found that they had more time to learn their craft, and their managers had more time to teach them imagery research. As their NPIC predecessors had experienced, the new imagery analysts learned what it was like to have a limited amount of imagery, how to research issues from past imagery, and what if felt like to have pending important questions in their heads waiting for collection to give them new information. But across NPIC, their anxiety was not universally shared.

In the development group, there was actually some relief. The delays in the satellite launch schedule might provide time for the Upgrade contractors to overcome some technical challenges before the volume of imagery increased. Also, the reduced amount of imagery intelligence generated every day meant less strain on the overloaded NPIC data system.

The risky nature of space launches became visible to the world months later when the Challenger space shuttle exploded shortly after takeoff. NPIC provided photo scientists and imagery analysts to assist NASA with its accident investigation.

As a result of the launch failure, during the fall and winter of 1985, the NRO began a crash program to retrofit a testbed KH-9. This was not an existing satellite, but a collection of satellite subcomponents previously used for testing. These components had to be assembled and integrated, and critical missing components had to be manufactured as quickly as possible. Even though the NRO and its contractors worked on an accelerated schedule, the process of manufacturing, assembling, testing, integrating, and pre-launch testing of all these subcomponents still took nearly six months. In that interval, the collection of search imagery nearly ceased. The haste to convert the KH-9 testbed into an operational satellite resulted from the knowledge that it was approaching three years since parts of the Soviet Union had been searched. The previous KH-9 had only flown for less than four months from late June to early October 1984, and only fifty-seven percent of its total film was recovered. In its review of the mission, NPIC criticized the limited amount of imagery collected against the SS-20 base construction areas.

On 18 April 1986, the last KH-9, the former testbed, the one for which all the planning had been done to search for the SS-20 bases, was launched. Its flight did not last ten seconds. The launch vehicle exploded at such a low altitude that the debris and the large amount of instantly ignited rocket fuel destroyed the satellite and severely damaged the launch pad at Vandenberg Air Force Base.

Some parts of the Intelligence Community seemed to operate in a business-as-usual fashion without any understanding what this loss would mean. Nine days after the KH-9 launch failure, the first word about a Soviet nuclear accident came to the Priority Exploitation Group. The nuclear accident at Chernobyl, and the loss of the KH-9 got William Casey's attention. The director of Central Intelligence was infamous for mumbling and being hard to understand, but his guidance about imagery was clear: "Fix collection."

While Casey and other CIA leaders had been aware that the imagery collection process was bureaucratic, Chernobyl and the loss of the KH-9 caused them to act. After consulting with CIA leadership, Rae Huffstutler persuaded CIA to direct two senior officers into critical assignments. The chief of COMIREX and the chairman of the COMIREX Operations Subcommittee (OPSCOM), who managed day-to-day imagery collection, were replaced. Wayne Strand, a former OIA imagery analyst and director of that office, became the new chairman of COMIREX in July 1986. Jim Simon, a CIA Soviet expert who had worked for Rae as a SOVA division chief, was recruited to manage the COMIREX Operations Subcommittee (OPSCOM).

By this time, eighteen months after his arrival at NPIC, Rae had already changed the NPIC senior leadership team and had selected his own group chiefs. John Westcott was managing the Priority Exploitation Group at the ground station; Ted Clark was managing the Imagery Exploitation Group in Building 213, and Nancy Bone had moved from managing the Graphics and Publications Division in the Exploitation Support Group to become Rae's Executive Officer. These personnel moves had started to address NPIC's leadership needs and to influence NPIC's position in the imagery collection community. And Rae had also taken measures to increase the Intelligence Community's visibility into NPIC's database and reporting.

The Data Base Audit

As a former customer of NPIC, Rae Huffstutler knew that NPIC's expertise with imagery analysis led to its sense of exclusivity about its imagery calls. Sometimes this exclusivity spilled over into righteousness. The pride that NPIC felt in its imagery analysis, rightly or not, led to an attitude that had to be managed. Rae managed it with analytic customer input and a database audit.

At first, customer input was provided informally. Rae had spent almost all his intelligence career as a Soviet military analyst and analytic manager. Over the years, as NPIC progressed from discovering locations, to comprehending targets, to tracking strategic issues, its analytic contributions to intelligence were growing far beyond providing facts about Soviet installations. The tradecraft developed by the analysts was providing credible warning of impending activities and strategic developments, and demonstrating that imagery analysis could accurately provide information about the status of Soviet strategic weapons systems on a schedule that enabled treaty monitoring with increasing confidence.

But much of this external reputation had not been widely known or shared inside Building 213. Customers from the policy community or other parts of the Intelligence Community did not routinely come to southeast Washington to provide feedback to NPIC. NPIC's imagery analysts were aware of their peers' reputation, but Rae was able to use his all-source network from CIA/DI and the arms control community to provide more regular and specific customer feedback. He had been calling analysts personally to tell them how their analysis and reporting was used, and what he learned in community meetings from senior leaders in the intelligence and policy communities.

Along with informal customer feedback, Rae started another method, a database audit to reinforce the value of good target monitoring. From an informal beginning, he developed a formal process for monitoring the quality of NPIC's imagery analysis.

Rae created an ad hoc team of NPIC managers for the audit. In late 1984, he brought in Gary Holmberg, on rotation from FBIS, to change how NPIC audited its reporting on the database. The audit started at Building 213 as an internal Imagery Exploitation Group exercise as part of its General Improvement Plan. IEG managers had put together their own team to check the completeness, accuracy, and timeliness of its work. But, any internal audit done by the NPIC imagery analysts would always be subject to questions of subjectivity. Target monitoring was a key NPIC mission and most reporting about national targets was written into the NPIC data system. By 1988, the NPIC Installation Data File had about 15,000 targets worldwide. The number of national targets had stayed relatively constant at about 10,000 worldwide from 1975 through 1984, when producing the annual baseline for each target became an analytic practice.

The growth in the NPIC database concerned the director. The quality of the target descriptions, and the imagery analysts' ability to put target observations into context were far more important to the Intelligence Community than the total number of targets. To ensure that the quality of the NPIC reporting and subsequent analysis remained high, Rae asked analysts from a DoD command, SAC, the CIA Arms Control Staff, DIA, and OIA to critique NPIC's work. The audit focused on Soviet strategic and air defense targets, then the most critical for these organizations. The revised NPIC database audit brought in all-source and imagery analysts who compared the existing written record with a new review of what the imagery showed. This was done on a sampling of some of the most important targets that mattered to the Intelligence Community.

The initial results showed that NPIC had the most accurate database of information in the community on targets related to a number of strategic issues. While not uniformly excellent, the quality of the database was very good. Initially, this audit was restricted to the NPIC information and reporting, but in subsequent iterations it was extended to review the reporting of other intelligence agencies.

The database audit helped NPIC emphasize the value of using the database to record target monitoring for imagery analysts and managers. The database critique also heightened the imagery analysts' awareness of the Intelligence Community's reliance on their reporting. The audit also reinforced that their work was done in a competitive environment. NPIC analysts re-learned that their work would have to be good enough to gain the attention of other organizations. This lesson was important, as other agencies and commands received copies of the imagery as well, and often reviewed the same targets. NPIC's imagery analysis was valued, and the audit taught managers and imagery analysts that value could not be taken for granted and would have to be continually earned. While the audit process started building and measuring customer confidence in NPIC's Soviet reporting in 1984, the community's confidence in NPIC's approach to strategic issues would be tested in the summer of 1986.

New Leadership in Collection
While Rae Huffstutler was able to influence leadership changes at NPIC and COMIREX, senior leadership changes alone would not "fix collection." Rae had a number of discussions with the NPIC leadership team about how to support the changes at COMIREX. They recognized that, to manage collection more efficiently and effectively, NPIC would have to direct individual officers from IEG and PEG into rotational assignments at CIA and into the Intelligence Community.

Two NPIC officers from PEG took new assignments. Lew Moon was detailed on a rotation to CIA to help its collection organization learn how to use and task imagery more effectively. Part of his charge was to coordinate CIA's collection process with NPIC's, so CIA better understood NPIC capabilities, and NPIC had a better understanding of CIA priorities during this era of limited collection and increased requirements. And Rae created the NPIC Senior Requirements Officer, a GS-15 position that reported directly to him. Phil Lago returned from a rotational assignment to the CIA's Arms Control Intelligence Staff to take this new position.

Collectively and cooperatively, these newly assigned officers set about making imagery collection faster and more responsive to important issues, rather than focusing on managing the traditional formula that focused on standing collection that averaged the number of collected targets against the total number of targets. Their long NPIC experience with managing imagery analysis and devising collection strategies, as well as their strong informal network, ensured that the bureaucracy and the process did not get in the way of national priorities or common sense. But to drive collection, NPIC still needed more than changes at COMIREX.

COMIREX's practice of using the collection management system to stall another organization's request for imagery by putting it into "rework" was discontinued, as was the cumbersome voting process that could not keep up with fleeting events or near-real-time imagery collection. The tenor of the daily COMIREX collection meetings changed drastically. When organizations made unreasonable collection requests or nominations, Jim Simon dismissed them. Simon was able to do this because he had backing through the director of Central Intelligence. The frequency and rapidity with which he dismissed frivolous or ill-conceived collection requests, or "noms," often from DoD organizations, led to the summation "That nom(ination) got Simonized."

Two additional personnel changes were made. Mary Ellen Keene went to the Ad Hoc Collection Branch at PEG, and Michelle (Mitch) Root managed the IEG Requirements Branch. Both were experienced at conceptualizing and managing collection. Mary Ellen, an imagery analyst, had worked Eastern European and sensitive Middle East issues. Mitch had been a support and collections officer at both IEG and PEG. Both brought much skill at successfully negotiating contentious requirements and a sophisticated understanding of priority intelligence issues, collection processes, and NPIC's imagery analysis capabilities and needs. And, in their work in support of the NPIC imagery analysts, neither shied away from conflict.

With their daily operational support, the new NPIC senior requirements officers effectively centralized NPIC collection management to ensure that it met national collection priorities. As they had the backing of the two new exploitation group chiefs, they changed NPIC's collection approach to reflect the near-real-time mindset that grew out of the PEG culture. In addition, the two new exploitation group chiefs were of one mind about reducing the sniping and conflict between the two exploitation groups, PEG and IEG. While the sniping did not disappear entirely, it was very much reduced. These changes, driven by the risk that Chernobyl exposed, turned out to be fortuitous.

The SS-20 Questions

Figuring out the legitimacy of Gorbachev's January offer to eliminate the SS-20s was NPIC's highest priority. In March 1986, the Soviet Union returned to the negotiating table for the Intermediate Nuclear Forces treaty talks, which they had suspended in 1983. The Soviet Union also resumed discussions on Strategic missiles (START I) and other space issues. This meant that the US arms control community quickly needed more information on the current state of the SS-20 force, and for that information it turned to NPIC.

Under pressure from the DCI, the Intelligence Community wanted to be certain it knew the location and status of all the Soviet SS-20 regiments. For

NPIC, this question meant it had to search more than sixty percent of the Soviet Union as quickly as possible to make sure that Gorbachev's SS-20 offer was not deceptive. And now, it had to accomplish this without the KH-9 and with very limited imagery collection options. Additionally, 1985 and 1986 were the years when the US Intelligence Community was losing all its human sources in the USSR. At that time, no one in the Intelligence Community knew what and why this was happening. The espionage of Aldrich Ames and Robert Hansson would not be discovered until the 1990s.

Since Rae Huffstutler's arrived in 1984, NPIC had been increasing its analytic efforts at tracking the SS-20s. It had built up its knowledge of the SS-20 bases, and then, through a series of intensive periods of collection, it began to learn how units at these bases operated. Although collection issues caused NPIC to delay its analytic initiatives, the imagery analysts used this interval when new collection was scarce to research older film and to develop more in-depth knowledge about existing deployed forces. This effort was not without cost. For some branches that worked less critical regional or functional issues, it was not uncommon at that time for these branches to receive only one or two frames of imagery a day. One imagery analyst, Charlie Nations, became so good at discovering new SS-20 deployments that he was sent through every Soviet branch to teach his methodology. For many younger imagery analysts, the relief from the large volume of daily information meant that they could learn to work "like the old guys."

NPIC created an SS-20 study team and brought to it additional imagery analysts who had been studying Soviet short-range strategic missiles. The extra imagery analysts, along with their new methodology and new computer tools, increased NPIC's knowledge of the operational SS-20 force. But when the last KH-9 blew up in April 1986, the collection and research plans had to be shelved. But the SS-20 questions remained.

The KH-9's capability for collecting search imagery was extraordinary. To get a sense of the scale of its capacity, envision an American football field, without its end zones. That area, one hundred by fifty yards, has 5,000 one-square yard blocks. If each of those blocks were a thousand square miles in area, that would approximate the size of the area that had to be searched for the SS-20s. Optimally, the largest KH-9 frame could cover nearly five of these blocks (4800 square miles) at a resolution at which individual military vehicles could be identified. Of course, intelligence issues are not rectangular.

The areas to be collected are often not contiguous; they are not evenly distributed; the likelihood of clouds always varied; and the orbital limitations, sensor limitations, time of year, weather, and probability of successful collection all have to be factored in. As a result, the number of planned KH-9 images was in the thousands.

The loss of the KH-9 area collection changed the community's collection priorities. Rather than trying to answer all the SS-20 questions raised by the January surprise, the community decided that the most important questions were: how many deployed SS-20 bases and how many missiles did the Soviet Union have?

NPIC's arms control staff, led by Tim Sample, devised a search strategy for the one operating satellite. Ted Clark, the IEG chief, briefed the strategy to the Intelligence Community. Lacking other options, NPIC devised this search strategy that was full of technical, operational, analytic, and political risks.

From an operational perspective, the proposed new search strategy would strain the NPIC requirements officers in ways that they had not foreseen. The KH-9 had been designed and could be programmed to cover large areas sequentially over weeks and months, and that is how the NPIC requirements officers had planned to use it. To get a sense of the scale of their task using the KH-9, imagine planning to cover a football field with rolls of paper towels until its entire surface was entirely covered at least once. And this could only be done on clear days and the towels would have to be placed in locations where no roll touched another roll. Accomplishing this would require a way to track what areas had been covered and what areas remained. And a way to return and fill in the coverage gaps would be needed. Now, all the planning would have to be redone.

Now imagine having to cover the same football field under the same constraints but with postage stamps. The differences in scale are analogous to the increase in collection planning, tasking, and re-tasking required by this new plan. Everyday, all this additional work would have to be re-keyed into the collection system. This process introduced a large possibility of error and operational risk. But the operational risk, while large, was far less than the intelligence and political risks. And, the intelligence risk was going to grow rapidly with the new strategy.

Inside NPIC, the scale of this effort was explained at an unprecedented meeting. Ted Clark, the IEG group chief, pulled together the arms control staff, the collections officers, and the fifteen branch chiefs from three divisions working the Soviet issue that would do this search. Ted outlined the collection challenge, and then challenged the branch and division chiefs: "We have to be able to tell Director Casey with high confidence that we know where all the Soviet SS-20 missiles are so that he can tell the president he can be confident signing the treaty."

The increased area coverage could be collected only by looking far less frequently at Soviet point targets or known facilities. In some cases, the risk of not looking could be mitigated by including these point targets in a larger area collection at a lesser resolution. But, for some areas of the Soviet Union, area collection would be obtainable only by not collecting any of these important point targets. This decision would infuriate the Intelligence Community.

When the NPIC search plan for the Soviet Union was ready, Rae Huffstutler set up preliminary, private briefings for the chairman of COMIREX and the chairman of the OPSCOM to gain their approval and to assuage their concerns. Rae also enlisted their direct support in helping manage the risky plan.

A number of targets in the Soviet Union were deemed so important that they warranted a high level of attention—they were looked at for indications and warning. These targets presented the most critical threats to the United States and our allies. They were supposed to be looked at frequently, which for some targets was every possible opportunity. But, the need to search the Soviet Union to answer the SS-20 questions outweighed the risk of temporarily not collecting some of the Soviet indications and warning targets. Some members of the Intelligence Community, in particular the uniformed services in the Department of Defense, did not feel the same way. Both in and outside the COMIREX meetings they protested loudly.

When the military services and DIA were briefed at the OPSCOM, they were furious that COMIREX had accepted the SS-20 search proposal. When they learned that their protests would have no effect, the rest of the imagery analysis community tried to make the case that the risk of not looking at the Soviet's indication and warning targets was unacceptable. In particular, the army, the air force and the navy were outraged.

The driver for the NPIC search strategy was the need for the arms control community—the Departments of State and Defense, the National Security Council, and ultimately the president—to be able to assess the credibility of Gorbachev's offer to eliminate the SS-20 force and to negotiate an INF treaty.

For the United States to negotiate securely, the Intelligence Community would have to verify the Soviet statements about the size of the SS-20 force, and it could not do that without searching the Soviet Union. NPIC had past experience in doing verification using a strategy it had employed in past work on the SS-20.

Part of the confidence shown by the creators of this collection strategy grew from the NPIC's research experience with an earlier intense collection of selected Soviet SS-20 garrisons. This intense ad-hoc collection, nicknamed a "blitz," incorporated both the near-real-time and film return systems. But it took place in a much smaller, single geographic area. It resulted in a much larger amount of information and intelligence that allowed for important, detailed research.

After the earlier SS-20 blitz, imagery analysts reviewed all this imagery to get a sense of how the bases operated, and what routine operations looked like. This review was important, as it enabled an awareness of when activity differed from the norm. Although this analysis could have been developed without the standing collection being changed so radically, it would have taken much longer.

The other outcome related to the localized SS-20 blitzes was an effort to use first-phase imagery analysis to tip off other intelligence sources. This proof of concept was a development that allowed one intelligence agency to make use of NPIC to gain additional information for its own collection. And, NPIC would make use of the information from other intelligence sources to refine its imagery collection. In particular, the 24/7 environment of PEG, with its ability to contact the community and re-task imagery quickly was essential for this strategy.

The new, experimental effort with the SS-20 missile units challenged imagery analysts in a new way. Previously, weapons systems reporting had been indexed to one location. Now, when these missiles left their bases, imagery analysts had to re-task rapidly, search expeditiously, and record temporary locations even though these new targets had no unique physical attributes other than a latitude and longitude—in other words, just a location. In the beginning, the imagery analysts were able to track and keep records of the kinds of activity they saw, but the cumulative number and record of observations at different locations, over time, soon strained the capability of their memories and the NPIC database system. As Rae had foreseen, the long

NPIC practice of "indexing activity to the story" became insufficient for the challenge of this kind of strategic, re-locatable target. Imagery analysts working on mobile missiles needed a tool that could record locations, times, dates, observations, and any other information that an imagery analyst thought significant.

The Improved NPIC System had contained locational databases of installations, but they were essentially flat files or sequential notebooks that could not be easily searched or cross-indexed. While queries could be written, they required a programmer's assistance, and they took far too long to get written, programmed, tested, debugged, and delivered. As often happened at NPIC, imagery analysts were forced to create their own tools.

The imagery organization that directly supported CIA's Directorate of Intelligence, OIA, was still in Building 213. OIA had invested in a software package called Analyst, a program originally programmed in Smalltalk, a computer language invented by Alan Kay at Xerox's Palo Alto Research Center. This early object-oriented language was flexible enough to enable the creation of a relational database. An NPIC imagery analyst, Ken Whitson, met with his OIA counterpart, Donny Armistad, who had been experimenting with this program. Between them, they developed an early version of a relational database to track the SS-20s. The beauty of their effort was that the form that captured the input could easily be modified as their observations sharpened. As a result, the program could pull information from the NPIC database, and output the new information in a structured format that could be sent back to the NPIC computer system to be disseminated in a standard cable format.

More importantly than the tracking and reporting of daily activity, the records kept in Analyst could be queried, and imagery analysts and NEL statisticians could ask different questions of the data over time, over distances, and at different locations. After a large number of observations were compiled, imagery analysts began to discern patterns of activity. This was one of the first digital examples in the NPIC analytic tradition of inventing and/or modifying its own tools. Whitson's and Armistad's efforts meant that NPIC analysis could go out more quickly and accurately to the arms control community. Like the programming work done by Mark Baker a decade earlier, Ken's effort was so well done that many contractor programmers who came to study it left both impressed and befuddled.

This different kind of database allowed imagery analysts to focus more on issues than targets, and to discover and understand the relations among different targets. This change in focus helped them see when activity at one target was a precursor for future activity at another target. Whitson's and Armistad's work accelerated the discoveries of the relationships among targets, and enabled analysts to learn more about the operations of the force more quickly. Their software development greatly eased the challenge of applying statistical or terrain analysis to NPIC 's reporting and imagery analysis.

The work done with this second SS-20 blitz was one of the first examples where imagery analysts developed digital tools. These tools allowed them to develop methodologies that could be refined to apply to other problems where re-locatable targets were involved. Not all imagery analysts welcomed these computer tools, as they required the ability to anticipate questions before the observations were made, and they required some understanding and tolerance of the challenge of developing new computer scripts. Looking at film as it arrived sequentially would no longer suffice for imagery analysis. These tools also required discipline in the reporting and analytic workflow. But the tools, which many of the younger imagery analysts took to, led to discoveries and reporting that helped convince the community that NPIC was successfully tracking the SS-20 force.

The SS-20 search took most of the summer of 1986. Initially, some collection adjustments had to be made. The earliest collection reduced the resolution too much and only very large geographic features, such as rivers, were recognizable. Imagery analysts and managers had to figure out a standard accounting process across all three of NPIC's Soviet divisions and the fifteen participating branches. While imagery analysts and collections officers could get collection information from the tasking system, it had to be matched with the information that the imagery analysts saw. This matching process let the collection manager know if the collected area was clear, cloud covered, or partially cloud covered. That information had to be discerned quickly in case the area had to be re-imaged. Once an area had been imaged successfully, the requirements officers could cease collecting this area and resume collecting known point targets. But this decision was possible only with accurate geographic information.

At this time, the NPIC computer system was not capable of visually displaying this amount of information or this frequency of change, so the accounting method across all fifteen branches was hand drawn everyday with colored markers on acetate overlays taped over paper maps. Each one of the tens of thousands of images was outlined by hand with rulers and triangles on the overlay in different shading to reflect if the collected image was clear and interpretable. While primitive and inexact, this method provided a visual and revisable indicator of the work that had been done and the work that remained.

When the film to be searched arrived at Building 213, the number of pieces or chips of film was daunting. Often it took most of a morning for multiple imagery analysts in each branch just to sort and file these hundreds of pieces of film. In one branch, a new imagery analyst had the idea to design a sorting system like the postal service. Although Sarah Lance had only been in NPIC and her branch less than a year, she took her drawing to the model shop, which designed a Plexiglas prototype that was quickly replicated. Her idea, now called the "tower of power" and "the towering infilmo" by the imagery analysts, reduced branch sorting and filing time to less than an hour.

Looking at the low-resolution imagery during the SS-20 search was a harsh experience for younger imagery analysts. They had grown accustomed to looking at imagery of much better resolution. The resolution of the SS-20 search imagery was so low that individual buildings could be identified only with difficulty. The old timers who grew up with the KH-4 recalled when all satellite imagery looked like this. But for the duration of this SS-20 search, all the Soviet imagery analysts worked this one issue with imagery, which they described as "crappy."

Through June, July, and August 1986, hundreds of imagery analysts worked overtime, nights, and weekends, but when the search was over, NPIC could verify that no new SS-20 bases were under construction in the Soviet Union. NPIC finished the search just before the August/September arms control meetings held in preparation for the October Reykjavik meeting where President Reagan and Soviet Premier Gorbachev agreed to the limits of the new treaty.

As a result of the SS-20 search, NPIC provided the information and the confidence necessary for the United States to judge that the Soviet's proposal was made in good faith. While the the SS-20 search was not as dramatic or as public as the Cuban missile crisis, NPIC again combined search and discovery under tight deadlines, with comprehensive analysis and tracking to provide confidence for the US arms control negotiators to negotiate a treaty. President Reagan went to Reykjavik knowing in advance that NPIC had seen, located, and counted the entire SS-20 force. The October 1986 summit at Reykjavik led to the agreement in principle about the INF treaty, and to its signing in December 1987 by the Soviet Union and the United States.

CODA

MANY LEADERS, ONE ORGANIZATION

Before going onstage that January afternoon in 1987, Art Lundahl had been briefed about NPIC's efforts with arms control, the plans for the NEL, and the digital technology that was starting to be used for imagery analysis in Building 213. During his talk, Lundhal told the imagery analysts how NPIC started at the Steuart Building; how he spoke directly to President Kennedy; and how he briefed President Eisenhower about the intelligence NPIC discovered with programs started in his administration—the U-2, the SR-71, and the KH-4 imaging satellite. As he finished his talk, Lundahl encouraged the young people in the NPIC auditorium to continue to make intelligence from photographic imagery. At the end, overcome by emotion, he burst into tears. As Arthur Lundahl received his last standing ovation, many in that audience also wept.

One year later, Rae Huffstutler was selected as the CIA's Director of Administration. He turned NPIC over to Frank Ruocco, its next director. But, he also turned over a workforce that had absorbed the lessons of his leadership style and the culture of Art Lundahl. NPIC continued under the guidance of three more directors—Frank Ruocco, Leo Hazlewood, and Nancy Bone—to produce critical intelligence until 1996 when it was absorbed into the new DoD National Imagery and Mapping Agency (now the National Geospatial-Intelligence Agency). Within this new intelligence agency, and in many other places in the intelligence community the residual NPIC culture and influences continued to produce leaders. That combination of influences, over thirty years, produced more senior executives than any other office in CIA.

APPENDIX

THE ONE DAY

Between Thanksgiving and Christmas each year, there was one day when the hallways of Building 213 were far more crowded than usual. The annual NPIC Open House was usually on the first Saturday in December. For parts of the previous weeks, every NPIC group in the building, along with the OIA, army, DIA, and air force tenants, would prepare to show their workplaces to their families who on that one day were allowed to come into Building 213.

The preparation was far more than cleaning up and storing classified materials out of sight. The support components had been preparing for this day on their lunch hours for weeks before. The model shop would dip into their coffee fund to buy the materials for a dollhouse, or a toy train layout to be raffled off on that Saturday open house. It too was built over their lunch hours. The graphics artists would draw coloring books and prepare memento giveaways for the kids. The print shop would take remnant paper stock and make notepads for the visitors. And, Security Division would set up a fingerprint station for parents and a mock polygraph to ask the kids if they were naughty or nice, and if they obeyed their parents.

The computer room would be open so the kids could see the technology, and all the libraries would also have displays. Santa Claus would be in the main library, with candy and a photographer so that the families could get souvenir photos. The Training Division would broadcast cartoons on its display screens, and the kids could look at the models of military equipment kept under plexiglass covers.

Usually, an unclassified briefing was presented in the auditorium, often by the legendary NPIC storyteller, Dino Brugioni, and the director's office was open and stocked with punch and cookies. The director, deputy director, and the executive officer would all attend. They opened their offices so everyone could see the US Capitol though the windows in the director's sixth floor office.

Every year during the open house, there were branches of analysts who had to work a hot issue on that Saturday, and the visitors would be blocked from entering their vaults. The exploitation group would set up unclassified film demonstrations on light tables in another vault and show sanitized analyst workspaces.

The NPIC open house tradition was long-standing. It was the only day each year that Building 213 employees could give their families some sense of where they spent the long hours. Many younger employees would arrange to have their families visit that weekend from out of town visit that so that they could bring their parents and siblings into the building and share their pride in their work and their colleagues. The other purpose was charitable.

Starting in November, there would be a series of branch and division chili cook-offs. Division coffee bars would sponsor gift raffles, and the quilters and bakers would raffle off their crafts and sell cakes and cookies. All these efforts raised money for the Washington Children's Hospital. This effort spread throughout NPIC and Building 213 over the years. In the 1980's, a Washington Post columnist, Bob Levey used to list holiday donations to the Washington Children's Hospital from various government charities. This was the only time that the people who worked in Building 213 did not mind being mentioned in the newspaper.

The author's share of any royalties from this book will be donated to the Washington Children's Center and the Children's Hospital of Philadelphia.

REFERENCES

1: Nearly Missing Chernobyl

p. 2   " at 1:23 in the morning,",, David E. Hoffman, *The Dead Hand: The Untold Story of the Cold War Arms Race and its Dangerous Legacy*. (NY: Doubleday, 2009), henceforth *The Dead Hand* pp. 245-53; Wikipedia "Chernobyl Disaster", viewed 25 February 2015; James Mahaffey, *Atomic Accidents: A History of Nuclear Meltdowns and Disasters from the Ozark Mountains to Fukushima*, (NY: Pegasus, 2014) pp. 357-75.

p. 3   "The COMIREX watch officer told Phil. . ." e-mail, Phil Lago to author , 4 March 2010

p. 4   "Kursk, Kola, Leningrad .""Russian Nuclear Powerplants, "Nuclear Power in Ukraine, Nuclear Power in Russia," Wikipedia, viewed 25 February 2015.

p. 4   "a rocket exploded . . . "Barrows, William. *Deep Black: Space Espionage and National Security.* (NY: Random House, 1987) p. 303

p. 4   "other parts of the Intelligence Community," E-mail, Lago to author 4 March 2010; author's conversations M. Rains and J. Westcott

p. 4   "both branch chiefs attended . . . author's conversation with Mike Rains, 2012

p. 5   "All this was done . . . " author's conversation with Mike Rains

p. 6   "For nearly 40 years," Barrows, William. *Deep Black*. p. 303; Richelson, Jeffrey T. *The Wizards of Langley: Inside CIA's Directorate of Science and Technology.* (Boulder Colorado: Westview Press, 2001) henceforth *Wizards* p.197

p. 6   "He was relieved . . . e-mail Phil Lago to author, 4 March 2010

p. 7   "the IDEX 1A workstation, Authors conversation with Dee Hunsucker, 2012 "None of the PEG managers . . ." author's conversation with Mike Rains, 2011.

pp. 7-8   "Fosmark," Hoffman, *The Dead Hand*. p. 249 Chernobyl Disaster, Wikipedia

p. 8   "But visible evidence of the evacuation ." Richelson. J. *Wizards*. pp.231-33

p. 9   "Later in the year . . ., " author's conversation with Jim Richey, May 2013

p. 10   "He called Rae Hufffstutler," E-mail Steve Irish to author, March 2014

2: Art Lundhal—The First to See the Secrets

Most of the material in this chapter comes from the *Reminiscences of Arthur C. Lundahl.* (henceforth *ROACL*) a series of ten audiotapes that Art Lundahl made in 1981 with the assistance of Fredrick Peterson (Peter) Jessup. The interview may be accessed in the Columbia University Center for Oral History collection housed in the Butler Memorial Library.

p. 13   "On Monday December 13th", *ROACL* pp. 199, 217

p. 13   "The U-2 Spy plane" Pedlow and Welzenbach. *The U-2 Program 1952-1972*. CIA Center for the Study of Intelligence. pp. 33-39; Evan Thomas, *Ike's Bluff: President Eisenhower's Secret Battle to Save the World*, p. 150

p. 13   "Less than a month earlier," Pedlow and Welzenbach, p. 82

p. 14   "Tilden Technical School," *ROACL* pp. 35-6, 43

p. 14   "artwork for professors, " *ROACL* pp. 43-44

p. 14   "After analyzing them with Lundahl," *ROACL* pp. 38-42

p. 15   "masters thesis" *ROACL* pp. 43-5, 54-5, 186-7

p. 15   "Mammoth Cave." *ROACL,* p. 45

p. 15   "Millington", ROACL pp. 58-60

p. 16   " While the test was being graded," *ROACL* pp. 60-65

p. 16   "petitioning the principals," *ROACL* pp. 62-73

pp. 16-17   Adak activities *ROACL* pp. 93, 116, 118-27, 151-55, 163-67

p. 18   Stop in Chicago and work in Washington, D.C., *ROACL* p. 174, pp. 178-79

p. 18   "After the Pacific war ended" *ROACL* pp. 86-87, 187-88

pp. 18-20   "Operation Crossroads", Wikipedia, viewed 16 January 2015; Phillip Taubman: *Secret Empire: Eisenhower, the CIA, and the Hidden Story of America's Space Espionage*. (NY: Simon and Schuster, 2003)

p. 19   Col Paul T. Cullen USAAF, p. 99 "Friday Afternoon Session, January 24, 1947, in *Photogrammetric Engineering*, Vol XIII, March 1947, pp 94-102

pp. 19-20   "Introduction to Project Crossroads film, p. 101, "Friday Afternoon Session, January 24, 1947, in *Photogrammetric Engineering*, Vol XIII, March 1947, pp. 94-102

p. 20   "His scientific reputation," *ROACL* pp. 193-94,

p. 20   "to attend the first postwar International Photogrammetry course," *ROACL* pp. 225, 360

p. 20   "publications editor for *Photogrammetric Engineering*," *ROACL* p. 225

p. 21   " After his December 1954 meeting," *ROACL* , pp. 198-99

p. 22   "Land's advocacy of the U-2 design," Pedlow and Welzenbach, pp. 29-31, 50

pp. 22-23   "The technological problems," Pedlow and Welzenbach, pp. 49-55

p. 23   "Geneva," Sheehan, Neil. *A Fiery Peace in a Cold War: Bernard Schreiver and the Ultimate Weapon.* (NY: Random House, 2009). pp. 280-83; Evan Thomas: *Ike's Bluff*, p. 172

p. 23   "Lack of news" E-mail from R. M. Huffstutler to author, 4 December 2013.

p. 24   "to become a national center" *ROACL* pp. 215, 326-27

p. 25   "the demands of CIA security," *ROACL* pp. 215, 326-7

p. 25   "Foreign technology," *ROACL*, pp. 221-6, 245, 374-8

p. 25   "One of the tenants on the lower floors," *ROACL* p. 221

p. 25   "for a total of 90 photo-interpreters, " "Alice Davy Sheldon" *ROACL* pp. 223-24, 216

pp. 25-26   levels of Service participation. *ROACL*, pp. 226-28

p. 26   "Lundahl designed PID to have shared management and leadership . . .," *ROACL* pp. 229-30

3: The Most Valuable Slum Property in America

The primary sources for this chapter are *The U-2 Program 1952-1972*. CIA Center for the Study of Intelligence, henceforth (U-2). For the history of the aircraft development and construction, see Kelly Johnson, *Kelly: More than My Share of It All* (Washington D.C.: Smithsonian Institute Press, 1985) Rich, Ben and Leo Janos. *Skunk Works: A Personal Memoir of My Years at Lockheed* (NY: Little Brown, 1996); and *The Reminiscences of Arthur C. Lundahl, (ROACL).*

p. 27   "training missions started,"*The U-2 Program 1952-1972.* CIA Center for the Study of Intelligence.

p. 27   *ROACL*, pp. 229-30 PID became PIC

pp. 27-28   *ROACL* pp. 221-2, 247, 296-7, 302-3; Moorhus, Donita. "The Cuban Missile Crisis: Personal Stories from NPIC" in *Geospatial Intelligence Review*, Vol 2, No. 1. May 2003 (Unclassified) (Springfield, Va. National Geospatial-Intelligence Agency. p.15 Carpools to stay late.

p. 28   "Automat," *ROACL*, pp. 202, 230-31, 311, 379

pp.28-29   This material has its source in Pedlow and Welzenbach's *The CIA and the U-2 Program 1954-1974*

p. 29   The role of Eastman Kodak in the U-2 and the film-return satellite programs is very well captured *in Bridgehead: Eastman Kodak Company's Covert Phototreconnaissance Film Processing Program*, ed. Msgt. Lorraine M. Jacobs, (Chantilly, VA: Center for the Study of National Reconnaissance, 2014)

p. 29   " Jim Reber," *ROACL*, p. 236

pp. 29-30   "President's approval*,"* *ROACL* pp. 208-9

p. 31   *Bridgehead*, pp. 13-17

p. 32   "photointerpreters had to be briefed . . ." *ROACL* pp. 223-5

p. 33   "called collateral information" *ROACL* pp. 222, 224-5; Brugioni, Dino A. *Eyes in the Sky: Eisenhower, the CIA, and Cold War Aerial Espionage.* Ed. Doris G. Taylor (Annapolis, MD: Naval Institute Press, 2010), henceforth (*EITS*) pp. 124, 395

p. 33   "1500 factories were relocated," in Mikhail Heller and Aleksandr Nekhrich, *Utopia in Power: The History of the Soviet Union from 1917 to the Present*, (NY: Summit Books, 1986), p. 376

p. 33   "when the 10-day war between Egypt and Israel began (Suez) *U-2* pp. 112-21

p. 34   "Semipalatinsk," *U-2,* pp.137-39

p. 34   and shoot down every flight," *U-2* pp. 124-27

p. 34   "Sensitivity about a shootdown . . " *U-2*, pp. 122-3, 127-8

p. 35   "contracts restricted to many fewer people," Greer "CORONA" p.6 Kenneth Greer, "CORONA" in *Studies in Intelligence* Supplement, 17 Spring 1973, reprinted in Ruffner, Kevin C. ed. *CORONA: America's First Satellite Program*, in CIA's Cold War Records Series, History Staff, Center for the Study of Intelligence (Washington, D.C.: Central Intelligence Agency, 1995) p. 4

pp. 35-36 "Civil Defense plans," Brugioni. *EITS* pp 245-6. *ROACL* p. 255

p. 36   Mahaffey, James. *Atomic Accidents:* p. 283; Kysthym Disaster. Wikipedia; Brugioni. *EITS*. pp. 240-41

p. 36   "U-2 anti-radar device," *U-2* pp. 143-44, 147

p. 37   "when the US air force started a series of balloon overflights" *U-2* pp. 145, 147

p. 37   "Khrushchev publicly boasted . . . " Michael Bechloss, *Mayday: Eisenhower, Khrushchev, and the U-2 Affair.* (NY: Harper Collins, 1986); *U-2.* p. 164 "250 missiles with hydrogen weapons"

p. 37   "Bissell's program worked . . . ," Greer history of CORONA pp.10-14

pp. 37-38 "But these great technological achievements . . . ," Sheehan, Neil. *A Fiery Peace in a Cold War: Bernard Schreiver and the Ultimate Weapon.* (NY: Random House, 2009) pp. 426-27. The January 21, 1959 attempt was considered Discoverer 0 by the program. The second-stage Agena nearly fired its motor on the pad. While the launch was stopped, the satellite and the Thor first-stage were damaged.

     Discoverer I, launched in late February was the first success-ful polar-orbiting satellite. The decision not to count Discoverer 0 was followed by 11 unsuccessful missions with success finally coming with a capsule recovery on Discover XIII, and Discover XIV returning 3,000 feet of film on August 18, 1960.

p. 39   "Many targets on the list. . ." Reber memo in Ruffner, *CORONA*, p. 50 Ruffner, *CORONA*, p. 106

p. 39   "Only two penetration missions . . ." *U-2* pp. 162-3

p. 39   "by some in the US government. . ." Brugioni, *EITS*, pp. 336, 339, 384-5

p. 40   "by the time Lundahl finished . ," Brugioni *Eyeball to Eyeball: The Inside Story of The Cuban Missile Crisis,* henceforth *ETE*, p. 467. *EITS*, pp. 349-50

p. 40 " On August 10, 1960, " ed. Ruffner, *CORONA* p. 2

pp. 40-41 " you would find a city," Doyle Retirement *NPIC Update* 1994 ", Brugioni, *EITS*, p. 365

pp. 41-42 "64 new airfields and 26 new SAM sites" *CORONA* p. 2

p. 43 "made maps from low resolution oblique imagery . . ." *ROACL* p. 42

p. 44 "As the early camera models changed." "CORONA satellite" Wikipedia, viewed 25 February 2015

p. 44 "more than 300,000 hours of overtime ' *ROACL*, p. 230

p. 47 "By 1961, the areas . . . ," *CORONA*. pp. 6, 127

p. 47 "specialized equipment purchases." *ROACL* pp. 243-46.

4: Cuba—Opportunity Wrapped In Crisis

The literature on the Cuban Missile Crisis is voluminous. The primary documents for this chapter are found in *CIA Documents on the Cuban Missile Crisis 1962*, ed. Mary S. McAuliffe. Central Intelligence Agency. CIA History Staff, October 1992;

p. 49 "for planning what became known as the Bay of Pigs," *U-2*, pp. 197-98

p. 49 "more than doubled the amount of information," Greer, Kevin, in Ruffner, *CORONA* pp. 24-26.

p. 50 Brugioni, Dino A. *Eyeball to Eyeball: The Inside Story of the Cuban Missile Crisis*. Ed. Robert F. McCort. (NY: Random House, 1991) (EtE) Graham Allison. *Essence of Decision. Explaining the Cuban Missile Crisis*, (NY: Little Brown, 1971)

p. 50 "Military activity in Cuba had been increasing,"McAuliffe. *CIA Documents on the Cuban Missile Crisis,* p. 13

p. 51 "Taiwanese shootdown" Brugioni *EtE*," p. 133

p. 51 SNIE in Mary McAuliffe. *Documents on The Cuban Missile Crisis*. pp. 9-13

p. 51 Resumption of overflights, *U-2*, p. 201.

pp. 52-54 Most of the narrative of the discovery of the missile canisters is taken from Moorhus, " The Cuban Missile Crisis: Personal Stories from NPIC"
Geospatial Intelligence Review. pp. 11-12; henceforth "Personal Stories,"

pp. 53-54   "Leon Coggin," Moorhus "Personal Stories" p. 15

p. 54   "precast concrete arches," Brugioni, *ETE*, pp. 539-48

p. 54   "Not the only Nuclear Weapons in Cuba,"Fursenko and Naftali. *One Hell of A Gamble: Khrushchev, Castro, and Kennedy 1958-1964*. (NY: Norton, 1997), pp. 188, 211, 217

pp. 54-55   "Rudolph Anderson," Moorhus, "Personal Stories" p. 20; Brugioni, *ETE*, pp. 461-62

p. 56   "the increasing squalor" ROACL, pp. 201-02. 205

p. 56   Interview Red White *Studies in Intelligence*; *ROACL* pp. 304-05, "Cost of refitting 213 and the use of Marble, "

5: Buckets of Discovery

The primary documentation for this chapter comes from the NRO declassi-fied versions of the CORONA, GAMBIT, and HEXAGON histories.

p. 59   "About 400 people," Red White Interview. *Studies in Intelligence.*

p. 60   "Kistiakowsky quote" *ROACL* pp. 300-301

p. 61   " NPIC used the higher resolution . . . ," *CORONA, GAMBIT, HEXAGON histories.*

p. 62   "As a consequence . . . ." *The GAMBIT Story*, p. xv

p. 63   "The NPIC Mission Assessment cables, "*CORONA*, p. 41

p. 63   CORONA, GAMBIT, HEXAGON histories. Lundahl's partici-pation in the Purcell Panel is cited in *Critical to National Security: The Gambit and Hexagon Reconnaissance Systems Compendium* pp. 82-139.

p. 64   "What does NPIC think?" author's conversation with T. Maddox, 2014

p. 64   Lundahl knew the leaders. . . ,"ROACL pp. 244-46, 376-78 p. 95, "Richelson. *The Wizards of Langley*. (Wizards) p. 123

p. 64-65   "The NTP. . . " *The Hexagon Story*, p. 134; O'Connell *in Studies in Intelligence*

p. 65   "10,000 targets" Geoff Langsam in Moorhus," Achieving Recognition: From Photo Interpreter to Imagery Analyst," hence-forth "Achieving Recognition," pp.10-11. *Corona*, p.38

p. 66   "A great briefer. . . "*ROACL*, pp. 286-87

p. 67   "Names of Soviet Military Locations," Wikipedia: "Strategic Missile Troops," viewed 25 February 25, 2015

p. 68   "By March 1964 . . .,"*CORONA*, p. 37

p. 68   "After considerable wrangling … "*The HEXAGON Story* pp. 27-29 (KH-4 area with KH-7 resolution)

p. 69   "Along with the report," Brugioni *EITS*. Pp. 395-96; SS-9 silo measurements; Baker conversations with author, 2013, 2011.

p. 70   "in the late 1960s,"Graham and Hanson, *Spy Satellites and Other Intelligence Technologies. ROACL* pp. 319-21

p. 70   "Soviet Submarine Construction,"Brugioni, *EITS*, pp. 395-96. *CORONA,* pp. xiv, 253-59

p. 70   Scoville quoted in Newhouse. *Cold Dawn:The Definitive History of SALT* pp. 15-17

pp. 70-71 "2500 people needed,"Brugioni, *Studies in Intelligence*, Red White Interview

p. 71   "Duckett." Richelson, *Wizards*, p. 163

pp. 71-72 "staffing with younger people," *ROACL*, pp. 86, 300-01, 328-29

p. 72   "we didn't have job descriptions back then," Jolien Mierke, *NPIC at 30*

p. 72   "Bill Hanlon," *NPIC at 30,*: veterans reflect, p. 14

p. 73   " he would be sent to get the training, " *ROACL* p. 330

p. 73   "they were taken to NPIC, "*ROACL* pp. 331-3

pp.73-74   "Opportunities for minorities,"*ROACL* p.333; NGA A&P Monthly Vol 3, Issue 5, p. 4 "George Brown and Floyd Short."

p. 74   "the higher, the whiter,: author's conversation with Mike Betts and e-mail from Danny Neal, 3 August 2010

p. 74   "Women are rarely mentioned," Alice Davy Sheldon was one of Lundahl's original hires, but she resigned in 1955 to go to college. A former air force photo interpreter in World War II, she wrote a study of the German photo-interpretation organization after the war. After her death, it was learned that she had been publishing science-fiction under a man's name, James Tiptree." *ROACL*, p. 216, Wikipedia, "Alice Davy Sheldon," viewed 25 February 2015

p. 75   "Reduction in force," *ROACL* pp. 340-1

p. 76   "the increasing volume, reliability, and security of overhead" Lindgren *Trust But Verify: Imagery Analysis in the Cold War*, henceforth *TBV* pp. 124-25

pp. 76-77   "worked closely with NPIC," E-mail RM Huffstutler to author 4 December 2013

p. 77   "Buckets were soon to become," Richelson, *Wizards*, pp. 166, 171

6: A Divided Center

p. 79   "buckets of useful satellite film," Wikipedia, articles on KH-4, KH-7, KH-8, and KH-9; CORONA, GAMBIT, and HEXAGON histories.

p. 79   "The film and its chemical emulsion," *Bridgehead,* pp. 91-95

p. 79   "to prepare NPIC for this new technology," Richelson, *Wizards,* p 166

pp. 80-81   "National Imagery Interpretation Rating Scale, " Brugioni, *EITS,* p. 407, NIIRS, e-mail to author from Bill Forster. 24 March 2014

p. 120   "NIIRS" *The HEXAGON story.* pp.138-93; *The GAMBIT Story,* pp 137-   39.

p. 81   Bob Kohler in McDonald, Robert A. ed. *Beyond Expectations— Building an American National Reconnaissance Capability: Recollections of the Pioneers and founders of National Reconnaissance.* (Bethesda, MD: American Society for Photogrammetry and Remote Sensing, 2002. pp. 222-23

p. 83   "Imagery analysts were now expected," Lindgren, *TBV,* pp 11-12, Richelson, *Wizards.* p 230 Moorhus, "Achieving Recognition," pp. 12, 15-16

p. 85   "Hicks continued Art Lundahl's workforce development, " *ROACL* pp. 333-4

p. 85   "Center for Creative Leadership,": telephone conversation between author and Larry Steffy, 2011

p. 86   "Feet of film, "*GAMBIT and HEXAGON Stories*, p. 133; *A history of the HEXAGON program, Appendix A.* p. 282

p. 87   " As it scanned an area, . . ." *The HEXAGON story.* p. 176; note to author from Bob Mihalik

p. 87   "By the later KH-9 missions, . . ." author's note from Tom Maddox, 2014

p. 89   "National Imagery Analysis Course, " *NPIC 30ᵗʰ anniversary,*

p. 90   "the air instructor . . ." author's conversation with B. Salvatore, 2012, Will Hopkins, 2011

p. 91   "Batch processing," *NPIC 30ᵗʰ Anniversary*

p. 93   "An unexpected challenge for the imagery analysts. . ." author's conversation with Mark Baker, 15 July 2010

pp. 94-95   *NPIC 30ᵗʰ Anniversary,* Richelson, *Wizards.* p. 229

pp. 94-95   "A Sperry 1110 . . ." *NPIC 30ᵗʰ Anniversary*

p. 95   "No one had a real sense . . ." author's conversation with Mark Baker, 2010

p. 96   "database discrepancies arose," Conversation between author and Mark Baker, 2010

p. 97   "the number would only double,"Richelson, *Wizards.* p. 244

p. 98   "largest single line item," Leo Hazlewood, e-mail to author 12 November 2010,; *ROACL* p. 243 "forty thousand dollars, " author's e-mail from Kurt Miller, 24 January 2010

7: The Slammer and Uptown

p. 100   "that challenged their organizational positions" "Richelson, *Wizards*, p. 230

p. 102   "When in 1972 "Moorhus, "Achieving Recognition", p. 12

p. 103   "But as more satellites began to fly, "Richelson. *Wizards.* p. 123, *ROACL*, pp. 208-09, 234-36

p. 103   "The ARC had been reorganized," *The GAMBIT story*, p. 120

p. 103   "COMIREX managed the competition," Richelson. *Wizards.* p. 157

p. 104   "with natural obstructionist tendencies,"Conversation D. Doyle with author 1990

p. 105   "Under COMIREX's National Tasking Plan, *The HEXAGON Story* pp. 134-35

p. 106   Burrows. *Deep Black* pp. 3-11

p. 106   "The National Tasking Plan focused," *The HEXAGON Story.* p. 134

p. 107   "that same cooperation did not extend," Brugioni. *EITS* pp. 245-46; *ROACL* p. 255; Lindgren *TBV.* pp. 141-143

p. 109   "each new level of hierarchy,"Moorhuis, "Achieving Recognition" in *Geospatial Intelligence Review*. March 2004, pp. 14-5, March 2004. pp. 7-11.

p. 109   "the film-return process still shaped their thinking," e-mail, John Westcott, 2010

p. 112   "These managers emphasized NPIC's obligation . . . "author's conversation with Mark Baker, 2010

p. 114   "a more formal pass-to," E-mail from Mary Ellen Keene to author, 1 July 2011

p. 115   "at the end of a long night shift," Note to author from Tom Maddox 2014

p. 115   "NPIC imagery analysts recognized ahead of the COMIREX staff, " author's conversations with John Westcott 2010 and Mark Baker 2010

p. 116   "While NPIC still created large format boards," author's conversation with Mark Baker 1992

pp. 116-17 "The difference in production schedules " author's conversations with M. Baker, 1992, and Bob Honold, 1990

p. 117   "pencils and yellow legal pads," author's conversation with Mike Hinkle, 1992

pp. 117-18 "in the first few months of 1977" Richelson. *Wizards*. pp.205, 208

p. 118   "the 40-year sentence," Richelson. *Wizards*. p.205-08; Wikipedia, "William Kampiles"

p. 120   "This imagery analyst " author's conversation with Dave Sullivan, 2012

p. 120   "Excess baggage," author's conversations with Mike Rains, 1993 and Dave Sullivan 2012

p. 120   " the rift between imagery analysts," author's conversation with Jack Elberti

p. 121   " They remained under-represented,"author's conversation with M. Betts, 2013; e-mail to author from D. Neal; e-mail to author from James Green, 1 July 2011

p. 121   "A number of female imagery analysts. . . " author's conversation with M. Gaughan, 2011; e-mail from M.E. Keene, 1 July 2011

8: Rae

p. 141   "their briefing had set him off on" author's conversation with John Green, 1987

p. 142   "Both had worked together," Richelson. *Wizards*. p. 196, p. 175

p. 143   "Because the SS-20 was mobile, " Wikipedia

p. 143   "While deployment of this missile posed," Wikipedia: "SS-20;" *The Dead Hand*. p. 211; *Reagan and Gorbychev*. pp. 38-41

p. 146   "He eliminated NPIC's traditional military-based hiring test . . ." e-mail, R. M. Huffstutler to author, 4 December 2013

9: The Third Typhoon

p. 147   "Frank Douglas," author's conversation with Tom Maddox, 2014

p. 148   "the Typhoon-class submarine," Sontag, Sherry and Christopher Drew with Annette Lawrence Drew. *Blind Man's Bluff: The Untold Story of American Submarine Espionage.* (NY: Harper, 1999) p.330; Wikipedia," Typhoon-class Submarine, "viewed 25 February 2015"

p. 148   "NPIC had tracked," Brugioni. *EITS*. pp. 242, 396; *CORONA*. pp. 253-60; *GAMBIT*. p. v-vi

pp. 148-49 In late December 1983," *Blind Man's Bluff*. p.330; Brugioni, *EITS*. p. 396.

p. 149   "OVER THE BLACK LINE?" author's recollection

p. 150   "NPIC believes," Richelson. *Wizards*. p.230; Moorhuis. "Achieving Recognition." pp. 6-7

p. 151   "When in April 1984,"Wikipedia: "Typhoon-class submarine"

p. 152   "not playing to NPIC's strength, Moorhus "Achieving Recognition," p. 5

p. 153   "NPIC never published . . .," author's conversation with John Oswald, 2010

p. 154   " The U. S. Navy had devoted,"*Blind Man's Bluff*. pp. 330, xiv-xx

10: The Impresario of Port Deposit

pp. 156-57 "they delegated the applicant review," E-mail to author from K. Pomeroy, 3 March 2010

p. 157   "Ron Snyder," author's conversation with Dave Sullivan, 2011

p. 158   Author's recollection; author's conversations with Jimmy R. Greene and Kathleen Aucoin, 2012

P. 160   "who had been at NPIC for only two years," e-mail to author from M. Kenney, 6 January 2011.

p. 160   "prove their calls to be right" author's e-mail from M. Dial, 3 July 2010.

p. 160   "I started out as an imagery analyst," E-mail to author from Dale Hutchinson.

p. 160   "bean counters," author's conversation with Cynthia Strand, 2012

p. 161   For a portrait of Donaldson Brown, see Peter Drucker. *Adventures of a Bystander* (NY: Harper and Row, 1980).

p. 165   "driving back to work," author's conversation with Lisa Spuria, 2010.

11: Managing By the Book

p. 167   "how many hits they got the previous night," author's conversations with P. Usowski, 2011, and T. Maddox, 2014

p. 170   "he introduced an informal award," author's conversation with Stephanie Danes Smith, 2010

p. 172   "Casey's decision," Moorhus, "Achieving Recognition", p. 13

p. 172   " an administrative upgrade," Moorhus, "Achieving Recognition", p. 14

pp. 173-74   "reorganization details" NPIC Update 1985

p. 174   "reorganization addressed critical structural issues," Moorhus, "Achieving Recognition," p. 15

pp. 175-77   Much of the material in this chapter is drawn from the *NPIC Supervisors Handbook of Personnel Policies and Procedures* 1985.

p. 178   "some managers tried to game the system,"author's conversations with Mark Baker, 2010, and Will Hopkins, 2013

p. 178   "Rae himself wrote the first draft," author's conversation with Jack Elberti, 2012; e-mail from R.M. Huffstutler to author 4 December 2013

p. 178   "A history of NPIC," author's conversation with Tom Jarvis, 2011.

p. 179   "be like me," author's conversation with Kristen Wood, 2005, author's conversation with Ken Pomeroy, 1993

pp. 180-81 "Some supervisors would be needed," Moorhuis. "Achieving recognition: From PI to IA": *Geospatial Intelligence Review*, p. 15

12: Every Upgrade is a Setback

p. 183   "a large problem for the Director," Richelson. *Wizards*. pp. 229-31

p. 185   "as a result of this recovery process," *NPIC at 30*

p. 185   "Beacon Precision Enlarger," *Bridgehead*, pp.118-19

p. 186   Wikipedia: Computer Memory, viewed 25 February 2015

p. 188   "NPIC continued working with Wang Laboratories . ," Authors e-mail from Bryan Aucoin, 8 September 2010

pp. 189-90 "he tailored each briefing . . .," author's conversation with Jack Elberti 2010

pp. 193-94 "a million dollars," E-mail from Kurt Miller to author, 24 January 2010

pp. 195-96 "Dennis Fitzgerald," Richelson. *Wizards*. p.212; E-mail from R.M. Huffstutler to author, 4 December 2013

p. 199   "focused on areas of interest to imagery analysts," Richelson, *Wizards*, p. 231

13: Verify then Trust--The SS-20 Search

p. 203   "the January surprise,' Wikipedia, "The Intermediate-Range, Nuclear Forces Treaty," viewed 21 February 2015

p. 204   "January through March," author's conversations with Michelle Root, Anne Arnold, and Lillian Taylor, 2011, 2013; KH-9 HEXAGON Wikipedia "The last KH-9 mission, viewed 25 February 2015

pp. 205-06 "Only fifty-seven percent" Waltrop, David W. "Recovery of the Last GAMBIT and HEXAGON Film Buckets from Space, August—October 1984," *Studies in Intelligence*, Vol 58. No. 2 pp.19-34

p. 206   "On 18 April 1986," Richelson, *Wizards* p. 197; Barrows, *Deep Black*, pp. 304-5, Phil Pressel, *Meeting the Challenge, The Hexagon*

KH-9 Reconnaissance Satellite, (Reston, VA: American Institute of Aeronautics and Astronautics, 2013) pp. 243-250

p. 206   "Simon," author's conversation with M. E. Keene, E-mail, Michelle Root to author 11 March 2014, "Wayne Strand," Moorhus, "Achieving Recognition", p. 2

p. 208   "to assure that the quality, " Richelson, *Wizards*, p. 231

p. 209   "a GS-15 position," E-mail Phil Lago to author 4 March 2010; author's e-mail from John Westcott, 4 March 2010.

p. 210   "that nom got Simonized," author's conversation with Michelle Root, 2011

p. 210   "to the ad hoc collection branch," author's conversation with M.E. Keene, 2011

p. 210   "neither shied away," author's conversation with J. Westcott, 2010

p. 210   " In March 1986," Wikipedia, "The Intermediate-Range, Nuclear Forces Treaty," viewed 21 February 2015

p. 211   "Charlie Nations, E-mail from Phil Lago, 5 March 2010; author's conversation with Mark Anderson, 2014

p. 211   "NPIC created an SS-20 study team," author's conversation with Tim Hays, 2010

p. 212   "Tim Sample " E-mail Phil Lago to author, 2011

p. 212-13   "Ted outlined " E-mail Michelle Root to author, 11 March 2014

p. 213   "the army, the air force, and the navy," E-mail Michelle Root to author, 11 March 2014

p. 215   "Smalltalk" E-mail Ken Whitson to author, 2012; author's conversation with Ann Dee Reiter, 2002

pp. 216-17   "Acetate overlays," author's conversations with Dave Lang, 2012, and Lillian Taylor, 2011

p. 217   "the towering infilmo" author's conversations with Dave Lang and Sarah Mangs, 2012

BIBLIOGRAPHY

Books

Appleby, Charles Albert, Jr. *Eisenhower and Arms Control 1953-1961*. (unpublished thesis) Johns Hopkins University, 1987.

Bechloss, Michael, *Mayday: Eisenhower, Khrushchev, and the U-2 Affair.* (New York: HarperCollins, 1986)

Brugioni, Dino A. *Eyeball to Eyeball: The Inside Story of the Cuban Missile Crisis*. ed. Robert F. McCort. (NY: Random House, 1991)

Brugioni, Dino A. *Eyes in the Sky: Eisenhower, the CIA, and Cold War Aerial Espionage*. ed. Doris G. Taylor (Annapolis, MD: Naval Institute Press, 2010)

Budiansky, Stephen. *Blackett's War: The Men who Defeated the Nazi U-Boats and Brought Science to the Art of Warfare.* (New York: Knopf, 2013)

Burrows, William E. *Deep Black: Space Espionage and National Security. (*NY: Random House, 1987)

Drucker, Peter. *Adventures of a Bystander*. (NY: Harper and Row, 1980)

Gardner, John W. *No Easy Victories*. (NY: Harper Colophon, 1968) ed. Helen Rowan.

Graham, Thomas Jr. and Keith A. Hanson. *Spy Satellites and Other Intelligence Technologies That Changed History*. (Seattle: University of Washington Press, 2007)

Heller, Mikhail and Aleksandr Nekhrich. *Utopia in Power: The History of the Soviet Union from 1917 to the Present* (NY: Summit Books, 1986)

Hoffman, David E. *The Dead Hand: The Untold Story of the Cold War Arms Race and its Dangerous Legacy*. (NY: Doubleday, 2009)

Jacobs, MSgt. Lorraine, M, ed. *Bridgehead: Eastman Kodak Company's Photoreconnaissance Film Processing Program*. (Chantilly, VA: Center for the Study of National Reconnaissance, 2014)

Johnson, Kelly, *More Than My Share of It*. (Washington, D.C.: Smithsonian Institute Press, 1985)

Lindgren, David T. *Trust But Verify: Imagery Analysis in the Cold War*. (Annapolis, MD: Naval Institute Press, 2000.)

Mahaffey, James. *Atomic Accidents: A History of Nuclear Meltdowns and Disasters From the Ozark Mountains to Fukushima*. (NY: Pegasus Books, 2014).

Matlock, Jack F. Jr. *Reagan and Gorbachev: How the Cold War Ended*. (NY: Random House, 2004)

McAuliffe, Mary S. ed. *CIA Documents on the Cuban Missile Crisis, 1962*. History Staff, Center for the Study of Intelligence (Washington, D.C.: Central Intelligence Agency, 1992)

McDonald, Robert A. ed. *Beyond Expectations—Building an American National Reconnaissance Capability: Recollections of the Pioneers and founders of National Reconnaissance*. (Bethesda, MD: American Society for Photogrammetry and Remote Sensing, 2002)

NPIC Supervisor's Handbook of Personnel Policies and Procedures, (1985)

Newhouse. John. *Cold Dawn: The Definitive History of SALT*. (NY: Holt, Reinhart, and Winston, 1973).

Outzen, James. ed. *Critical to US Security: The Gambit and Hexagon Satellite Reconnaissance Systems Compendium*. (Chantilly, VA: Center for the Study of National Reconnaiassance, 2012.)

Pedlow, Gregory W. and Donald E. Welzenbach. *The CIA and the U-2 Program: 1954-1974*. History Staff, Center for the Study of Intelligence (Washington, D.C.: Central Intelligence Agency, 1998)

Pressel, Phil. *Meeting the Challenge: The HEXAGON KH-9 Reconnaissance Satellite*. (Reston, VA: American Institute of Aeronautics and Astronautics, 2013)

Rich, Ben and Leo Janos. *Skunk Works: A Personal Memoir of my Years at Lockheed*. (New York: LittleBrown, 1996)

Richelson, Jeffrey T. *The Wizards of Langley: Inside CIA's Directorate of Science and Technology*. (Boulder, Colorado, Westview Press, 2001)

Ruffner, Kevin C. ed. *CORONA: America's First Satellite Program*, in CIA's Cold War Records Series, History Staff, Center for the Study of Intelligence (Washington, D. C.: Central Intelligence Agency, 1995)

Sheehan, Neil. *A Fiery Peace in a Cold War: Bernard Schreiver and the Ultimate Weapon*. (NewYork: Random House, 2009)

Sontag, Sherry and Christopher Drew with Annette Lawrence Drew. *Blind Man's Bluff: The Untold Story of American Submarine Espionage*. (NewYork: Harper, 1999)

Thomas, Evan. *Ike's Bluff: President Eisenhower's Secret Battle to Save the World*. (New York: Little Brown, 2012)

Treverton, Gregory F. *Reshaping National Intelligence for an Age of Information*. (Cambridge: Cambridge UP, 2003)

Articles

Hanrahan, James. "An Interview With Former Executive Director Lawrence K. "Red" White. (U). *Studies in Intelligence*. Vol. 42, No. 3 (Washington, D.C. Central Intelligence Agency)

Moorhus, Donita. " The Cuban Missile Crisis: Personal Stories from NPIC" in *Geospatial Intelligence Review,* Vol 2, No. 1. May 2003 (Unclassified) (Springfield, Va. National Geospatial-Intelligence Agency)

Moorhus, Donita. "Achieving Recognition: From Photo Interpreter to Imagery Analyst," in *Geospatial Intelligence Review*, Vol 3, No. 1. March 2004 (Unclassified) (Springfield, Va. National Geospatial-Intelligence Agency)

"Conversations with Two Former Directors: Arthur C. Lundahl. R. M. Huffstutler. in *Thirty and Thriving*, NPIC, December 1991

"Time Flies: Veterans Reflect on Three Decades at NPIC," in *Thirty and Thriving*, NPIC, December 1991

Waltrop, David W. "Recovery of the Last GAMBIT and HEXAGON Film Buckets from Space, August-October 1984." *Studies in Intelligence.* Vol 58, No. 2, June 2014 UNCLASSIFIED

Acknowledgements

More than five years ago, in late 2009, I started what I thought would be a six-month project, when I tried to answer the question: What was it about NPIC that produced so many senior leaders in the intelligence community. While I am obviously inaccurate about scheduling writing projects, one of the joys in the project has been connecting and reconnecting with NPIC veterans and learning more about the Center and their parts in the story. More than 200 of them have helped me with this book, and I would like to recognize their contributions. Many have suggested other NPIC alumni and veterans and have helped me connect with those I did not know. This book would be much less accurate and interesting without their help. Sadly, one of my regrets about taking so long is that a few of the contributors are now no longer with us.

I wish that I was able to incorporate more stories into the book. Storytelling was a large part of the NPIC culture, and a great number of the stories I was privileged to hear or read had to be cut. Their omission is not meant to slight any of the contributors, but reflects the illustrative rather than exhaustive nature of the book. As more and more information about the 1970s and 1980s is declassified, it will be possible to tell more of those stories.

My thanks go out first to the following NPIC alumni and veterans who have shared their stories and insights:

John Agatone, John Allison, Mark Anderson, Anne Arnold, Craig Arrighetti, Bryan Aucoin, Kathleen Aucoin, Judy Bailey, Mark Baker, Bob Ballance, Rebekah Barrish, Ron Beavers, Jon Beckman,

George Beck, Bob Berkebile, Gail Betts-Anderson, Janet Betts, Mike Betts, Bette Black, Steve Blohm, Geoff Boehm, Nancy Bone, Bruce Boslaugh, Dennis Bowerman, Mike Brennan, M.L. Buchannan, Keith Burgess, Diana Burgess, Lisa Burns, Ashley Brogden, Patty Cameresi, Tom Caroscio, Charlotte Carter, Tony Cherico, Earl Chidester, Ann Marie Clark, Dave, Clark, Steve Clark, Greg Conradi, Gary Craig, Jennifer Daniel, Steve Davila, Dan Deyo, Mark Dial, Dave Delia, Dave Doyle, Shawn Dilles, Ted Donaldson, Diane Dunnegan, Harold Dunnegan, Dan Dueweke, Don Durand, John Edwards, Jack Elberti, Dan Ernst, Jack Fahy, Ken Feichtl, Randy Ferryman, Jack Fletcher, Alan Florkowski, Jim Forster, Bill Forster, Joan Gartin, Joe Gartin, Monica Gaughan, Alan Gill, Barbara Gould, James Green, Jimmy R. Greene, John Green, Ed Grimes, Julie Grimes, Ron Hale, Craig Haney, Ellen Harley, Kim Harley, Frank Hart, Andy Hayden, Penny Hays, Tim Hays, Leo Hazlewood, Bill Henry, Nancy Hervey, Mike Hinkle, Shirley Hogan, Jim Holden, Tim Holden, Tricia Holden, Bob Holt, Bob Honold, Will Hopkins, Vicki Howard, Dee Hunsucker, Dale Hutchinson, Steve Irish, Jeanie James, Eileen Janas, Tim Jarvis, Donna Jung, Russ Johnson, Venus Jones, Sue Kalweit, Mary Ellen Keene, Kevin Kelleher, Matt Kenney, Dawn Keenan, Jeff Kerridge, Tim Kirkpatrick, Jim Knittle, Phil Lago, Joe Lambert, Kenny Lane, Dave Lang, Cara Lauler, Karen Lewis, Carolyn Little, Geoff Lockwood, Tom Logan, Matt Long, Bruce Louie, Peter Lund, Mike Lutjen, Jimmy Lynch, Sean Lyons, Skip Mabry, Tom Maddox, John Magee, Mark Majoros, Mary Majoros, Leona Maluzzi, Dave Mangs, Sarah Mangs, Steve Martin, Teresa Martin, Cindy Marisch, John Matson, Bill McGeorge, Hank Messick, Paul Mekkelson, Clay Meyers, Pauline Meyers, Ed Milligan, Kurt Miller, Jay Moeder, Lew Moon, Marie Morrell, Chris Morris, Bill Mugford, Judy Murphy, Tommy Murphy, Charlie Nations, Danny Neal, Leanne Nielson, Greg Nida, Chuck Norville, Jim Novak, Brian Orlick, Marlene Orlick, John Oswald, Joe Ozefovich, Lynn Paulson, Terry Peckarsky, John Peele, Tony Perillo, Bill Petersen, Cathy Petersen, Elissa Plylar, Ken Pomeroy, Karen Pratzner, Tom Purcell, Jessica Rasco, Mike Rains, Jim Rattray, Ann Dee Reiter, Robin Richard, Jim Richey, Ledia Rivera, Craig Roberton, Steve Roberts, John Robson, Terry Rogers, Josh

Rooksby, Dennis Rooney, Mitch Root, Debbie Ruehl, Ron Ruehl, Karen Hayes Ryan, Barbara Salvatore, Peter Salvatore, Jeff Sanford, Jennifer Schnarre, Chris Sills, Dave Silvernale, Betsy Simms, Leah Lamba Skidmore, Tad Skidmore, Lisa Spuria, Bill Smith, Stephanie Danes Smith, Larry Steffy, Renee Steffy, Cynthia Strand, Dennis Suddarth, Dan Sullivan, Dave Sullivan, Tom Swanson, Tonya Tatum, Doris Taylor, Gordon Taylor, Lillian Taylor, Lori Ternes, Leslie Tharp, Joe Thomas, Linda Thomas, Kim Thompson, Mark Thompson, Howard Toomey, Tolpa, W. Glenn Turner, Peggy Tuten, Jane Tyler, Mark Tyler, Peter Upton, Peter Usowski, Terry Vernier, John Westcott, Kennith Whitson, Saundra Whitson, Bill Wilder, Lynne Wilder, Tom Wahl, Kristen Wood, Randy Wood, Steve Wood, Sammye Woods. I have tried very hard to keep track of the conversations and e-mails, but if there are any contributors I have inadvertently omitted, please let me know.

Along with the stories, I received a great deal of help in accessing what has been written about NPIC and some of the topics I mention. I would like to thank Chuck Appleby for letting me read his unpublished thesis about Arms Control in the Eisenhower Administration. I'd also like to thank Jim Goslee for informing me about the role of General Schreiver in developing the missile programs that enabled space reconnaissance.

My thanks and appreciation also goes to the Columbia University Center for Oral History. In particular I would like to recognize Breanne LaCamera for her assistance in my reading of The Reminiscences of Arthur C. Lundahl. The staff at the American Society for Photogrammetry and Remote Sensing have also been very helpful in providing access to their archives of Photogrammetric Engineering, in particular the issues during the years when Arthur Lundahl was the President of their association and editor of their journal. I would like to thank Dr. Michael Hauck and Jesse Winch for their open assistance. I would also like to acknowledge the public release staff of the National Geospatial-Intelligence Agency, in particular Betsy Smith and Paul Polk for their review of the photographs. Finally, to the unsung warriors of the intelligence community, the librarians at the Central Intelligence Agency and the National Geospatial-Intelligence Agency. I would also like to express my appreciation to the Fairfax County Public Library, in particular the John Marshall Branch.

The Publications Review Board of the Central Intelligence Agency has been very responsive and professional in their reviews of my manuscripts. I would like to express my appreciation to David Ventrello in particular. The PRB brokers the review with other federal agencies, and I would like to express my appreciation to the readers at the National Geospatial-Intelligence Agency and the National Reconnaissance Office. While I did not always agree with all their decisions, they collectively were responsive to my requests.

I would also like to express my gratitude to those who have helped create this book. Over the past five years a number of friends and colleagues helped by reading parts or whole earlier drafts: Terry Joseph Busch, Jim Goslee, Tim Holden, Jack Elberti, Tom Maddox, Mike Mears, Frank Miller, John Oswald, Josh Rooksby, Stephanie Danes Smith, Brian Tarallo, Vicki Tarallo, Peter Usowski, John Westcott, and Terry Vernier all provided very useful suggestions. Additionally, at times when the project would look overwhelming, a number of people helped keep me engaged and focused, and I would like to thank them for their support. Mike Mears, who started the Leadership Academy at CIA, sharpened my thinking about leadership in the intelligence community, and provided much encouragement and advice as well. My ongoing conversation with Stephanie Danes Smith about NPIC and other topics has been a very helpful source of ideas and encouragement. I am indebted to two generations of the Tarallo family, Vicki and Brian, for thoughtful questions, ideas, and encouragement. Peter Usowski was the first person with whom I discussed my observations of all the former NPIC names in the executive promotion announcements and he provided a critical review with several insightful questions. Over the past five years every encounter with my estimable colleagues in Georgetown Leadership Coaching Cohort 24 and the coaching community in which I have been privileged to work has recharged me and encouraged me.

This book has been aided inestimably by the work of three people. First, Terry Peckarsky pointed out important ideas, areas for development, and observations in an earlier draft. Terry, who copy-edited the NPIC Supervisors Manual, all those years ago, provided great help and encouragement and I am grateful.

Bob Mihalik was the editor every writer hopes for. Bob's sharp mind and eye, honed through experience as a senior Intelligence Community official and manager, improved the book through his questions, suggestions, and organizational changes. His uncanny sense of what the book could be and what must be added or changed were an essential help. Because he is in such demand, I consider myself fortunate to have received the great benefit of his insights, humor, and editorial skills.

Finally, the design and layout of this book, its cover, and my website are the work of Marti Spaulding. Marti has the uncanny ability to take a concept and design the visual emblem that captures its essence. And she can accomplish this in digital as well as traditional media. Her ability to organize and communicate information is exceptional, and a number of government agencies have benefited from her talents. While I have admired her design work for a decade, and wondered how she accomplished so much, I have been fortunate that she took on this project.

Finally, while I am humbled and grateful for all the help I have received, I alone am responsible for any errors in this book. In writing a book about the intelligence community, I have attempted to explain some history without revealing the intelligence tradecraft that made that history possible. That goal, and my decisions along the way, necessitated the omission of some of the detail in the stories. Imagery analysts, more than any other group of intelligence officers, know the importance of the details. If I have distorted any of the history by my omissions, I ask forgiveness.

Finally, I would to thank my wife, Kathy, who has her contributed her own NPIC experiences, who has supported my long hours for many years, and tolerated my obsession with this story.

ABOUT THE AUTHOR

Jack O'Connor retired from CIA in 2013, after more than 31 years of service, most of it managing and leading support, analysis, and staff organizations. He spent his first 15 years at NPIC, and the remainder of his career serving in NIMA and NGA (The National Geospatial-Intelligence Agency) which is now responsible for national imagery and geospatial intelligence. Throughout his career, Jack received numerous awards, including the National Intelligence Medal of Achievement in 2004 and the Office of the Director of National Intelligence Galileo Award in 2005. Prior to his government service, Jack taught at colleges and universities in the Philadelphia area. He holds degrees from Delaware County Community College, St. Joseph's University, and an M.A in English from Bryn Mawr College.

Jack's post-retirement career focuses on his lifelong interest in developing analysts and leaders. He has been actively coaching leaders and executives since 2008, and is an ICF-certified graduate of the Georgetown Leadership Coaching Program. He now incorporates his experience leading in environments of risk, volatility, and significant consequence in his work as a coach, consultant, and researcher. He is available for talks and presentations, and can be reached at jpkoconnor554@gmail.com

Index

H